Strategic XML

W. Scott Means

201 West 103rd St., Indianapolis, Indiana, 46290 USA

Strategic XML

International Standard Book Number: 0-672-32175-0

Library of Congress Catalog Card Number: 2001089627

Printed in the United States of America

First Printing: September 2001

04 03 02 01 4 3 2 1

Trademarks

Warning and Disclaimer

Associate Publisher
Michael Stephens

Acquisitions Editor
Carol Ackerman

Development Editor
Tiffany Taylor

Managing Editor
Matt Purcell

Project Editor
George E. Nedeff

Copy Editor
Cheri Clark

Indexer
Rebecca Salerno

Proofreader
Marcia Deboy

Technical Editor
Robert Brunner

Media Developer
Dan Scherf

Interior Designer
Aren Howell

Cover Designer
Anne Jones

Page Layout
Octal Publishing, Inc.
Gloria Schurick

Contents at a Glance

Contents

About the Author

W. Scott Means has been a professional software developer since 1988, when he joined Microsoft Corporation at the age of 17. He was one of the original developers of OS/2 1.1 and Windows NT, and he did some of the early work on the Microsoft Network for the Advanced Technology and Business Development group. Most recently, he served as the CEO of Enterprise Web Machines, a South Carolina–based Internet infrastructure venture. He is currently writing full-time and consulting on XML and Internet topics. This is his second book. He may be reached via email at `smeans@moonlightideas.com`.

Dedication

To my grandparents Madeline & Fred Means for being a constant source of love and inspiration in my life (without ever using a computer).

Acknowledgments

As with any book, there are many people to thank. And odds are, unless you're one of those people, you'll probably skip right by this section. But if you are, and by some amazing quirk of fate you do read this and don't find your name mentioned, I assure you that it was not from lack of appreciation. It is actually a lack of organization on my part.

First, as always, I need to thank my lovely wife, Celia, for the super-human patience she displays each time I "stay up just a couple more hours to finish this chapter." She has the sometimes (ok, always) thankless job of taking care of two small children as well as one much larger one from time to time. And I need to mention my daughter Selene and my little son Skyler. Maybe after seeing this Selene will stop telling her friends at school that "Daddy doesn't go to work."

I'd like to thank Mike Bodie ("It's pronounced 'body'"), an excellent programmer and ruthless reader. He provided consistent, high-quality comments that kept me honest the whole time.

I'd also like to thank Mr. Bennett Norell of LG Electronics U.S.A. for taking time out of his busy schedule to help me obtain copyright clearance for the VCP Manual used throughout the example chapters. After I had called around in circles for weeks, Mr. Norell kindly took the time to listen to my somewhat unusual request and do something about it.

Another reviewer who deserves praise for going above and beyond the call of duty is Judy Livingston. Judy is my friend, an IT professional, and our next-door neighbor. She has also been a good sport about being made into an involuntary manuscript reviewer.

Another person who deserves mentioning here is Elliotte Rusty Harold, my authoring role-model and mentor (even if he doesn't know it). He has helped me in so many ways I can't even begin to list them here.

I also need to thank David Setzer and the team at VirtualConnect.net for providing me with Web hosting, great graphic designs, and everything else that the hard-core programmer needs (and can't do for himself).

And I owe a huge debt of gratitude to the management and employees of the Barnes & Noble bookstore on Harbison Boulevard here in Columbia, South Carolina. They provided an ideal working environment complete with free electricity, fresh coffee, and as many reference books as any tech writer could need.

I need to thank my agent, Neil Salkind, and the rest of the staff at Studio B. They've provided consistent support and encouragement throughout this project.

This book also wouldn't have been completed so rapidly without the support and assistance of my programming "minion," Jess Males. Without him as my strong right hand, I would have been left with one (hand, that is).

Robert Brunner, the technical editor on this project, deserves kudos for playing the devil's advocate on numerous occasions where I was tempted to give short shrift to potential solutions I didn't personally favor.

And last (but certainly not least), the great people at Sams who had the hard job of taking what I wrote and turning it into an actual, honest-to-God, book; Carol Ackerman, Tiffany Taylor, George Nedeff, and Michael Stephens have all worked hard to make this book come together.

Tell Us What You Think!

As the reader of this book, *you* are our most important critic and commentator. We value your opinion and want to know what we're doing right, what we could do better, what areas you'd like to see us publish in, and any other words of wisdom you're willing to pass our way.

As an Associate Publisher for Sams Publishing, I welcome your comments. You can fax, e-mail, or write me directly to let me know what you did or didn't like about this book—as well as what we can do to make our books stronger.

Please note that I cannot help you with technical problems related to the topic of this book, and that due to the high volume of mail I receive, I might not be able to reply to every message.

When you write, please be sure to include this book's title and author, as well as your name and phone or fax number. I will carefully review your comments and share them with the author and editors who worked on the book.

Fax: 317-581-4770

E-mail: `feedback@samspublishing.com`

Mail: Michael Stephens
Associate Publisher
Sams Publishing
201 West 103rd Street
Indianapolis, IN 46290 USA

Pervasive XML

PART
I

IN THIS PART

Introduction

CHAPTER 1

"The History of every major Galactic Civilization tends to pass through three distinct and recognizable phases, those of Survival, Inquiry and Sophistication, otherwise known as the How, Why and Where phases. For instance, the first phase is characterized by the question 'How can we eat?' the second by the question 'Why do we eat?' and the third by the question 'Where shall we have lunch?'"

—The Hitchhiker's Guide to the Galaxy

Extensible Markup Language (XML), as a technology, has definitely passed beyond the "How?" stage. Now it is time for programmers and managers alike to ask themselves the "Why?" and "Where?" questions, and come up with answers that make sense.

The incredibly rapid acceptance of XML throughout the Information Technology community reflects one fundamental truth: XML makes sense. Before XML, there was an entire class of problems that each programmer had to solve in his own way. Without a simple, rigorously defined, and widely supported format for representing structured data, data incompatibility was the rule, not the exception.

The growth of the World Wide Web combined with the legacy of the Standard Generalized Markup Language (SGML) led to the approval of the XML recommendation in February 1998. Since then, countless XML applications have been defined, and numerous parsers, tools, and libraries have been released for use by programmers around the world.

The question is no longer whether an organization will adopt XML within its internal and external systems, but when and where. This book attempts to explain the types of applications for which XML is best suited. It also provides a series of fully developed and tested IT projects that incorporate XML or an XML-based technology such as the Simple Object Access Protocol (SOAP).

Who This Book Is For

This book is meant for senior technical users, system architects, and technical managers who want to understand the impact XML can have on their organization and its systems. A shortage of skilled IT personnel, combined with tight IS budgets, means that every new project must be justified and a business case must be made. Large organizations are based around evolution, not revolution. Attempting to use a great technology to solve the wrong problem is a recipe for frustration and failure. This book shows how XML can be integrated with existing systems in a long-term, controlled fashion.

Readers of this book should already have a solid foundation in Internet technologies and protocols. There are many good books on the market that explain the workings of the HTTP protocol, SOAP, and TCP/IP. Although in-depth knowledge of these topics is not required, some familiarity with the plumbing of modern Internet applications is helpful.

Most organizations are forced to deal with heterogeneous systems, so this book gives examples for both Microsoft and open source platforms. XML provides an excellent mediator between systems that previously had no "common ground." With an XML-based RPC protocol, such as SOAP, it is conceivable that a Microsoft ASP script could call an Enterprise Java Bean, which might then in turn read XML data from a legacy application running on a mainframe. This type of integration used to be costly and difficult to implement, but the adoption of XML by most software vendors means that interoperability is becoming easier all the time.

What This Book Is About

Large organizations are slow to adopt new technologies and standards. This book attempts to show where an organization can spend its limited development resources to leverage the power of XML. When it's used properly, converting a proprietary application protocol or data format to XML actually reduces the burden on software developers and users alike. When critical business data is available in XML, off-the-shelf tools and technologies can be used to view it, maintain it, transform it, and share it.

XML's rapid acceptance is indicative of its tremendous potential as a fundamental enabling technology. New versions of office productivity applications (such as the open source `Openoffice.org` suite) save and load files natively in XML. Banking transactions, Web page requests, and even SEC filings are moving to XML. This ubiquity provides various challenges to already-overworked development teams.

Selecting when, where, and how to implement XML within a large enterprise is crucial to ensure that maximum benefit achieved with minimal effort. Should organizations think about replacing their RDBMS systems (such as Oracle or Microsoft SQL Server) with XML files? Of course not. XML is not fundamentally well suited to storing and retrieving large amounts of data. It also does not lend itself to building relations between different records on-the-fly. Knowing where XML is appropriate is as important as knowing where it is not.

How to Use This Book

This book is organized into three distinct parts. Each part is intended to be self-contained, and each can be read out of sequence (or skipped entirely).

Part I, "Pervasive XML," is a cursory introduction to (or refresher of) XML and its related technologies. It gives a rapid tutorial in the basics of XML, namespaces, DTDs, and schemas. It lists the other XML-related technologies (such as XSLT), what they are used for, and where they can be found. It also explores some of the tools available to XML developers from various software vendors, as well as the large number of open source XML implementations currently in use.

Part II, "XML Zones," develops the concepts outlined at the end of Part I. A chapter is devoted to each of the enterprise "zones" where various applications of XML technologies are explored. Selected applications from these chapters are fully implemented in Part III.

Part III, "Applying the Technology," builds a set of complete IT projects that incorporate XML technology to solve common business problems. The projects are taken from the problem definition stage, through the gathering of requirements, implementation, and deployment phases. Full source code for every project is available on the book's Web site, `www.strategicxml.com`.

Throughout the book, the 🔗 symbol indicates that more information about the topic in question (including hyperlinks, sample code, corrections, and comments) can be found on the book's Web site. Go to `www.strategicxml.com/chapter??` (where ?? is the chapter number) to see the list of links for that chapter. The ➥ symbol indicates that a single line of code continues to the following line.

The sample projects include the following:

Web Content Publishing (Chapter 12)

By authoring Web content in XML, and linking it with presentation information in XSL, corporate Webmasters can shift some of the responsibility for site maintenance to nontechnical users.

Automating Workflow (Chapter 13)

Large companies generate massive amounts of paperwork, everything from purchase orders to ISO 9000 training records. XML can provide the leverage needed to automate processing of documents in a cost-effective manner.

Offline Order Processing (Chapter 14)

Despite the near-100% connectivity of large companies and their workforce, store-and-forward technologies (such as e-mail) still have a place when real-time connectivity is not practical.

Customer Self-Service Web Application (Chapter 15)

Massive quantities of information about users and accounts are stored in legacy systems, data warehouses, and data marts. Building a self-service application that presents information to users on the Web can cut costs and increase customer satisfaction.

B2B Transactions (Chapter 16)

In theory, communicating directly with the IT systems of partners, customers, and suppliers can greatly improve the accuracy and timeliness of information available to a company. In fact, the implementation details quickly become overwhelming. SOAP and the HTTP protocol can help companies quickly establish lines of communication without having to move heaven and earth (not to mention the corporate firewall).

Migrating Legacy Data (Chapter 17)

Terabytes of data are still stored and maintained in legacy information systems. The death of legacy languages such as COBOL has been greatly exaggerated. The good news is that XML technology has made its way onto the big iron, and can make life for the typical developer much simpler.

Unifying Product Documentation (Chapter 18)

Many types of documentation generated by large corporations are available on the Web. Many of these documents are also available in print. Unfortunately, these two sets of documentation frequently don't overlap. XML can provide a company with the leverage it needs to effectively communicate with its customers on *their* terms.

Where to Go from Here

If you are not familiar with XML and the tools that support it, you should read the rest of Part I before proceeding. It will rapidly give you the knowledge necessary to understand the applications discussed throughout the rest of the book.

If you are already familiar with XML but are not completely familiar with the latest developments in related technologies and tools, skip Chapter 2, "XML Tutorial." This chapter gives a rapid but thorough introduction to XML and its related standards for users who have never used XML before.

If you are well versed in XML, XSLT, XSL-FO, and tools such as Xalan, Xerces, and SAXON, you should skip Chapter 4, "Tools and Technologies." It gives a high-level roadmap of the various popular commercial and open source development tools and libraries that support XML, XSL, and other related standards.

If you have a particular problem to solve or need to learn a particular XML technology in a hurry, you should start with Chapter 11, "About the Applications." It explains the structure of the sample chapters and gives a brief synopsis of each application, including the tools used to build it.

XML Tutorial

CHAPTER 2

There's an often-quoted excerpt from a letter by Blaise Pascal that reads, "I have made this letter longer than usual, because I lack the time to make it short." When I started planning this book, everyone questioned my intention to include a single-chapter XML tutorial. The most common observation was this: "If people (like you) have written entire books explaining XML, what good can you do in a single chapter?"

My answer to that rests in my belief that XML is a simple technology at heart. One of the reasons I was so attracted to it in the first place was that it could be grasped in its entirety in a single afternoon. It is powerful, flexible, and simple. There is no way I can fully cover every intricate detail of XML, namespaces, and schemas in a single chapter. But I do believe that it is possible to include enough information to allow someone to immediately begin reading and understanding the examples that are included in Part III, "Applying the Technology."

Before we can discuss advanced applications of XML, a basic understanding of the technologies involved is required.

A Simple Document

The easiest way to understand what XML is and what it can do is to work with a concrete example. Listing 2.1 shows a simple lunch menu (`LunchMenu.txt`) saved as a plain-vanilla text file.

LISTING 2.1 A Simple Lunch Menu

```
SNL Diner
Lunch Hours: 11:00AM - 2:00PM

Lunch Items
================================
Cheeseburger* .......... $2.50
Chips .................. $1.25
Pepsi .................. $.75

Special Combo (Cheeseburger,
  Chips, & Pepsi) ...... $4.50

* Soy burger available on
request.
```

This text file is clearly designed to be read by humans. The actual information content (such as item names and prices) is mixed in with characters and whitespace that serve only to make the layout more aesthetically pleasing. But what if this same information needed to be presented on the World Wide Web, or had to be stored in a database? Keeping a single text file up-to-date is no problem, but keeping three or four copies of the same data synchronized becomes cumbersome in a hurry.

This type of application is precisely what XML was designed to do. Listing 2.2 shows the information from `LunchMenu.txt` reformulated as an XML document.

LISTING 2.2 XML Version of Lunch Menu

```
<?xml version="1.0" encoding="UTF-8"?>
<restaurant>
  <name>SNL Diner</name>
  <menu type="Lunch" start-time="11:00AM"
      end-time="2:00PM">
    <items>
```

LISTING 2.2 Continued

```
      <item id="L1">
        <name>Cheeseburger</name>
        <price>$2.50</price>
        <note>Soy burger available on request.</note>
      </item>
      <item id="L2">
        <name>Chips</name>
        <price>$1.25</price>
      </item>
      <item id="L3">
        <name>Pepsi</name>
        <price>$.75</price>
      </item>
      <combo id="C1">
        <name>Special Combo</name>
        <item ref="L1"/>
        <item ref="L2"/>
        <item ref="L3"/>
      </combo>
    </items>
  </menu>
</restaurant>
```

Several things become immediately apparent when comparing the XML document to the original text file:

- The XML version is twice as long.
- The text version is much more attractive.
- The XML version includes information that is obviously not for human consumption.

It is important to realize that XML documents are not intended to be read by humans. XML syntax was designed to be extremely easy for machines to parse. Other technologies (such as XSLT or CSS) are provided to make the raw XML presentable to human beings. Using a transformation language like XSLT, it is possible to convert the XML document from Listing 2.2 into a text file (like the one in Listing 2.1), an HTML document, a series of SQL statements, or any other text-based language.

Markup Versus Content

When you're looking at the XML document in Listing 2.2 for the first time, it is easy to become overwhelmed by its apparent complexity. But fundamentally, every XML document is a combination of some content with its associated markup.

Content is the unique information that needs to be conveyed by the document. The names of the menu items, their prices, and the name of the restaurant are all examples of document content.

The markup is the set of tags and other XML syntax features that give structure to the content. In general, anything appearing between <> characters in an XML document is considered to be markup.

All About Elements

The most important (and frequently encountered) type of markup is the element tag. An element consists of an element open tag (for example, `<name>`), which is possibly followed by character data and additional elements, and an element close tag (`</name>`). Unlike HTML, XML requires that element open and close tags must match. This means that if an element begins with a `<name>` tag, it must end with a matching `</name>` closing tag. Mismatched tags will generate a well-formedness error (like a syntax error) in an XML parser. For example, the following tag sequence would generate an error if it were used in an XML document:

```
<p>This is the first line,<br>and this is the second.</p>
```

Although this is a perfectly valid HTML tag sequence, XML does not automatically close the `<br>` tag upon parsing the `</p>` close tag. To fix this, either the `<br>` tag must be closed with a `</br>` end tag or the empty element syntax must be used.

The empty element syntax is simply a shortcut for encoding elements that contain no character data or markup. This is the empty element syntax:

```
<tagname/>
```

This is a normal open tag that ends with a `/` character before the closing `>`. To an XML parser, this is equivalent to an empty open and close tag combination, like this:

```
<tagname></tagname>
```

Adding Attributes

Within the sample document (Listing 2.2), there are several open tags that include extra information in the form of

```
name="data"
```

These name/value pairs are called *attributes*. An attribute is generally a piece of information that is related to an element, but is not necessarily part of the content. Deciding what content should be encoded as an attribute and what should be left as element content is a topic that still generates a great deal of discussion among XML experts. Without digging too deeply into the various attribute philosophies, treating attributes as “keys” to the underlying element content is a fairly standard practice among experienced XML document authors.

You should keep a few restrictions in mind when using attributes to encode information:

- Attribute names must be unique (that is, you cannot have two attributes with the same name on a single element).
- Markup characters (such as <>) cannot appear directly in attribute values. It is possible to include them using the built-in character references `<` and `>`, which are covered later in the chapter.
- The sequence of attributes in an element cannot be guaranteed. If an element is written as `<el a1="foo" a2="bar">`, the attributes may be returned by the XML parser as `a2` followed `a1`. Don't depend on attribute ordering for the logic of your application.

Attributes usually consist of simple character data. When a document is validated using a document type definition (DTD), attributes can be declared to contain special types such as IDs, entities, and name tokens. These special types are used by a validating XML parser to enforce the contents and relationships between attributes. For more information about advanced XML topics such as attribute declaration, an excellent XML reference book to consult is *XML in a Nutshell*.

Whitespace and Comments

In XML documents, as in most other types of documents, whitespace serves to improve the readability and organization of textual content. XML defines the characters in Table 2.1 to be whitespace and considers them to be interchangeable.

TABLE 2.1 XML Whitespace Characters

ASCII Value	*Description*
32 (#x20 hex)	Space
9 (#x9 hex)	Tab
13 (#xD hex)	Carriage return
10 (#xA hex)	Line feed

The formal grammar for XML outlines exactly where whitespace may and may not occur. In practical application, it can appear anywhere that common sense dictates that it could. It cannot appear in the middle of a name token, for instance, but it can appear between an attribute name and its corresponding = sign.

Comments are a different matter. In some programming languages, comments are syntactically equivalent to whitespace. This is not the case in XML. The simplest way to think about it is to consider a comment to be another markup tag (like an element or entity declaration). A comment cannot appear inside another markup tag, but can appear inline with it. For example, instead of

```
<!ATTLIST myelement
  attr CDATA #IMPLIED <!-- should this be required? -->
>
```

you would need to rewrite it this way:

```
<!ATTLIST myelement
  attr CDATA #IMPLIED
> <!-- should the attr attribute be required? -->
```

Character References and CDATA Sections

XML documents are considered to be written using the Unicode character set. This is true no matter what character encoding is used to store or transmit them at the operating-system level. After the document is parsed by an XML parser, the character data is made available to the client application in Unicode. The full Unicode specification defines tens of thousands of characters, many of which cannot be generated directly using a normal Qwerty keyboard. XML provides the character reference facility to allow a document to include any Unicode character, even when the underlying character encoding or physical input method doesn't support it. For more resources and references to Unicode characters, see `www.unicode.org` (the Unicode Consortium's home page).

Character References

Character references reference a Unicode character by number. For example, the following XML snippet shows the character encoding for the copyright symbol (©) using both decimal and hexadecimal syntax variants, respectively:

```
&#169; &#xA9;
```

This syntax can be used to include any Unicode character, although that doesn't guarantee that your display device and other text-processing software will be able to display it. You can include the reference for the Greek capital letter sigma (`&x3A3;`) in your document, but that doesn't mean that the character will be visible (or even legal for your OS) on output.

CDATA Sections

In some cases, the special significance of the various XML markup characters (<, >, and `&`) can place an unacceptable burden on document authors. For example, imagine including the following fragment of Java code within an XML element:

```
if (a < b && b >= c) {
```

To make this acceptable to an XML parser, the special characters would need to be escaped, like so:

```
if (a &lt; b &amp;&amp; b &gt;= c) {
```

To simplify the task of including large blocks of text with characters that need to be escaped, XML provides the `CDATA` section. Using `CDATA`, the preceding Java code could be included in an XML document like this:

```
<![CDATA[if (a < b && b >= c) {]]>
```

The only restriction is that the escaped text cannot contain the `CDATA` closing delimiter (`]]>`), which would ordinarily be a problem only when quoting XML data itself. To get around this restriction, it would be necessary to close the `CDATA` section, include the delimiter text using XML character references, and then reopen the `CDATA` section:

```
]]>]]&gt;<![CDATA[
```


Creating a Valid Document

The document in Listing 2.2 can be successfully parsed by any XML parser because it doesn't violate any of XML's well-formedness constraints. But just because a document is well-formed doesn't mean that the contents are useful for a particular application. For instance, what if the restaurant owner made a mistake when he was updating the menu and accidentally gave an item two prices:

```
<item id="L3">
  <name>Pepsi</name>
  <price>$1.00</price>
  <price>$.75</price>
</item>
```

The document would still be parsed without generating errors, because it is still well-formed XML. But in the context of the actual application, having an item with two prices is definitely an error. At best, this would generate incorrect output (a menu with two prices on one item), and at worst it could cause a custom-written program to crash.

Fortunately, various mechanisms can be used to ensure that a particular document is valid for a given application. The validation scheme that is defined as part of the XML 1.0 specification is the DTD. The DTD provides some basic capabilities for limiting the type and number of elements within a document. It also allows the document author to control the names and, to some extent, the contents of element attributes. But it does not allow authors any control over the character content of elements, making it a poor choice for sophisticated applications.

NOTE

Not every parser reads and enforces the rules set out in a document's DTD. Parsers that do are called validating parsers. And in most cases, validating parsers can be configured to behave like nonvalidating parsers (that is, ignore the DTD and simply check for well-formedness). If you are building a custom application, be sure to check the documentation of the XML parser you choose to see whether it is a validating parser (if you need that functionality).

Besides the basic DTD validation method, other technologies have evolved to provide greater control over the content and structure of XML documents. The XML Schema standard was developed by the W3C to provide much finer control over the placement and contents of elements within a document. Schemas will be covered in greater detail later in this chapter.

The `<!DOCTYPE>` Declaration

To make a document valid, it must be associated with a document type definition. The `<!DOCTYPE>` either directly contains or points to the element and attribute declarations that make up a DTD for a particular XML application. For instance, adding the following line to the document in Listing 2.2 instructs a validating parser to read the declarations in `restaurant.dtd` and ensures that the contents of the document obey the constraints given:

```
<!DOCTYPE restaurant SYSTEM "restaurant.dtd">
```

The `SYSTEM` keyword tells the parser to read the contents of the file referenced by the relative Uniform Resource Identifier(URI) `restaurant.dtd`. The contents of this external file are called the *external subset*. Besides the external subset, the `<!DOCTYPE>` syntax allows declarations to be included directly within the XML document, like so:

```
<!DOCTYPE restaurant SYSTEM "restaurant.dtd"
[
  <!ENTITY name "SNL Diner">
]>
```

The markup included within the `[]` characters is called the *internal subset*. To simplify the job of XML parser developers, the internal subset doesn't support the full range of declarations and instructions that can appear in the external subset. For most document authors, this difference is not significant. Consult a complete XML reference for a discussion of internal versus external DTD subsets.

The <!DOCTYPE> markup must appear after the XML declaration (<?xml ...>) but before the single top-level document element. Refer to ValidLunchMenu.xml to see the exact placement of the <!DOCTYPE> markup tag within a document.

Element Declarations

Now that you know how to associate element and attribute declarations with a document, you need to understand what these declarations look like.

The <!ELEMENT> markup tag is used to declare what type of content is permitted for a particular element. For example, the following declaration from restaurant.dtd defines the markup that can appear inside an <item> element:

```
<!ELEMENT item (name, price, note?)?>
```

The first token following the <!ELEMENT> markup is the name of the element being declared (in this case, item). Following the name is either a simple regular expression that dictates the contents of the element, or a special keyword such as ANY (the element may contain any combination of other elements and text) or EMPTY (the element must be empty).

The regular expression syntax is somewhat similar to UNIX or Perl regular expressions. In lieu of a full formal description of the language, Table 2.2 gives a few sample expressions with valid (matching) and invalid (nonmatching) content.

TABLE 2.2 Sample Element Declarations

Regular Expression	*Valid Content*	*Invalid Content*
(a, b, c)	<a/><b/><c/>	<a/><c/>
(a | b | c)	<a/>	<a/><b/>
	<c/>	
(a | b | c)*	<!--empty element-->	<d/>
	<b/>	
	<a/><a/><c/>	
(a)+	<a/>	<!--empty element-->
	<a/><a/></a>	
(a, c)?	<!--empty element-->	<a/>
	<a/><c/>	<c/><a/>
(#PCDATA | a | b)	This <b/> is <a/> text.	<c/> text.

Although none of the elements in this example have content of their own, in an actual application they would have element declarations of their own. Parent element declarations don't have any effect on the legal content of their children.

A Quick Note About NOTATIONs

Before discussing attributes, it is necessary to briefly touch on one of the least-understood (and least-frequently used) parts of XML 1.0: the `<!NOTATION>` declaration. The `NOTATION` facility is essentially a way of associating an XML name identifier with a `PUBLIC` ID and/or a `SYSTEM` ID (a.k.a. URI). The specification does not dictate that an XML parser actually do anything with the IDs in a notation declaration, other than pass them to the client application.

Notations can be associated with external unparsed entities (such as binary image files) using the `NDATA` keyword in an entity declaration. They can also be associated with particular elements, by using the `NOTATION` attribute type (discussed below). A third use is to categorize processing instructions (by declaring a notation name that matches the processing instruction target name).

Besides these "official" uses, it is possible to declare notations for some other use within your application. Because information from all notation declarations is made available by an XML parser to the client application, an application is free to interpret them any way it wishes. But in most cases, a standardized approach would be preferable.

Declaring Attributes

Just as the element declaration limits the contents of a particular element, the attribute declaration controls which and what type of attributes can be included in a particular element.

The `<!ATTLIST>` markup tag is used to control the attributes that can be included in a particular element. As an example, here's the attribute declaration for the `item` element:

```
<!ATTLIST item
  id  ID    #IMPLIED
  ref IDREF #IMPLIED
>
```

The first name token after the `<!ATTLIST>` markup is the name of the element associated with this declaration. Following the element name is a list of attribute name, type, and default-value triples. Multiple `<!ATTLIST>` declarations can be given for a single element throughout the DTD. The result is the same as if all the declarations were combined into a single large declaration.

Looking at a single triple, the first token is the name of the attribute to be declared. The second token is the attribute type, which must come from the following list:

- CDATA—Plain-character data
- ID—A document-unique ID
- IDREF, IDREFS—A single value or list of values that must be equal to the value of an ID attribute within the document
- NMTOKEN, NMTOKENS—A single XML name token or list of tokens, respectively
- ENTITY, ENTITIES—A single declared entity name, or a list of names
- NOTATION—A single name from an enumeration of declared notation names

Besides these types, it is also possible to declare an attribute that is limited to a list of valid values. The full attribute declaration syntax is very complex and would require an entire chapter in itself. For a full explanation of valid attribute declarations, consult a complete XML reference. However the most frequently used attribute types by far are CDATA, ID, and IDREF.

CDATA Attributes

The CDATA type indicates that the attribute can contain an arbitrary string of character data. Character references (such as &) are recognized and expanded within the string, as are entity references. Attribute strings cannot contain unescaped markup characters (such as <, >, and &). Also, as in most programming languages, because the attribute value is quoted, it cannot contain unescaped quote characters (for example, "He said "Boo"" would not be valid). In some cases using the alternative quote character (' instead of ") can be simpler than using the " built-in entity reference: 'He said "Boo"'.

ID and IDREF Attributes

The ID and IDREF types are complementary. The XML ID mechanism is intended to give document authors a way to uniquely identify elements within a document. The IDREF attribute type indicates that the attribute may contain only a value that matches an ID value within the same document. Here are a few points to remember about ID and IDREF attributes:

- ID values must be valid XML names (that is, start with a letter or underscore [_], and contain only letters, numbers, and certain punctuation).
- No two elements (even of different element types) can have the same value in an ID attribute. For instance, having two elements <person id="ID20"/> <company id="ID20"/> in a single document would make that document invalid.

- Every IDREF attribute must match the value of an ID attribute somewhere in the document. IDREFs are like one-way links to elements, and it is illegal to have a document with broken links in it.

NMOTOKEN Attributes

The NMTOKEN type indicates that the corresponding attribute must contain a value that is a valid XML name token. There is a fine difference between XML names and XML name tokens: name tokens may start with any valid name character, instead of being restricted to letters and the underscore (_) character (or colon, which should not be used in order to minimize namespace confusion).

Referencing External Entities

ENTITY attributes are provided to allow XML documents to include references to data that is not valid XML, and possibly not even textual. The basic usage of an entity attribute is to declare an external unparsed entity using an <!ENTITY> declaration (covered in the next section), and then use the entity name as the value for an entity attribute. One common application of this is to include image data in an XML document, as shown in Listing 2.3.

LISTING 2.3 An Entity Attribute Example

```
<?xml version="1.0" encoding="UTF-8"?>
<!DOCTYPE picture [
  <!NOTATION gif SYSTEM "images/gif">
  <!ENTITY flowers_gif SYSTEM "flowers.gif" NDATA gif>
  <!ELEMENT picture EMPTY>
  <!ATTLIST picture
    src ENTITY #REQUIRED
  >
]>

<picture src="flowers_gif"/>
```

Although this approach has some advantages, such as associating notation information with external entity references, many XML experts recommend against using entity attributes for this purpose. More familiar and full-featured solutions such as the XLink standard should be used instead.

NOTATION Attributes

The NOTATION attribute type provides a mechanism for associating an XML notation name with a particular element. In the declaration, a list of possible valid notations is given, like so:

```
<!ATTLIST picture
  src   ENTITY #REQUIRED
  type  NOTATION (bmp | gif | jpg) #REQUIRED
>
```

Within the document, every `<picture>` element must have a `type` attribute that contains one of the notation names given in the list (`bmp`, `gif`, or `jpg`). When the document is parsed, the XML application can use the notation name to access additional information about the element type from the associated `<!NOTATION>` declaration.

Attribute List Types: IDREFS, ENTITIES, and NMTOKENS

The plural forms of the `IDREF`, `ENTITY`, and `NMTOKEN` types can be used to declare an attribute that contains a list of values, instead of a single value. The values in the list must be separated by whitespace and must conform to the same restrictions as the singular form (discussed earlier).

Using Entities

When one is authoring complex documents or creating multiple related documents, certain content fragments tend to be repeated over and over again. For example, a series of XHTML Web pages might share a set of common footer tags. Entities are provided as a primitive macro facility to allow commonly repeated sequences of document content and even DTD declarations to be defined and referenced by name.

Listing 2.4 shows a simple entity declaration and reference.

LISTING 2.4 A Simple Entity Example

```
<!DOCTYPE message [
  <!ELEMENT message (#PCDATA)>
  <!ENTITY my_message "Hello, world." >
]>
<message>&my_message;</message>
```

First, the entity is declared using the `<!ENTITY>` markup, and then the associated text (`"Hello, world."`) is included in the target document using a normal entity reference (`&my_message;`). The actual syntax of entity declarations and references changes based on the following:

- Where the replacement text comes from (an inline string or an external file)
- Where the entity will be referenced (within the DTD or the document)
- Whether the resulting replacement text will be read by the parser

Internal Versus External Entities

In Listing 2.4, the replacement text of the entity is contained in a string within the <!ENTITY> markup itself. For short, simple entities this is very convenient. For longer, multiline replacements, storing the entity value in an external file would be more appropriate. The XML entity syntax provides this capability by using the SYSTEM keyword (in place of a string) within the entity declaration, like so:

```
<!ENTITY wp SYSTEM "war_and_peace.txt">
```

Within the document, every occurrence of the ℘ entity reference would be replaced by the contents of the file war_and_peace.txt. The XML parser would then continue parsing, beginning with the text that was just included. This means that entity text can, in turn, contain entity references.

General and Parameter Entities

The second criteria (where the entity will be used) affects both the entity declaration and reference. The entity shown in Listing 2.4 is called a general entity, because it is referenced within the body of the document. If the entity is to be referenced within the DTD, it is called a parameter entity. For parameter entities, it is necessary to add a % character to the <!ENTITY> markup:

```
<!ENTITY % base_att_list 'xml:lang CDATA "en-us"'>
<!ELEMENT message (#PCDATA)>
<!ATTLIST message %base_att_list;>
```

NOTE

The rules about where and how parameter entities can be declared and used are arguably the most complex part of the XML 1.0 specification. For instance, the preceding XML snippet is perfectly valid if it is included in the external DTD subset (stored in a file separate from the main document). It is not valid, however, if it is included directly in the internal subset (the portion of the <!DOCTYPE> declaration between the [and] characters). If you plan to rely heavily on parameter entities in your documents, it would be a good idea to use a comprehensive XML reference.

The benefit of using a parameter entity to declare attributes like this is that if multiple tags have a common base set of attributes, the base set can be changed in a single location.

Parsed Versus Unparsed Entities

Earlier, I mentioned that the XML parser will continue parsing the text that is included as the result of reading an entity reference. The only time this is not true is in the case of the external unparsed entity. This special case is the result of including the NDATA keyword with a notation name in a normal general entity declaration, such as the flowers_gif entity declaration from Listing 2.3:

```
<!ENTITY flowers_gif SYSTEM "flowers.gif" NDATA gif>
```

Unparsed entities cannot be referenced within a document using the &*entityname*; syntax. The only way to refer to unparsed external entities is through the ENTITY attribute type. See the "Referencing External Entities" section of this chapter for an example of referencing an external unparsed entity.

NOTE

There is no such thing as an unparsed parameter entity. Because the only use for a parameter entity is to help construct the DTD, there was no apparent use for including nonmarkup content in the DTD.

Additional XML Features

There are a few other features of XML that are not commonly used by document authors. This section discusses each of them briefly, along with their intended usage.

Processing Instructions

As with any data format or programming language, there will always be applications that were not foreseen by the language designers. The processing instruction provides an "official" escape hatch for developers who need to work beyond the constraints of XML itself. This is the basic syntax of a processing instruction:

```
<?target_name [app. specific data]?>
```

The only part of the processing instruction that is recognized by the XML parser is the target name. This must be an XML name, and it may be associated with a declared XML notation (see the earlier section "A Quick Note About NOTATIONs"). The only restriction on the name is that it cannot match the case-insensitive string "xml" (which is used in the XML declaration).

Special Attributes

Two special attributes are documented in the XML 1.0 recommendation: xml:space and xml:lang. The first, xml:space, provides a way for a document author to indicate that whitespace is significant for a particular element. The xml:lang attribute allows an ISO 3166 country and language code to be associated with an element.

Although the XML specification defines how these two attributes must be declared and how they should be used, no special action must be taken when they are parsed by an XML parser. It is up to the application (Web browser, stylesheet processor, and so on) to recognize them and interpret their meanings.

Conditional Sections

Within large DTDs, it is sometimes convenient to conditionally include and exclude blocks of declaration markup. The special <!IGNORE> and <!INCLUDE> markup tags are provided for this purpose. The following example illustrates how include and ignore are used to select one version of an element declaration over another:

```
<![INCLUDE[ <!ELEMENT message (#PCDATA)> ]]>
<![IGNORE[ <!ELEMENT message (#PCDATA | comment)*> ]]>
```

To select the alternative declaration of the <message> element, simply switch the INCLUDE keyword with the IGNORE keyword:

```
<![IGNORE[ <!ELEMENT message (#PCDATA)> ]]>
<![INCLUDE[ <!ELEMENT message (#PCDATA | comment)*> ]]>
```

Although it is possible to use the IGNORE and INCLUDE keywords directly, it is much more common to use parameter entities to allow multiple sections to be switched by changing a single set of entity declarations:

```
<!ENTITY % production "INCLUDE">
<!ENTITY % debug "IGNORE">
<![%production;[ <!ELEMENT message (#PCDATA)> ]]>
<![%debug;[ <!ELEMENT message (#PCDATA | comment)*> ]]>
```

That being said, this facility is still fairly cumbersome, and similar results can be achieved through the strategic use of parameter entity references to include declarations:

```
<!ENTITY % message_decl "<!ELEMENT message (#PCDATA)>">
<!ENTITY % message_decl_dbg
    "<!ELEMENT message (#PCDATA | comment)*>">

<!-- change following to %message_decl_dbg; for debug version-->
%message_decl;
```

Combining Applications with Namespaces

One of the obvious limitations of the original XML 1.0 recommendation was the lack of a mechanism for dealing with the inevitable naming collisions that would occur as more and more XML applications were defined. For example, imagine how many different documents would include a <name> element. If large, complex documents were to be built using shared libraries of markup declarations, some definitive way for grouping and separating markup elements had to be developed.

The W3C Namespaces in XML recommendation serves this purpose. It allows XML document designers to mix elements from different applications without the possibility of confusing one with another. This is done by associating each element and attribute name with an XML namespace.

Namespace URIs

Logically, an XML namespace is simply a Uniform Resource Identifier. Most commonly, the URI is a simple HTTP URL (such as `http://www.strategicxml.com`). Because domain names are guaranteed to be globally unique (thanks to their hierarchical nature), applications can depend on well-known published namespace URIs to make assumptions about element contents.

For example, the URI `http://www.w3.org/2001/XMLSchema` is the official namespace for elements that define an XML schema. A `<schema>` element associated with this namespace should conform to the XML Schema recommendation, and nothing else. So, the question remains: How are elements and attributes associated with namespace URIs?

The `xmlns` Attribute

The answer is that they are associated via the special `xmlns` attribute. Whenever an element has an `xmlns` attribute, it (and its descendants) belong to the namespace associated with the URI in the attribute value. For instance, adding the following attribute declaration to the `restaurant.dtd` example places every restaurant document into the `http://namespaces.strategicxml.com/restaurant` namespace:

```
<!ATTLIST restaurant
  xmlns CDATA #FIXED "http://namespaces.strategicxml.com/restaurant"
>
```

The root `<restaurant>` element and (by default) every child element and attribute now belongs to the globally unique namespace associated with the URI given previously. But setting the default namespace doesn't help us combine elements from different XML application vocabularies. To combine elements, you actually need to change the structure of the element tag names themselves.

Qualified Names

To support mixing namespaces, the "Namespaces in XML" recommendation defines the idea of a qualified element name. A qualified name consists of a regular tag name with a namespace prefix, like this:

```
<prefix:localpart/>
```

The part of the name to the left of the colon is the namespace prefix. The part to the right is called the local part. When different prefixes are used, elements with the same base name can be combined in a single document. Take, for example, the following XML snippet that contains three different elements that have the same name but belong to different namespaces:

```
<a:localname>
  <b:localname/>
  <c:localname/>
</a:localname>
```

Without the namespace prefixes, all the tags would be called <localname> and would be indistinguishable. But the prefix by itself is not what distinguishes one element from another. The prefix is merely shorthand for the actual namespace URI that must be declared using a special xmlns: attribute:

```
<namespace-example xmlns:a="http://namespaces.strategicxml.com/example/a"
    xmlns:b="http://namespaces.strategicxml.com/example/b"
    xmlns:c="http://namespaces.strategicxml.com/example/c">
  <a:localname>
    <b:localname/>
    <c:localname/>
  </a:localname>
</namespace-example>
```

The three xmlns attributes on the <namespace-example> element declare the a:, b:, and c: prefixes. When a namespace-aware parser is comparing elements for equality, it doesn't do a simple text comparison of the two tag names, it actually compares the namespace URIs and local names. Therefore, the namespaces from the preceding example could be declared like this:

```
<namespace-example xmlns:a="http://namespaces.strategicxml.com/example/a"
    xmlns:b="http://namespaces.strategicxml.com/example/b"
    xmlns:c="http://namespaces.strategicxml.com/example/c">
```

In this case, all three elements would actually be equivalent to a namespace-aware parser, even though they all have different namespace prefixes. Although this kind of thing is possible, it is definitely not considered to be a good XML design practice, and should be avoided.

Better Validation with Schemas

The DTD mechanism that was included in the XML 1.0 recommendation allows fairly sophisticated document structures to be declared. But when programmers started to apply XML to rigorous data transfer applications (such as importing and exporting data from a relational database), the limitations of DTDs became quite obvious. DTDs cannot restrict what types of character data can be stored in an element, allowing anomalies such as this:

```
<phone-number>smeans@strategicxml.com</phone-number>
```

The XML Schema recommendation (which was finally approved on May 2, 2001) is intended to address the shortcomings of the XML DTD and provide capabilities for very strict document content validation. The remainder of this chapter attempts to give a very quick introduction to the concepts and facilities provided by XML Schemas. The full XML Schema specification is actually much longer and more complex than the XML recommendation itself, so if you plan to begin seriously developing schema documents, you should invest in a good schema reference such as *Sams XML Schema Development: An Object-Oriented Approach*.

Schema Overview

Interestingly enough, XML Schemas are actual standalone XML documents in their own right. The XML Schema language is a specialized XML application that is designed to describe allowable content in another XML document. Schema-enabled parsers read an XML document, read the associated schema document, and then compare the contents of the target document with the descriptions in the schema.

To illustrate how schemas differ from DTDs, Listing 2.5 shows a sample schema (`restaurant.xsd`) that duplicates (and extends) the functionality of the DTD located in `restaurant.dtd`.

LISTING 2.5 A Restaurant Sample Schema

```
<?xml version="1.0" encoding="UTF-8"?>
<xsd:schema xmlns:xsd="http://www.w3.org/2001/XMLSchema">
  <xsd:element name="restaurant">
    <xsd:complexType>
      <xsd:sequence>
        <xsd:element ref="name"/>
        <xsd:element name="menu" type="menuType" minOccurs="1"
            maxOccurs="unbounded"/>
      </xsd:sequence>
    </xsd:complexType>
  </xsd:element>

  <xsd:complexType name="menuType">
    <xsd:sequence>
      <xsd:element name="items" type="itemList"/>
    </xsd:sequence>
    <xsd:attribute name="type" type="mealType" use="required"/>
    <xsd:attribute name="start-time" type="xsd:dateTime" use="required"/>
    <xsd:attribute name="end-time" type="xsd:time" use="required"/>
  </xsd:complexType>
```

LISTING 2.5 Continued

```
<xsd:simpleType name="mealType">
  <xsd:restriction base="xsd:string">
    <xsd:enumeration value="Breakfast"/>
    <xsd:enumeration value="Brunch"/>
    <xsd:enumeration value="Lunch"/>
    <xsd:enumeration value="Dinner"/>
  </xsd:restriction>
</xsd:simpleType>

<xsd:complexType name="itemList">
  <xsd:choice maxOccurs="unbounded">
    <xsd:element ref="item"/>
    <xsd:element ref="combo"/>
  </xsd:choice>
</xsd:complexType>

<xsd:element name="item">
  <xsd:complexType>
    <xsd:sequence minOccurs="0">
      <xsd:element ref="name"/>
      <xsd:element ref="price"/>
      <xsd:element ref="note" minOccurs="0"/>
    </xsd:sequence>

    <xsd:attribute name="id" type="xsd:ID"/>
    <xsd:attribute name="ref" type="xsd:IDREF"/>
  </xsd:complexType>
</xsd:element>

<xsd:element name="combo">
  <xsd:complexType>
    <xsd:sequence>
      <xsd:element ref="name"/>
      <xsd:element ref="item" minOccurs="1" maxOccurs="unbounded"/>
    </xsd:sequence>
    <xsd:attribute name="id" type="xsd:ID" use="required"/>
  </xsd:complexType>
</xsd:element>

<xsd:element name="name" type="xsd:string"/>

<xsd:element name="note" type="xsd:string"/>

<xsd:element name="price" type="currency"/>
```

LISTING 2.5 Continued

```
  <xsd:simpleType name="currency">
    <xsd:restriction base="xsd:string">
      <xsd:pattern value="$\d*\.\d\d"/>
    </xsd:restriction>
  </xsd:simpleType>
</xsd:schema>
```

Schema Elements

The schema in Listing 2.5 shows examples of various elements that make up the XML Schema language. The following sections give a brief explanation of each element and what it is used for.

NOTE

Note that each of the following elements belongs to the schema namespace (`http://www.w3.org/2001/XMLSchema`), which is traditionally assigned to the `xsd:` namespace prefix.

`<xsd:schema>`

The `<xsd:schema>` element is always the top-level element of a valid XML Schema. It may contain top-level element and type declarations. It may also contain top-level attribute, group, and notation declarations, but this advanced usage is not covered here.

`<xsd:element>`

The `<xsd:element>` element is used to declare a concrete XML element that may appear in a document. In the preceding example, the first `<xsd:element>` markup that appears declares the top-level `<restaurant>` element. There are also top-level declarations for `<item>`, `<combo>`, `<name>`, `<note>`, and `<price>` elements.

NOTE

Although this schema is intended to validate a document that contains a top-level `<restaurant>` element, legally any element declared in a top-level `<xsd:element>` can appear as the single, top-level element:

```
<name xmlns:xsi="http://www.w3.org/2001/XMLSchema-instance"
      xsi:noNamespaceSchemaLocation="restaurant.xsd">SNL Diner</name>
```

The name attribute indicates the name of the element being declared. It may then contain additional markup (such as a complexType or simpleType element) that indicates what type of content it may contain. It is also possible to reuse type and element declarations through the use of the type attributes. In the declaration for the <menu> element, for example, the type attribute is used to point to the menuType complex type declaration:

```
<xsd:element name="menu" type="menuType" minOccurs="1"
             maxOccurs="unbounded"/>
```

The <xsd:element> element is also used within <xsd:complexType> declarations to indicate what type of sub-elements an element can contain (for example, the top-level <item> element declaration in the example).

<xsd:simpleType>

In schema terminology, a simple type is used to declare an element that does not contain other elements. Similar to most programming languages, the schema specification provides several built-in simple types, such as string, integer, boolean, and dateTime. These simple types can also be used to construct user-defined extended types (such as declaring restrictions on an integer value that forces it to be greater than 0 and less than 1000).

<xsd:complexType>

Unlike the <xsd:simpleType> element, the <xsd:complexType> element is used to declare elements that may contain other elements. If a complex type declaration appears at the top level (as a child of the <xsd:schema> element), it must have a name attribute. It can then be referred to by an element declaration that uses the type attribute.

It is also possible to declare anonymous complex types. The <xsd:element> markup that declares the <restaurant> element, for instance, uses an unnamed complexType element to declare a sequence of child elements that it must contain.

<xsd:sequence>

In some cases, it is necessary to declare that a list of elements must appear in a particular order. The elements declared in an <xsd:sequence> must appear in the order given (subject to minOccurs and maxOccurs values, explained later).

For example, the <xsd:sequence> element within the <item> element declaration is equivalent to the <!ELEMENT> declaration in the basic restaurant DTD:

```
<!ELEMENT item (name, price, note?)?>
```

The sequence is implied by the order of the <xsd:element> elements, and the minOccurs attribute is used to simulate the ? DTD syntax.

<xsd:attribute>

Like the <!ATTLIST> DTD markup, the <xsd:attribute> element is used to declare the names and valid content of element attributes. In addition to the special attribute types defined in XML 1.0 (such as ID and IDREF), schema attributes can be declared to contain any built-in or user-defined simple type (string, integer, and so on).

The attribute declarations contained in the menuType complex type declaration use type and use attributes to indicate what values they may contain and whether the attribute is required. By default (if no use attribute is given), all attributes are optional.

<xsd:restriction>

The XML Schema language allows types (both simple and complex) to be extended to create new types. The <xsd:restriction> element indicates what type is being extended (using the base attribute) and what additional restrictions are being imposed on the base type to create the new type.

NOTE

The various types of restrictions that can be applied are called *facets*. A complete list of facets and how and where they can be applied can be found in the schema specification itself. See this book's Web site for links to the schema specification.

<xsd:pattern>

The top-level simple type declaration for the currency type extends the built-in xsd:string type to restrict it to strings that reflect dollar amounts. Within the restriction element, a pattern element is used to provide a simple regular expression:

```
<xsd:pattern value="$\d*\.\d\d"/>
```

This expression indicates that any value that matches the currency type must consist of a dollar sign ($) followed by zero or more digits, a decimal point, and two digits to the right of the decimal point. The full schema regular expression syntax is similar to the Perl regular expression syntax. For a complete reference see the schema specification itself.

<xsd:enumeration>

Another restriction that can be placed on element or attribute content is that the value must appear in an arbitrary list of valid values. Multiple <xsd:enumeration> elements may be used within an <xsd:restriction> element to provide the permitted values. The mealType simple type declaration declares a string-based value that must contain one of the strings `"Breakfast"`, `"Brunch"`, `"Lunch"`, or `"Dinner"`.

`<xsd:choice>`

The `choice` element is equivalent in some ways to the `|` operator in the basic DTD element declaration syntax. It indicates that one of the elements within the `<xsd:choice>` block may appear at that point in the target document. Based on the values of the `minOccurs` and `maxOccurs` attributes, however, multiple elements from the list may occur one after another in the target document. The markup for the `itemList` complex type uses the `choice` element with `maxOccurs="unbounded"` to permit any number of `<item>` and `<combo>` elements to appear in any order in the target document.

`minOccurs` and `maxOccurs` Attributes

Throughout the sample schema in Listing 2.5, the `minOccurs` and `maxOccurs` attributes are used to control how many times a particular element, sequence, or choice of elements may appear. If these attributes are not present on a particular element, the implied values are `1` and `1` (meaning that the given structure must appear one and only one time). By setting these values to a positive integer or zero, the number of times certain document structures may appear can be controlled. Besides integers, the `maxOccurs` attribute may contain the special value `unbounded`, which means that an unlimited number of occurrences may appear.

Wrapping Up

This has been a whirlwind tour of basic XML syntax, namespaces, and schema usage. It is obviously far from a complete reference to each of these technologies, but it should contain enough information to provide a springboard for an experienced developer to read and understand sophisticated XML examples right away. For pointers to useful XML-related sites, standards, and additional tutorials, visit the 🔗book's Web site.

Standards and Applications

CHAPTER 3

The Information Technology industry is rife with acronyms, made-up words, and terminology that is uniformly confounding to the outsider. Another field that has a similar love of unpronounceable and obscure terminology is aviation. My grandfather was a commercial pilot for many years, amassing more than 10,000 hours of flying time over the Appalachian mountains of West Virginia, Ohio, and Kentucky. I spent many hours down on the ramp, listening to pilots talk to each other.

Naturally, I was subjected to the same torture that many of my non-IT friends must experience when they are forced to listen to a conversation between two programmers. Imagine being a 10-year-old boy and trying to decipher the following anecdote: "Well, I was PIC of a flight from CKB to CLT. We were IMC and I was trying to get ATIS when my left mag went Tango Uniform." Fortunately, aviation terminology evolves much more slowly than IT terminology. I guess the fact that a misunderstanding can cause the listener to impact a mountain at 250 knots instead of just crashing a Web site tends to suppress innovation for innovation's sake. . . .

Since the initial release of the XML 1.0 recommendation in February 1998, myriad related and complementary technologies have been developed. In XML parlance, any custom vocabulary of XML tags is called an *application*. But many of these "applications" are actually extensions to XML itself (such as XML Schemas).

To an XML neophyte, understanding how the various technologies interrelate can be a difficult task. Further complicating matters, many of the new XML-related technologies are actually implemented using XML. For instance, the Extensible Stylesheet Language standard is intended to provide a framework for formatting and displaying XML data. Of course, these stylesheets are themselves written in XML, introducing the possibility of interesting self-referencing applications.

Technology Roadmap

Before we explore each specific XML-related technology in detail, you'll find it useful to have a high-level overview of where these technologies come from. Figure 3.1 depicts several of the most widely used XML technologies, their interrelationships, and their current status.

The rest of this chapter gives brief descriptions of the standards and applications shown in Figure 3.1. For convenience and ease of understanding, these topics have been organized into three broad categories: core standards, standard applications, and general applications.

Core Standards

The core standards category is composed of the original XML 1.0 specification and the rest of the fundamental standards that are logically bound to it. Taken as a group, these standards form the foundation on which new standards and applications can be built. They are relatively stable and are widely supported by XML parsers and tools.

XML 1.0 Recommendation

This is the specification of the XML language itself. It lays down the rules for how XML documents can be constructed, how they can be validated (using the Document Type Definition method), and how they can be encoded using various character sets. All other standards and applications either extend or depend on this specification.

Namespaces in XML

In a perfect world, Namespaces in XML would have been incorporated directly into the XML recommendation itself. But, in the interest of market timing, the W3C wisely decided to release XML 1.0 without namespaces. Namespaces provide support for mixing the vocabularies from multiple XML applications together in a single document.

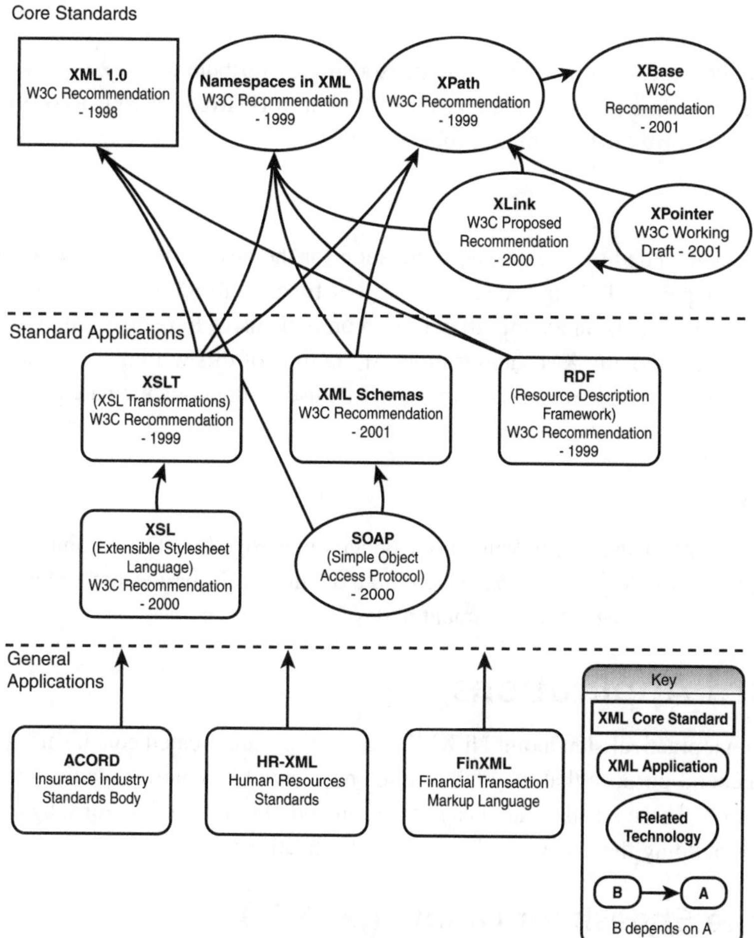

FIGURE 3.1
XML technology roadmap.

XPath

Many tools and standards that are intended to manipulate XML documents (XSLT, XML Schemas, and so on) need to be able to identify locations within and select portions of XML documents. Just as the Structured Query Language (SQL) supports selecting values from relational database systems, XPath supports selecting data from XML documents.

XBase

This is a very short recommendation that defines a special attribute called `xml:base`. This attribute serves the same purpose as the `<base>` element in HTML, which is to override the default base for relative URLs with an explicit base.

XLink

Because XML is intended to serve as the foundation for the next-generation "semantic web" on the Internet, hypertext linking is a critical piece of functionality it must support. The XML Linking Language effort is an attempt to define a comprehensive hypertext linking system that can be incorporated into any XML application. At the time of this writing, it has not yet been approved as an official W3C recommendation, but its use is already anticipated by standards such as XHTML.

XPointer

The XLink standard focuses on linking various documents together. The XPointer standard deals with locating single points or ranges within a document. It defines how XPath expressions may be used to locate XML document nodes.

Standard Applications

Although from a practical standpoint all XML applications are created equal, certain applications are so general-purpose that they fall into the purview of standards organizations (like the ISO or the W3C). These standard applications are intended to be used, in turn, by other developers who are building their own special-purpose applications.

Extensible Stylesheet Language (XSL)

One of the primary design goals of XML was to provide an environment where document content (such as a phone number) could be separated from presentation information (such as the formatting instructions making the phone number bold and italic). Although XML documents are very well suited to expressing information, at some point they generally must be formatted for human consumption. XSL is the W3C's solution to the problem of transforming and displaying XML documents.

XSL is actually a blanket term that covers two separate technologies—one for transforming XML documents into other formats and another for describing page layout and formatting in XML. These two technologies are called XSL Transformations and XSL Formatting Objects, respectively.

XSL Transformations (XSLT)

Oddly enough, the XSLT portion of the XSL recommendation is already a W3C recommendation (as of November 16, 1999). As with XML and Namespaces for XML, it was decided that the immediate need for an XML transformation language was too pressing to delay it until the entire XSL specification was complete. In operation, an XSLT stylesheet document is an XML document that contains templates that describe how a source document is to be modified to create a target document. Figure 3.2 shows an example of how this process works.

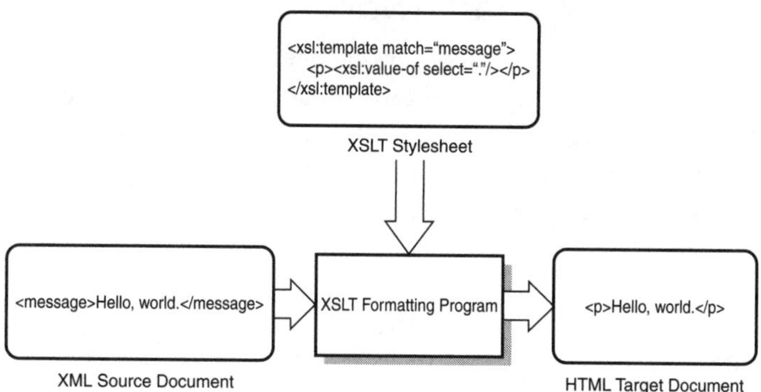

FIGURE 3.2
The XSLT transformation process.

Using this technique, the same source document might be rendered into half a dozen target formats (such as XHTML, XSL-FO, plain text, or a different XML application). Currently several full-featured standalone and integrated XSLT transformation programs are available. See the next chapter for a list and brief description of these tools.

XSL Formatting Objects (XSL-FO)

Unlike XSLT, XSL-FO does not specify how to transform XML into another format. Instead, it is a very sophisticated XML vocabulary for specifying how to lay out text and graphical information on a page (or series of pages). Although it is technically possible to author XSL-FO documents directly, the more common intended use is to use a transformation language (particularly XSLT) to transform an XML document into an XSL-FO document.

The XSL-FO portion of the XSL specification has still not been finalized, and there are presently no browsers or display programs that show XSL-FO pages directly. The current solution for testing and developing XSL-FO production systems is to use a translator program that converts XSL-FO documents into a more widely supported page-layout format (such as Adobe's PDF or PostScript).

XML Schema

One of the more controversial and widely discussed of the recent XML-related standards is the XML Schema recommendation. Schemas were originally intended to provide a more strongly typed and flexible language for validating the contents of XML documents. Like XSLT stylesheets, XML Schemas are themselves valid XML documents. Chapter 2, "XML Tutorial," includes a comprehensive introduction to both DTDs and schemas.

Resource Description Framework

As more and more content becomes available on the Internet, the need for some standardized method for cataloging and expressing information about a document's content becomes keener. Basically, the RDF recommendation defines an XML vocabulary for making informative statements about things. For instance, expressing the idea that "W. Scott Means is the author of Strategic XML" could be encoded in RDF like this:

```
<?xml version="1.0"?>
<rdf:RDF
  xmlns:rdf="http://www.w3.org/1999/02/22-rdf-syntax-ns#"
  xmlns:sxml="http://namespaces.strategicxml.com/example/bookinfo">
  <rdf:Description about="Strategic XML">
    <sxml:Author>W. Scott Means</sxml:Author>
  </rdf:Description>
</rdf:RDF>
```

As with XLink, the acceptance of RDF is considered to be an important part of the development of the semantic web. If more document authors take steps to provide meta-information about the information they publish, search engines will be able to provide higher-quality content to end users.

General Applications

The final category in Figure 3.1, "general applications," is meant to show a very small slice of the thousands of new XML applications being defined by end users and industry standards bodies every year. Whether it is a private markup language that is used only internally by a single company, or an approved language that is usable by an entire industry, this last category is what has truly driven the rapid growth of XML.

The one defining characteristic of applications that fall into this last category is that they are not really intended to be incorporated into other XML applications. Unlike a standard application, such as the mathematics markup language (MathML), a vocabulary for reporting quarterly financial results to the U.S. Government is not likely to become a widespread component of other XML documents. For a list of sites that act as repositories and listing services for these specialized applications, see this book's Web site.

Tools and Technologies

CHAPTER

4

One of my favorite workplace witticisms (those little sayings that are photocopied and posted on cubicle walls) is the saying "If all you have is a hammer, everything starts to look like a nail." This is painfully apparent in the IT world, where the cost in lost time and effort to learn a new tool means that the same old tools are often applied to problems to which they are not very well suited.

It is impossible for even the best-read, most up-to-date developer to have a thorough understanding of every new development in the IT field. And to be honest, there are a lot of new technologies that it wouldn't pay to learn (anybody want a copy of an old OS/2 programming book?). It's a foregone conclusion that XML is a new technology that is here to stay. But when you're surveying the XML landscape, it pays to have a broad understanding of the problems it can solve and the new problems it creates.

Technically, it's not necessary to ever actually *do* anything with an XML document. It can be a perfectly valid, well-formed document without your ever parsing it, transforming it, or transmitting it across the Internet. But real-world applications require that XML documents are actually used for something.

This chapter discusses some of the things that can be done with an XML document, and some of the tools that can do them. The lists of tools and products are by no means exhaustive. See this book's Web site for links to online resources for additional alternatives and more information.

XML Workflows

Figure 4.1 depicts a generic XML workflow. Not every application will involve all the steps shown, and many will include steps that are not present in this simple diagram.

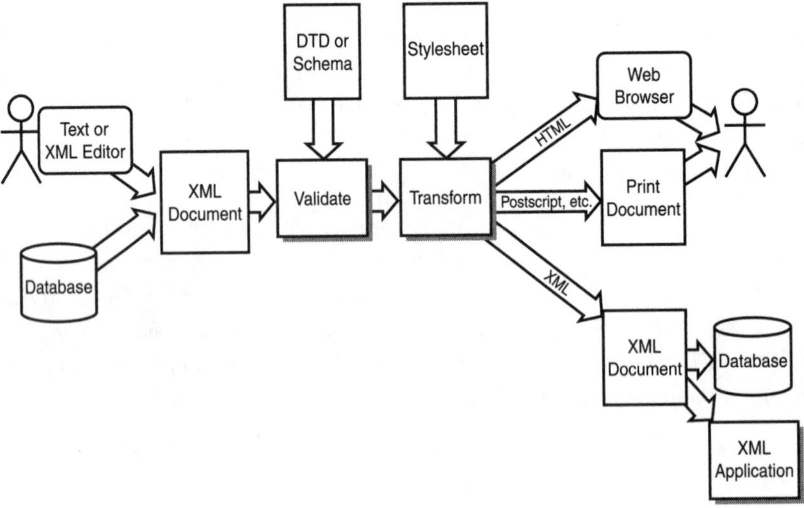

FIGURE 4.1
A basic XML document workflow.

The following sections discuss the various types of operations that are performed in a typical XML processing scenario.

Authoring Documents

Although many applications involve XML that is generated automatically (for example, the body of a SOAP message), there are at least as many instances in which the document is authored and maintained by a human being.

Text Editors

With the proliferation of massive Integrated Development Environments (such as Microsoft Visual Interdev and Borland's JBuilder 4.0), it is amazing how much can be accomplished with a lowly text editor. Unlike a sophisticated programming language with a large runtime library, an XML document has relatively few syntax structures to memorize. Without the need for online help and syntax completion, a simple text editor can provide a perfectly viable tool for writing XML documents. These are a few text editors you might consider:

- *Notepad* (shipped with Windows)—Really a terrible editor, but it is ubiquitous.
- *WordPad* (shipped with Windows)—Better than Notepad, but still not great for structured text editing.
- *SlickEdit* (`www.slickedit.com`)—A commercial programmer's editor. Has many features for integrating with software development processes (compilers, linkers, make programs, and so on). Good but expensive.
- *UltraEdit* (`www.ultraedit.com`)—A really good shareware editor with plenty of features for indentation, tab and space handling, and syntax highlighting.

For the record, all the XML sample documents in this book were written using UltraEdit. It has tons of features, is very inexpensive, and loads quickly (in under three seconds on my system).

WYSIWYG XML Editors

The idea of a what-you-see-is-what-you-get XML editor might seem to be an oxymoron. XML is not intended to be a presentation format, so what exactly does a WYSIWYG editor show you? In most cases, the high-end commercial editors are capable of displaying an XML document as a free-form prose view with embedded tags. The lower-end and freeware products usually provide only a tree view, showing nested tag relationships. These are some advanced features to look for:

- Integrated stylesheet editing (CSS and/or XSL)
- DTD and schema editing
- Good import/export facilities to non-XML data sources

A few dedicated XML editors available today are listed here:

- *XMLNotepad* (`msdn.microsoft.com/XML`)—A freely available tree-based XML editor. Awkward interface, but it is free.
- *XMetal Pro* (`www.xmetal.com`)—From the same company that produced HotMetal (a WYSIWYG HTML editor). Very full featured, has a nice free-form prose editing window that shows the XML tags as special icons embedded in the text (a la WordPerfect).

- *XMLSpy* (`www.xmlspy.com`)—Another GUI editor for XML document development. The latest version includes a graphical XML schema design view.

Opinions vary widely on the utility of visual XML editors. On one side, visual-editor fans like the fact that it is impossible to create a document that isn't well-formed and valid (if validation is being used). Text-editor aficionados, on the other hand, say that XML syntax is so simple that it is more efficient to edit it directly (despite the occasional syntax or structural error). In the end it comes down to a matter of personal preference, comfort level with XML syntax, and budgetary constraints.

Validating Documents

Whether developing new XML DTDs or schemas, creating new XML documents, or verifying that a program is generating correct XML output, being able to quickly validate an XML document is an important task. Every XML parser must at least be able to determine whether a particular document is well-formed. More sophisticated parsers can verify that the document's structure matches the formal description in a DTD or schema. The following sections discuss various tools that can be used to validate XML documents.

Web Browsers

After the initial breakneck race between Netscape and Internet Explorer for Internet domination, the rate of introduction of new browser features has slowed considerably. Microsoft has included some form of XML support in IE since version 5.0, although it didn't fully support the XSLT recommendation until version 5.5. The release of Netscape as an open-source product (Mozilla) did not appreciably accelerate the introduction of XML support. The most recent versions of Netscape and Mozilla do include support for displaying XML documents using CSS2 (no XSLT support is included).

The incorporation of XML parsing and validation into IE means that practically any Windows computer can be used to write and validate XML documents. To quickly validate a new XML document, simply display it using IE. Any well-formedness or validity errors will be flagged by the browser.

Standalone Validators

In many applications, it is desirable to independently check the well-formedness and validity of an XML document. Most XML parser packages provide simple standalone tools for parsing and validating documents from the operating-system command line. These tools always check for well-formedness, and they can also be configured to validate against the document's DTD and/or an associated schema file.

Web-Based Validation Services

Some Web sites provide tools for validating XML documents on the World Wide Web. Some of them require that the target document be hosted on another Web server, whereas others allow the user to upload a copy of the document. If you intend to perform a large number of validations, this type of tool can become cumbersome quickly. However, if you need to validate a document quickly and don't have a standalone tool or XML-enabled Web browser handy, these tools can be a useful alternative. These are two online validators available at the time of this writing:

- `http://www.ltg.ed.ac.uk/~richard/xml-check.html`
- `http://www.stg.brown.edu/service/xmlvalid/`

Viewing Documents

Although the focus tends to be on writing and validating XML documents, in the end the information in a document must be presented to a user. Although some Web browsers can display XML documents directly, most users would prefer not to have to interpret the raw XML source code. The mechanisms for making XML presentable to end users are generically called stylesheets.

One of the first (and most widely supported) stylesheet languages is Cascading Style Sheets (CSS). CSS was originally intended for use with HTML documents to allow authors to separate presentation information from the structural details of the HTML page. When XML began to be widely used, CSS was extended to support formatting and displaying XML documents. IE 5.0 included support for associating CSS stylesheets with XML documents. Unfortunately, because CSS does not support structural transformation of the target document, it is being deprecated as a display technique for XML documents.

Another, more common, method for displaying XML data is to transform it into HTML (using XSLT) and then present it using a Web browser.

Transforming Documents

Although XML is an excellent format for storing information, in many cases it is necessary to reformulate the information into another format for consumption by a particular application. The process of taking an XML document and reformulating it is called transformation.

The Extensible Stylesheet Language (XSL) is the de facto standard for transforming and displaying XML documents. The two branches of XSL cover transforming XML into another format (XSLT) and describing page layouts using a specialized XML vocabulary (XSL-FO). The most common way to present XML data to users today is to transform it (using XSLT) into HTML, which can be directly displayed by any Web browser. However, in the future, generating printed documentation (using a XSL-FO and tools such as FOP) will be at least as important as web presentation.

For the Web

Transforming XML for use by a Web browser is one of the most common tasks facing an application developer today. A few Web browsers (such as IE version 5.0 and above) can perform an XSLT transformation on the client. But because most Web sites do not want to limit their audiences, Web-site developers tend to perform transformations directly on the server and send HTML content to the browser. The sample application in Chapter 12, "Web Content Publishing," shows how this can be done.

For Printing

Although online viewing of XML data is a very common task, being able to generate both online and offline (printed) versions of a document is a very powerful concept. Keeping online and offline content synchronized is a difficult task for most companies, and integrating the two with XML can provide numerous benefits. The example in Chapter 18, "Unifying Product Documentation," shows how the data from Chapter 12 can be transformed (with XSLT) into a printable version using XSL-FO.

For Different Applications

As companies begin to share more and more information with their suppliers, customers, and partners, the need to transform from one XML format to another will increase. Take, for example, the following XML document that represents a simple parts order for Company A:

```
<?xml version="1.0" encoding="UTF-8"?>
<order>
  <item quantity="1" SKU="235144"/>
  <item quantity="2" SKU="519151"/>
</order>
```

As long as both parties in the transaction use the same precise XML format for orders, this can be sent directly from Company A to Company B for fulfillment. But suppose that Company B's order format looks like this:

```
<?xml version="1.0" encoding="utf-8"?>
<order>
  <SKU count="1">235144</SKU>
  <SKU count="2">519151</SKU>
</order>
```

The order from Company A would not be recognized by Company B's system. Because XSLT can be used to generate XML as well as HTML output, the first order can be automatically transformed into the second order using a simple XSLT script:

```
<?xml version="1.0" encoding="UTF-8"?>
<xsl:stylesheet version="1.1" xmlns:xsl="http://www.w3.org/1999/XSL/Transform">
  <xsl:template match="order">
    <order>
      <xsl:for-each select="item">
        <SKU count="{@quantity}"><xsl:value-of select="@SKU"/></SKU>
      </xsl:for-each>
    </order>
  </xsl:template>
</xsl:stylesheet>
```

When companies can tightly couple their key information systems, they become more competitive than before. XSL transformations can be used to facilitate this type of integration.

Storing and Retrieving XML Content

Because the XML recommendation makes a point of not dictating how documents must be stored, users are constantly coming up with new ways to use XML for data storage and retrieval.

Text Files

The simplest way to store an XML document is as a normal text file. The file can then be passed to an XML parser for processing, copied, or even served up by a Web server. The only technical issue that may need to be addressed is the character encoding of the file in question. The `encoding="..."` portion of the `<?xml?>` declaration is intended to tell an XML parser what character set was used to encode the document in question. By default, the encoding is assumed to be the UTF-8 encoding of Unicode. As long as your document contains only characters from the seven-bit ASCII character set, it is already compliant with the UTF-8 character set.

If you are authoring documents with a tool or on an operating system where text files are non-ASCII, you may need to change the `encoding` declaration to allow an XML parser to properly interpret it.

Database Integration

Many RDBMS systems (such as the latest versions of Microsoft's and Oracle's products) are incorporating the capability to transmit and receive data using XML. The most straightforward application of XML in a database application involves transmitting the results of a query as an XML document rather than as columnar text.

Unfortunately, there has been little effort at standardization of XML support among database vendors. Any application that wants to take advantage of these "special" features runs the risk of becoming tied to a particular database vendor's platform-specific extensions.

XML Servers

The XML server is a new class of database server that natively stores and retrieves data in XML format. What exactly an XML server comprises varies from product to product, but in most cases they support the following:

- Storing and retrieving XML documents
- Querying stored data using an XML selection syntax (such as XPath or the experimental XQuery language)
- Tight integration with XML programming APIs such as DOM or SAX

Some of these servers actually use a RDBMS system to store and retrieve XML content, further blurring the line between XML servers, database servers, Web servers, and general-purpose application servers.

Programming with XML

When it comes time to incorporate XML into a proprietary application, a few widely available open-source implementations of XML Application Programming Interfaces (APIs) are available.

Without going into language specifics, the major XML APIs are either tree-based or event-based. Depending on your specific application, understanding the difference between these two API types can mean the difference between a successful and an unsuccessful development project.

Tree-Based APIs

Tree-based APIs, such as the W3C's Document Object Model (DOM), parse an entire XML document and store the resulting information in a memory-based tree structure. This tree structure is then made available to the client application. The client can traverse, query, modify, and generally manipulate the memory model of the document as it pleases.

The advantage of this approach is that all the information in the document is available to the application at all times. For applications such as XML editors, this functionality is crucial. The disadvantage is that the entire application must be loaded into memory before any processing can be done. For very large documents, the system may not have sufficient virtual memory to allow a document to be stored.

Event-Based APIs

Unlike tree-based approaches, event-based APIs do not store the contents of a document in memory as it is parsed. Instead, notifications are sent to the client application as document structures are parsed and recognized. Because the document data is never stored in memory, very large documents can be processed in this way. It is up to the application writer to determine how much and which information from the document is to be saved, and which is to be discarded.

Summary

There are a staggering array of different tools, parsers, APIs, and editors available for working with XML data today. The discussions in Part II, "XML Zones" and the examples in Part III, "Applying the Technology" try to provide a broad survey of the various approaches and technologies that can be used to build XML solutions.

XML Enabling the Enterprise

CHAPTER 5

One of my favorite Monty Python sketches of all times is the so-called "Architect Sketch." In this sketch John Cleese plays an architect who "hadn't fully divined" his client's attitude toward their tenants. Whereas his clients wanted a simple block of flats, he had designed a state-of-the-art abattoir. And although they were very appreciative of his wonderful slaughterhouse design, it didn't do them a bit of good in solving their actual problem, which was housing tenants.

As with any other technology, it is possible to grossly misuse XML if you don't have a solid understanding of its strengths and limitations. By studying the various ways to use XML within a large company, you can prevent misunderstandings like the one above from ever happening.

Few technologies can be applied to such a wide variety of problems as XML can. One of the most unusual aspects of the XML phenomenon is how well it is suited to both programming and documentation applications. The same XML editor could be used to view a company's annual report and verify an XML message stream between two servers.

There are so many compelling applications of XML that it is easy to lose focus on where it can provide the most value with the least effort. No system lives in a vacuum, and it is impossible to adopt XML in one place without impacting systems and users in another.

Deciding where and when to implement XML support within an organization requires a thorough knowledge of how XML can be applied to various business problems. Data storage, content publishing, and transmission are three major areas that can immediately benefit from XML solutions.

Storing Data

The proliferation of cheap and powerful low-end servers and personal computers has inadvertently fueled the uncontrolled fragmentation of information. Within a large organization, important documents, spreadsheets, and data files are scattered across personal workstations and file servers. With each software vendor implementing its own proprietary file format, the problem of searching and indexing all of these scattered documents would be insurmountable.

Proprietary file formats also guarantee that information will be lost over time. As products evolve, old file formats tend to be left behind. Two or three versions later, frequently even the product that created a file is unable to read it. The widespread acceptance of XML by product vendors promises to alleviate this problem, and at the same time open documents to new, sophisticated search engines.

A long-term migration of corporate documents to XML-based formats is inevitable. But the timetable for such a migration is heavily dependent on the support of application vendors, such as Microsoft. In the interim, some pure XML editing tools are gaining acceptance, primarily in the Web publishing community.

Besides simple document storage, various structured storage products have implemented some form of XML support. Popular relational database systems (such as Microsoft SQL Server 2000 and Oracle 9i) now support the retrieval of query results in XML format. Unlike adopting new document standards, rebuilding existing applications to take advantage of XML storage products requires considerably more planning and effort on the part of the Information Technology organization.

Publishing Content

With the globalization of large corporations and the need to offer ever greater quantities of information on the Internet, content publishing has never been a more difficult proposition.

Traditional methods of content publishing require either duplication of effort (for instance, maintaining the same content in both HTML and Word document format at the same time) or a sacrifice in quality and expressiveness by offering content using the lowest common denominator (for example, offering a PDF file for download).

One of the major benefits of moving to XML as a corporate data-storage format is the ease of distributing data in different formats. The "extensible" part of XML means that your document formats can grow indefinitely as new types of information are required.

The availability of XSLT means that a single master XML document can contain enough information to generate online, printed, and even audio versions of its content. A single master document can be transformed into anything from plain text to a printable PostScript version, with no loss of fidelity or information.

Transmitting Content

Before the Internet, physical connectivity was the major road block to system integration. Each company operated as an island, with a local area network (LAN) connecting computers at a single physical location, and perhaps (but not necessarily) a wide area network (WAN) connecting multiple locations together. High telecommunications costs made this type of networking expensive and the cost of dedicated connections between different companies prohibitive. Then the rapid growth of the Internet drove connectivity costs down to the point where now every business can have an affordable network connection to every other business, at will.

After the network connectivity problem was solved, data formats become the primary issue. With rapid connectivity also came the need to protect sensitive corporate data from unauthorized users. Firewalls and proxy servers proliferated to keep hostile Internet users away from critical systems. Even within a single organization, mixed vendors and incompatible technologies made transporting data between systems impractical.

New standards such as XML-RPC and SOAP have greatly simplified the task of connecting otherwise-incompatible systems. The capability of XML to be encoded as UTF-8 (of which ASCII is a subset) means that almost every computer system developed in the past 40 years is capable of reading and writing messages sent in XML format. That coupled with the simple syntax of XML means that even the oldest legacy systems can support XML parsing and more sophisticated protocols that are built on XML, such as SOAP.

Enterprise Zones

When viewed in terms of the users it serves, every large corporation can be divided into well-defined zones. For our purposes, a zone is defined by the type of information consumer that is served, not necessarily by the information system that is used to do the serving. For example, the same Web server and database might be used to serve content to public Web users and connect with the supply chain automation systems of parts vendors. Although the same infrastructure is used for both, the types and applications of XML are decidedly different. Figure 5.1 shows a road map to the enterprise zones that are discussed throughout the book.

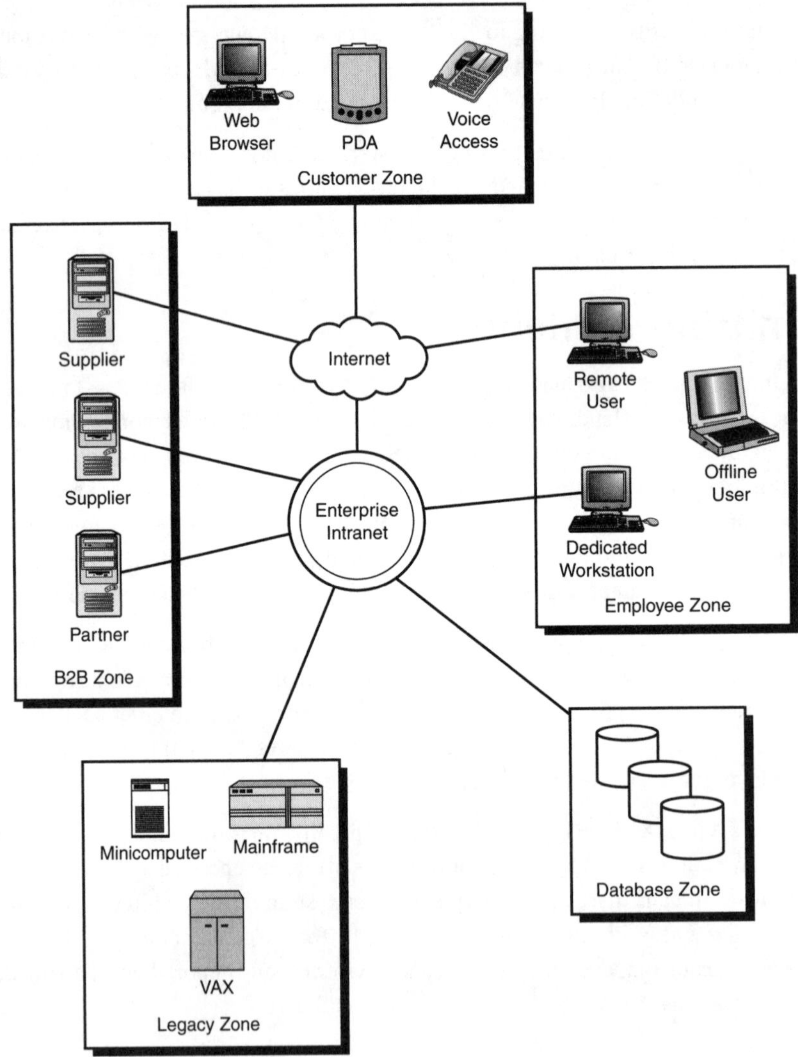

FIGURE 5.1
Dividing information systems into distinct zones.

Part II, "XML Zones," explores each of these zones in detail, and Part III, "Applying the Technology," gives concrete examples of XML-based applications for each zone.

XML Zones

IN THIS PART

The Customer Zone

CHAPTER

6

One day, my wife and I went to a local electronics superstore (that shall remain nameless) to resolve a problem with our credit statement. After waiting in line for about 30 minutes, we finally got to the service desk. The young lady at the desk listened patiently as my wife explained the problem, typed a few commands into her terminal, and then informed us without a trace of sarcasm, "We're just the customer service department—we can't help you here."

Her manager overheard this exchange and whisked her off to perform some pressing function in the back room. After some further discussion, we eventually resolved our problem. Every business relies on the patronage of its customers. Making sure that customers can get what they want, when they want it, should be everyone's job (even customer service's.)

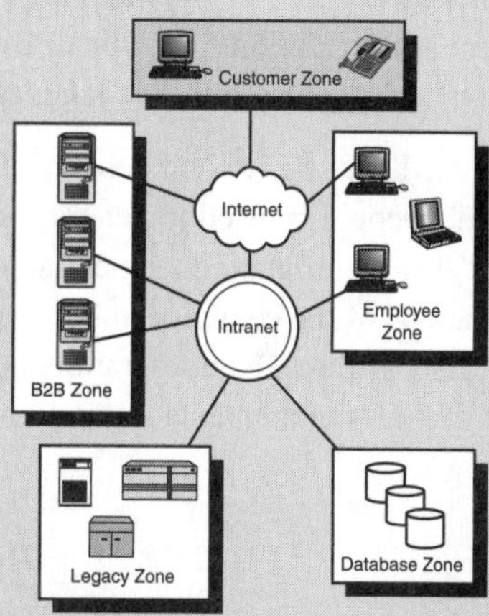

Within a large company's IT department, there is rarely (if ever) any interaction with actual customers. Although there is a tendency to characterize the managers in departments that depend on IT services (such as sales, marketing, customer support, and finance) as "customers," in reality, they lack the one attribute that true customers have: the ability to go elsewhere.

Despite all threats and dire warnings, the number of cases in which a company has actually disbanded its own internal IT department and outsourced its critical business functions are few and far between. So, whether you're building applications to serve your peers within the company or to serve the actual consumers of your company's products, the goal is still to build systems that are flexible enough to meet current and future as-yet-unidentified business needs.

What Is a "Customer"?

According to the *Oxford American Dictionary,* a *customer* is "a person who buys goods or services from a shop or business." But the alternate definition is "a person one has to deal with, *an ugly customer*." Keeping a person in the first category from becoming one in the second category should be a major goal of any organization. Whether dealing with users of internal IT systems or real customers in the outside world, offering relevant, up-to-date information in a useful format is the holy grail of any good IT group.

Of all the users of a company's IT systems, customers are the least tolerant of problems, perceived or real. In many cases, what the user reports as a problem is actually an intentional function of the system. Although employees and partners might be forced to use systems that are difficult to use, true customers likely will use their freedom of choice and will take their business elsewhere.

Systems that serve customers need to be simple and reliable. On the Internet, this means that customers need to be able to access the information they need in a format that they can use in a language that they can understand. In a perfect world, these goals can be met without the user ever realizing that it took any effort at all.

Customers don't adapt to poorly designed systems—they abandon them. Particularly on the Internet, where it is so simple to hit the Back button and try another site, delivering the right content at the right time is critical. But to keep supplying a site with fresh content in multiple formats and possibly multiple languages is a daunting task.

Using XML to receive and deliver information yields incredible flexibility. A single master document could be used to generate dozens of targeted Web pages with complete consistency. Modifying the original document automatically updates all the related pages. Foreign-language translations of the content can be stored within the document itself, using the standard `xml:lang` attribute. Nonprogrammers, using readily available XML editing tools, can perform most routine site maintenance and update content as required.

Types of Customer Interactions

Studying customer behavior is an entire subscience of product marketing. Although the IT department might not be directly involved with sales and marketing plans, the information systems that it provides must be capable of supporting the campaigns and promotions required to promote and sell the company's products.

Knowing what types of information must be presented to a customer at different phases of the acquisition cycle makes system design decisions simpler.

Unsolicited Advertising

What can a new technology such as XML offer to traditional advertising media such as direct mail, print, radio, and so on? Marketing and communications agencies are traditionally slow to adopt new technologies. The growing importance of the Web and Internet-based marketing has forced them to update their skills and systems to meet the demand for technologically sophisticated advertising campaigns.

One possible application of XML to product advertising and promotion is in the area of unsolicited advertising. The content of e-mail-based advertising and the content of direct-mail campaigns frequently overlap. Using a common XML format to contain the information for a particular promotion reduces the chances of erroneous or inconsistent information being disseminated to customers. Figure 6.1 shows how XML documents could be combined and transformed to produce targeted advertising collateral.

A single well-designed XML template can simplify building current and future promotions, while eliminating information replication errors. As customer relationship management (CRM) applications become more sophisticated, the need for automated tools to construct campaigns and promotions becomes readily apparent.

Company Information

Particularly on the Internet, being able to present accurate and easy-to-index information about your company is the key to good search engine placement. By storing financial information, press releases, and investor information in XML format and then generating HTML pages on demand, company information is guaranteed to be fresh and consistent. This also makes the job of the Web designers easier because they can focus on the look and feel of the site without having to be involved in the creation of the actual page content. Figure 6.2 shows how corporate information can be kept current through the use of a single, canonical XML document source. This document need not be a static file, but could draw content from other XML data sources (such as an XML-aware database).

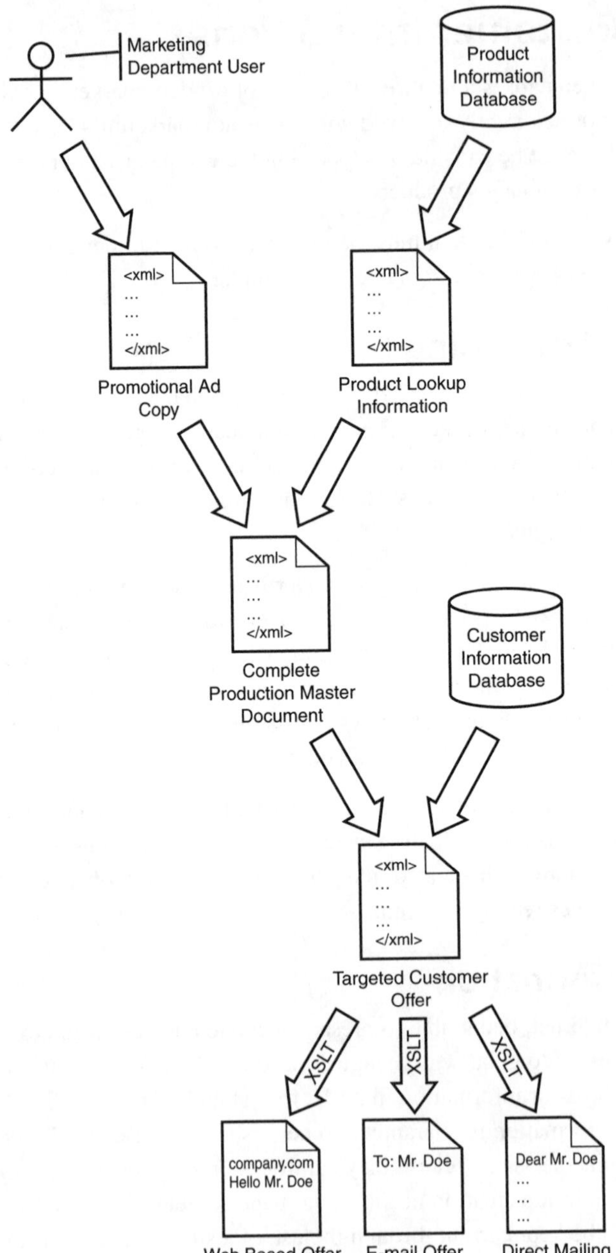

FIGURE 6.1
Merging XML data into targeted customer offers.

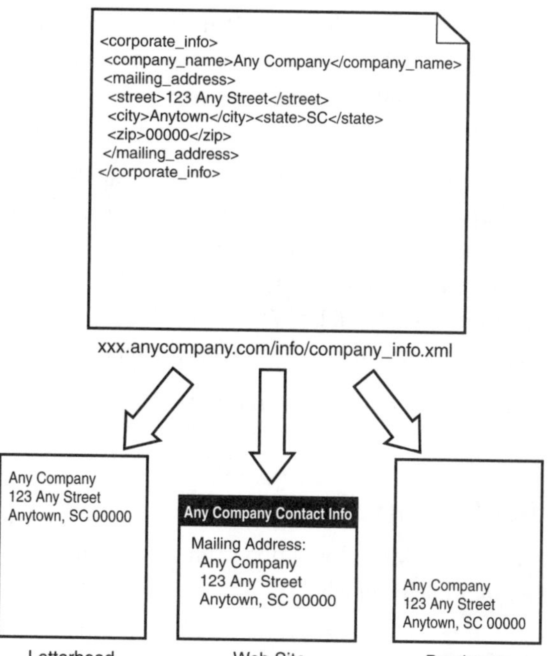

FIGURE 6.2
Retrieving corporate information from a central XML source.

Various government agencies are moving toward XML as a reporting format. The Securities and Exchange Commission (`www.sec.gov`) already allows companies to file their EDGAR documents in XML format. The U.S. Patent and Trademark Office (`www.uspto.gov`) is in the process of deploying new XML patent application forms. Although these programs are currently voluntary, the long-term trend toward eliminating paper-based forms cannot be ignored. Moving internal systems to XML can only help make that eventual transition less painful.

▶**See** Chapter 12, "Web Content Publishing" for an example of a system like this.

Product Documentation

Traditionally, product documentation is developed by a technical documentation team whose goal is to create attractive and complete printed documentation. As the demand for electronic and online documentation increased, hybrid approaches such as Microsoft's HTML help format were used with mixed results. One of the biggest problems facing documentation writers was that no single format was capable of containing all the information required for every possible output format.

HTML was ideal for displaying online help on the Web but was not suitable for producing high-quality printed documentation. Document-oriented formats such as PDF produced high-quality printed output but were too monolithic for use as a general-purpose online format. Compromises had to be made, and frequently the quality of the documentation suffered.

By building product documentation in XML, it is possible to satisfy not only current documentation requirements, but also future requirements. The open-ended nature of XML document construction makes it very easy to extend a basic document to incorporate additional information as it becomes necessary. Then, using XSLT, unnecessary information can be filtered out, depending on the target application. A public Web site could show content marked for general release, while internal reports could show additional proprietary information.

▶**See** Chapter 18, "Unifying Product Documentation" for an example of this type of application.

Product Technical Support

Figure 6.3 shows how the same XML information source can be used to deliver product support information through multiple channels.

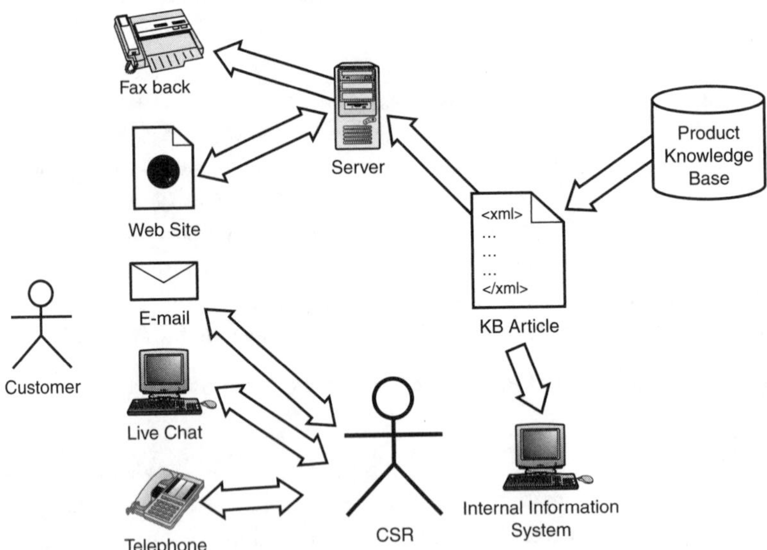

FIGURE 6.3
Delivering a single knowledge-base article via multiple channels.

Existing database solutions can be quickly adapted to XML delivery using new, XML-enabled versions of the underlying DB engine. The latest versions of both Microsoft's and Oracle's database products have built-in support for extracting SQL data in XML format. When the data is in XML format, XSLT transformations can be applied to produce content that is appropriate for Web, e-mail, or even fax delivery.

Premium support content can be maintained inline with free content using XML tags to differentiate. When the content is accessed by external users, the premium content is filtered out during the transformation process. Internal users and product support technicians can view the entire message, including any premium content.

▶**See** Chapter 18 for an example of this type of application.

Delivering Targeted Information

Before XML, complex Web sites that deliver targeted information to users were built using scripting and RDBMS technology. If a company wanted to host an online monthly newsletter, for instance, a programmer developed a database schema to contain the articles, advertisements, and editorial information. Then he developed a Web application that could display data from the database and possibly allow users to dynamically update the database. If the structure of the newsletter needed to change, the underlying schema had to be modified, and any scripts dependent on the schema had to be fixed as well.

This programmer/DBA intensive approach created several problems:

- Systems either lacked flexibility or were extremely complex.
- Programmers were forced to develop custom caching systems to improve performance as user loads increased.
- Database systems are inefficient for storing and retrieving static content.

XML combined with XSLT offers most of the power of script/database solutions with a fraction of the complexity and overhead. Rather than involving a programmer in structural changes, a user with a WYSIWYG XML editor can make any desired changes to the newsletter document type definition. Then a Web designer can update the XSLT transformation scripts so that the new content is correctly displayed. As a side benefit, the entire text of the newsletter is available in XML format for other applications (such as formatting for e-mail or print distribution).

Capturing Customer Data

So far, most of the customer-related XML applications have been one-way: from the company to the customer. But initiatives are under way (such as the XForms specification being developed by the W3C) for describing Web-based forms in XML. Unlike existing HTML forms, XML forms promise to help constrain data entry based on expected data types and application rules.

XML is a natural format for data collection, but the required tools and platforms are not yet available. Even after XForms becomes an official W3C recommendation, there will be a long wait for Web browsers that support the more sophisticated forms standard.

Although Web-based XML forms will not be available in the near future, proprietary vertical applications can begin incorporating XML right away. XML is an excellent format for storing responses to surveys, training records, status reports, expense reports, and so on. With the wide variety of XML parsers available, adding XML to existing applications is relatively painless.

Distributing Information in XML

Most of the publishing solutions mentioned so far involve transforming XML into another format for presentation to the user. But, in some cases, the final transformation step is not required.

For example, take the simple online banking site design shown in Figure 6.4.

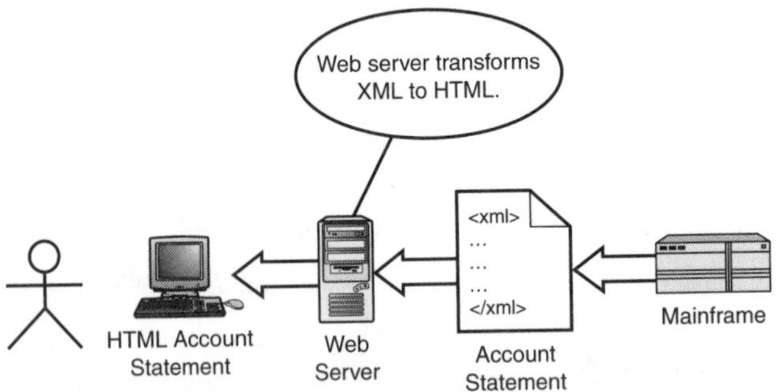

FIGURE 6.4
XML account statement transformed to HTML for Web access.

As more personal productivity software is XML-enabled, the demand for access to raw personal information in XML will increase. Many personal accounting packages already download financial information, but, for the most part, the protocols are proprietary and vary among financial institutions. Figure 6.5 shows how the raw XML could be delivered directly to an application running on the user's local workstation.

The best part of this type of functionality is that after the XML-based publishing system has been built, it is available for free. To offer access to the raw XML data, all that is required is for the Web server to pass the original data without applying any transformations to it. This is yet another argument in favor of moving to XML as a standard corporate data format.

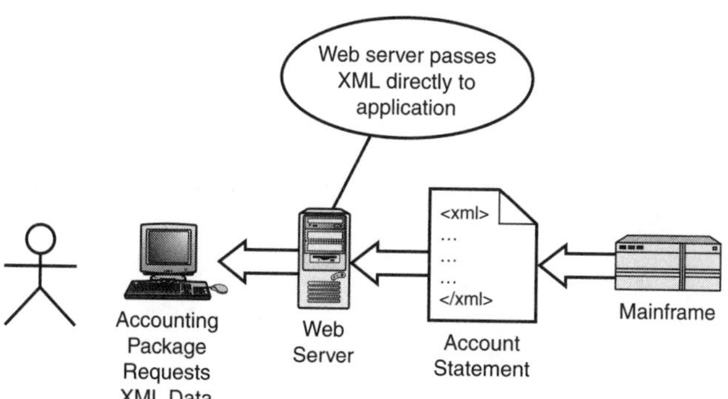

FIGURE 6.5
XML account statement delivered directly to an application on a client PC.

▶**See** the Automating Internal Processes with XML project (in Chapter 13) for an example of this type of application.

Conclusions

Technology that is considered to be a strategic benefit today will become par for the course tomorrow. As users become accustomed to using the Web to access information about their bank accounts, investment portfolios, and utility bills, they will begin to take that ability for granted. The challenge for IT systems architects is to build a system that can not only meet the needs of today, but anticipate the needs of tomorrow. Leveraging the power and flexibility of XML as an underlying data format can make this job much simpler.

The Employee Zone

CHAPTER 7

At one point in my career, I was working for a company that required its employees to file weekly time sheets outlining how much time they spent working on various projects. The system was DOS-based (this was in the early 1990s), slow, unintuitive, and prone to frequent crashes. One person in the entire organization really knew how to use it, and her time was monopolized by clueless engineers (like yours truly) who couldn't make the thing perform. It got to the point that time entry was given a project code of its own, to account for the time spent accounting for our time!

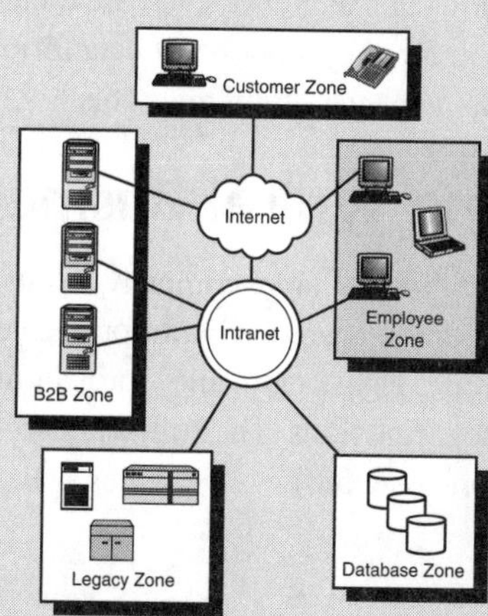

One area in which many otherwise good companies fall down is in the area of internal IT systems. Unlike an external Web site, internal systems are seldom seen by outsiders. The "if it ain't broke, don't fix it" mentality can become so entrenched that, unless the system stops working entirely (as many did during the Year 2000 watershed), it will never be upgraded.

Because internal users are a captive audience—and because monies spent on internal IT projects come directly out of the bottom line—the quality of internal systems is frequently not on par with that of production systems used by customers. The company's most experienced engineers are usually allocated to projects that bring in revenue, while less senior developers are tasked with building and maintaining systems that are truly critical to an organization's day-to-day operations.

Proprietary Systems

Most large companies have developed "home-grown" solutions to typical business problems. Particularly in software companies, the temptation to quickly throw together a fat-client application (using VB, Delphi, or other RAD tool of choice) backed by a database is almost overwhelming. The price tag on off-the-shelf enterprise applications can be intimidating, and when the costs for customization are factored in, build vs. buy becomes an attractive option.

Unfortunately, demands for new features frequently outstrip the development budget for these internal tools. After they have been implemented and deployed, the burden of developing, testing, and deploying upgrades is more than many IT departments can handle.

Also, sharing information between departments using different systems can be problematic. Incompatible database schemas, competing development platforms (Microsoft versus Java and open source), and file formats make connecting systems within the enterprise time-consuming (and money-consuming).

Replacing proprietary data formats and transports with XML-based solutions can ease the transition to more open solutions. Taking small steps, such as implementing XML data import and export functions, can pave the way for better interoperability. Adopting an Internet-ready RPC standard such as SOAP can ease connectivity problems between remote locations. In many cases, removing proprietary data format support and implementing XML can actually simplify the maintenance of internal tools.

Some Typical Business Systems

Although every large company has its own unique business model, the mechanics of day-to-day operations are fairly uniform. Every large company must deal with employees, financial reporting, legal compliance, project management, and a host of other mundane but critical business functions. The following sections give some examples of back-office systems that support basic business activities.

Human Resources

Between recruiting, professional development, benefits administration, and government compliance, corporate HR departments have significant data-processing requirements. Frequently, paper-based files are used to track various events in an employee's career, making the task of collecting aggregate information difficult. Although the utopian vision of a paperless office is still a very long way off, XML is definitely a step in the right direction.

The highly personal nature of information in HR systems dictates that access be strictly limited. A benefits administrator doesn't need access to an employee's stock option grant information. The payroll department doesn't need access to his performance reviews.

Storing information in XML and applying strategic transformations can help ensure that information is made available on a "need-to-know" basis. For instance, all employee files could be made available on an internal Web server. Different departments are limited by server-side transformations to see only the data that is relevant to the task at hand.

▶**See** the Web Content Publishing project (Chapter 12) for an example of a system like this.

Personnel Files

A typical employee's personnel file can contain large quantities of disparate information. Types of information located in a personnel file might include the following:

- Compensation information
- Personal contact information
- Performance reviews
- Benefits usage

Many companies use specialized vertical applications for tracking personnel information. By requesting that vendors implement XML for data import and export, you can help ensure that your critical information will be easily accessible in the future. One of the greatest features of XML is its self-documenting nature. Unlike binary file formats, XML makes the relationships between data elements explicit through the use of text-based tags. An XML document written today will be just as valid and easy to understand 20 years from now (although the actual physical media it is stored on may be obsolete by that time).

Corporate Directory

Maintaining contact information within a large organization is a full-time job. New employees are being added. Existing employees move. Keeping track of physical addresses, mail stops, telephone numbers, e-mail address, network connections, and so on is problematic. The need for rapid access to this information precludes storing and accessing this type of information directly in XML. However, for updating, storing offline, and transmitting directory information, XML is a natural choice.

Currently, technologies such as LDAP are used to integrate contact information with groupware applications (such as Microsoft Exchange, Novell GroupWise, and so on). XML can be used to bridge the gap between the online version of this information and Web and print media.

▶**See** the Unifying Product Documentation project (Chapter 18) for an example of a system like this.

Financial and Accounting

Reliable financial forecasting requires accurate information about corporate expenditures and income. One of the earliest XML applications was the Microsoft BizTalk language, geared toward automating financial systems and business-to-business transactions. Planning the migration to online record keeping with XML should be on every CFO's to do list.

Emerging standards such as the Extensible Business Reporting Language (XBRL) and EDGAR online promise to remove the need for labor-intensive filing of paper forms with regulatory agencies. When all the relevant corporate records are available in some XML dialect, it becomes a relatively trivial problem to transform them for use by analysts, auditors, and government agencies.

Time Sheets

Many service-oriented companies need to track time spent working on projects for specific customers. Particularly in service-oriented companies, accurately tracking employee contributions to billable projects is crucial to maintain profitability. Unfortunately, most time-reporting systems are based on proprietary legacy technologies.

Web-based time and accounting systems are gaining momentum. With recent advances in server-side XML technology, creating and storing time-sheet information in XML is becoming a valuable complement to database-oriented solutions. When employees are offline, geographically disbursed, or onsite with a customer, the capability to enter and submit time-sheet information in XML via e-mail is a welcome change to the error-prone fax-based method.

▶**See** the Offline Order Processing Using Store-and-Forward project (Chapter 14) for an example of a system like this.

Expense Reports

Spreadsheet-based expense solutions are difficult to assimilate into an automated framework. Even with powerful scripting languages (such as Microsoft's Visual Basic for Applications), developing reliable systems that integrate information from multiple documents into a single, coherent database is difficult. As more XML editing tools and forms packages become available, XML will become the format of choice for documenting and submitting incurred expenses.

Legal

Despite the somewhat antitechnology bias of the legal profession, XML is making inroads in selected applications. With the approval of the E-Sign Act, the U.S. government has opened the door to legally binding electronic documents. Major standards organizations are working on standards to integrate XML and digital signature information, such as the Internet Engineering Task Force's (`www.ietf.org`) XML Digital Signatures initiative. Legally binding electronic documents promise to greatly simplify the task of managing complex business relationships.

Patent Filings

The U.S. Patent and Trademark Office has implemented the Electronic Filing System, a system that enables users to submit patent applications over the Internet. Online collaboration between IP lawyers and engineers can streamline the process of protecting vital corporate technology.

Product Development

Creating a viable product for a given market in a timely manner requires clear communication among various groups. Most professional development organizations have some processes in place for writing product requirements, design specifications, implementation specifications, and product documentation. In many cases, these documentation requirements are fulfilled by using regular word-processing tools.

Product Documentation

Currently, the requirements, design, development, documentation, and support phases of a product have distinct (and often separate) documentation standards. Frequently, the marketing, design, development, and testing departments develop their documents in a vacuum, interacting only with their nearest neighbors in the development process. Figure 7.1 shows how separate documents limit interaction among the various groups.

Adopting a common XML framework for all product-related information keeps various internal groups "in sync." Encoding product information in XML enables a snowball approach to product documentation. Each group adds its own comments and content to the master design document, and the end result is an up-to-date and complete description of every phase of product development. Figure 7.2 illustrates this approach.

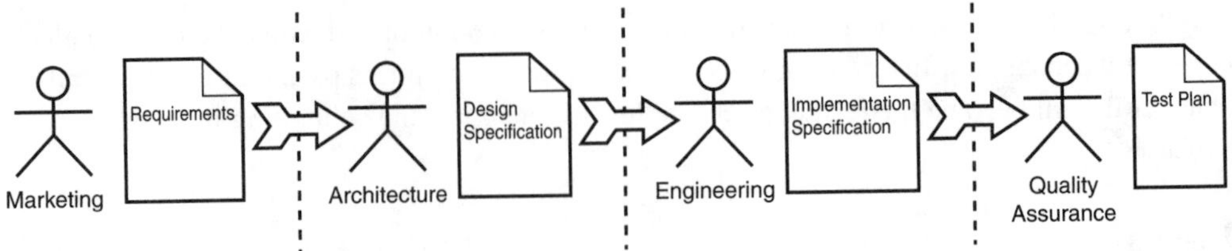

FIGURE 7.1
Compartmentalization leads to out-of-date information.

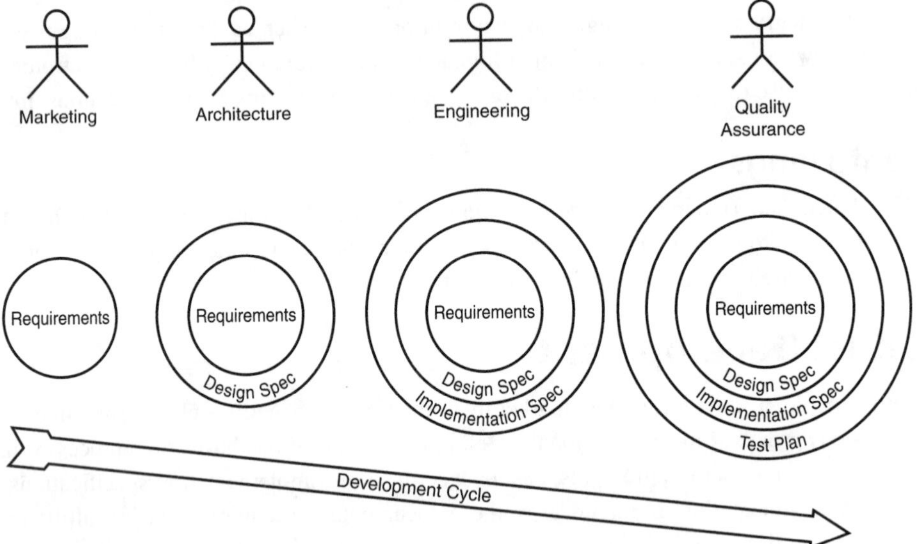

FIGURE 7.2
Combined product-development documentation.

By combining all product-related documentation in a single source, it is possible to answer queries as they arise. Test plans can link directly to the relevant portion of the implementation spec. Features can be linked back directly to the requirements they address. A more consistent view of the product as a whole can be achieved. Then, through XSLT, this information can be delivered in both human and machine-readable formats.

Customer Support

Constructing an accurate picture of a customer's status within a company's IT systems can be complex. Often transactional information from a legacy system must be combined with relational data stored in a database or data mart. Connecting these systems and combining the data that they provide has traditionally been very difficult. XML-based protocols such as SOAP promise to simplify the acquisition and presentation of real-time customer information. Figure 7.3 shows a typical IT back-office system, including the protocols used to communicate between systems.

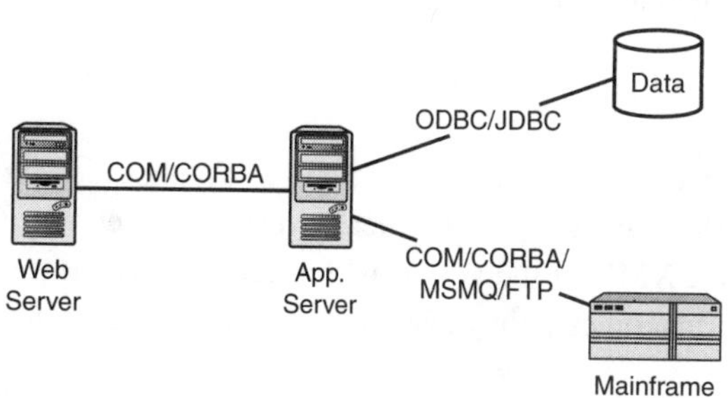

FIGURE 7.3
Typical tightly coupled IT system.

Proprietary binary protocols such as CORBA, DCOM, and RPC are difficult to access from foreign platforms, such as Web servers. Frequently, they require reliable network connections, tight integration between the host systems, and large amounts of custom development.

Standardizing on XML for intrasystem messaging makes it easier to provide real-time Web-based access to customer information. Geographically distributed applications become simpler because HTTP/SOAP solutions can pass directly through corporate firewalls. Also, when data can be submitted and retrieved in XML, new access methods can be developed rapidly. When standards such as XForms become more mature, it should be possible to build an application that reads and updates mainframe information directly from a client's browser. Figure 7.4 shows a more open system that relies heavily on SOAP and HTTP for communications.

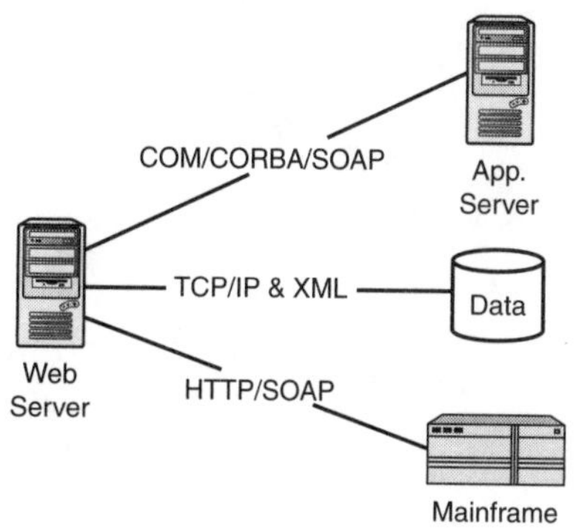

FIGURE 7.4
Loosely coupled IT system using HTTP and SOAP.

Simpler protocols and XML message formats reduce the amount of effort required to present information to end users. Frequently, data from the mainframe or database server can be reformulated as HTML directly using XSLT, without the need for custom coding. The network connectivity requirements for HTTP also are much less demanding than those for more sophisticated protocols such as RPC or DCOM.

Conclusions

The need for good internal systems will never go away. Whether they are purchased or home-grown, they will still need to integrate with other systems in the enterprise. Ensuring that new systems smoothly support XML, at the very least for data import and export, will extend their usefulness and act as an insurance policy against premature obsolescence.

The B2B Zone

CHAPTER 8

In late 1999, the hottest buzzword for new Internet startups was B2B. Business-to-business exchanges promised ultra-efficient global marketplaces for raw materials, goods, and services. One of my favorite movie scenes of all time is from the spoof-rockumentary This Is Spinal Tap. An interviewer was talking to one of the band members about his custom-made amplifier. The musician was explaining that although the volume control on most amps only go to 10, his went to 11. When the interviewer asked him why couldn't they just make the dial go to 10 and make that a little louder, the rocker could only respond, "These go to 11."

This obdurate belief in an idea is similar to that held by people who believed that B2B exchanges would change the economics of supply and demand overnight. The timeframe will be longer, but the capability of companies to implement efficient business-to-business transactions online will eventually become a critical factor in a company's profitability and long-term success.

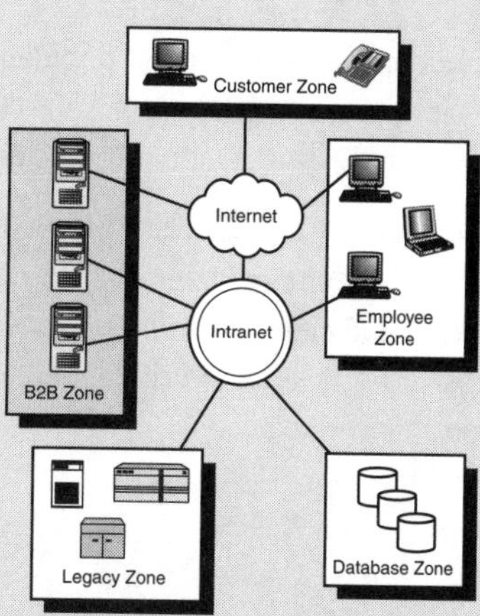

Partners and suppliers, driven by cost savings and competitive pressures, are prepared to invest some time and effort into integrating IT systems. But giving even well-established, trusted partners access to internal systems raises a number of interesting challenges.

Unless a single company is powerful enough to make demands on weaker companies, connecting IT systems involves compromise on both sides. Barring the unlikely event of parallel evolution, each company will have a completely unique mixture of technologies, tools, and applications to conduct its business. Fortunately, the wide acceptance of XML and the Internet is providing more common ground for companies that want to share access to information and systems.

Systems Integration Options

A surprising number of options exist for transferring data between foreign IT systems. Besides the traditional (and expensive) option of dedicated networks and custom protocols, several Internet protocols can be easily adapted for B2B transactions.

The appropriate solution for a given problem depends on various requirements:

- **Time frame**—How quickly must this message be processed?
- **Transactional support**—Does the calling system require immediate feedback? If the message fails, does the client need to know so that it can roll back any partially committed changes?
- **Security**—How sensitive is the information that will be exchanged? How likely is it that the communication could be compromised? How can the server protect itself from bogus clients?

Using only standard Internet protocols, communications solutions can be built on top of e-mail (SMTP), file transfer (FTP), and real-time object requests (HTTP/SOAP). The following sections detail the strengths and weaknesses of each approach.

Connecting Systems Using E-mail

E-mail is the oldest and most popular application on the Internet. In fact, e-mail actually predates the Internet. Before ARPANET(the precursor to the Internet), companies had access to internal e-mail systems and various bulletin board–based systems such as Bitnet.

E-mail is a store-and-forward protocol, which means that when a message is sent, the sender no longer has any control over it. This makes it unsuitable for transactional applications in which the client sends a request and needs some sort of immediate confirmation that the request was processed. For less time-critical applications, however, e-mail can provide a simple and robust transport mechanism.

To send and receive e-mail, a system must have access to a mail server. Two popular protocols for sending and receiving e-mail are (respectively) the Simple Mail Transfer Protocol (SMTP) and Post Office Protocol 3 (POP3). Another widely used mail client protocol is the Internet Mail Access Protocol (IMAP). Before committing to a particular technology, it is important to determine which protocols are supported by the available corporate mail servers.

E-mailing XML documents is one of the slowest but most robust ways to connect two systems. Figure 8.1 shows how two back-office systems can communicate using e-mail to send and receive application messages.

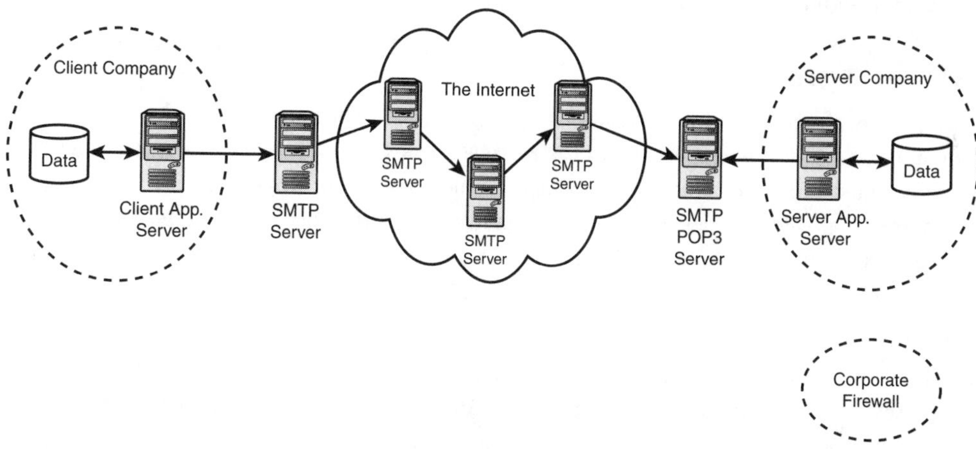

FIGURE 8.1
The client application sends a "blind" message to the server application.

Mail servers are programmed to continue trying to send messages over a period of several days, making it an ideal transport for solutions where network reliability is not guaranteed.

▶**See** Chapter 14, "Offline Order Processing Using Store-and-Forward" project for an example of a system like this.

Compatibility

Any operating system and programming language that supports opening, reading, and writing a TCP/IP socket can support e-mail transfers. Modern programming languages such as Perl and Java have built-in classes for interfacing with mail servers. Even if no explicit SMTP or POP3 support is available, the protocol used to send e-mail is very simple and can be implemented rapidly.

Reliability

Mail servers are very resilient to changes in network topography, temporary network failures, and so on. The Domain Name Server (DNS) system is used to resolve e-mail addresses to physical hosts for e-mail delivery. In most cases, sent messages can be delivered to the target host within a few minutes.

All that is required is a public e-mail address for each system that wants to participate. In a one-way message exchange, the client machine need not even have a message inbox. The only complications that might arise are related to modern SMTP security features that are designed to prevent unauthorized users from forwarding mail (spam) through public mail servers.

Data Integrity

Although it is possible for the contents of e-mail messages to become corrupted, this is not a frequent occurrence. If absolute integrity is an issue, checksums and secure message digests should be considered to ensure that a message has not changed or been tampered with. Again, many freely available libraries exist for implementing modern encryption and message digest functions for popular programming languages.

Security

Unfortunately, Internet e-mail is not a particularly secure medium. A message might pass through several servers before arriving at its final destination. To ensure that sensitive data is protected, consider using a public-key encryption system to encrypt the data before sending it to the mail server.

Transmitting Data via FTP

The File Transfer Protocol is one of the oldest and simplest methods for moving data from one machine to another. As a result, several FTP server and client implementations are available for most operating systems and programming languages. The wide availability of FTP software makes it ideal for cross-platform applications.

FTP is a connection-oriented protocol and requires that the two participating systems be capable of establishing a socket connection on port 21. This might not be possible in many cases because of corporate firewall and proxy server restrictions. Even if the FTP server is visible on the public Internet, the FTP client could be restricted in which ports it may connect to.

Unless you are willing to create a customized FTP server implementation, any processing to be performed on incoming data is asynchronous. Also, the transaction is one-way, with no feedback (other than successful receipt of the file) being sent to the client. This makes FTP useful for asynchronous updating of read-only information but unsuitable for transaction-oriented applications. Figure 8.2 shows a typical FTP messaging configuration between two companies.

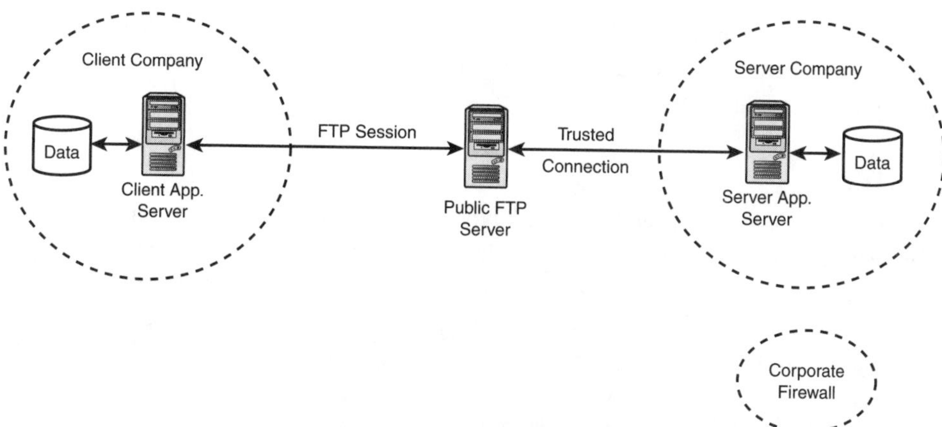

FIGURE 8.2
Client applications post XML message files to a public FTP server.

Compatibility

Most server operating systems provide a basic FTP implementation. Although the FTP server is used to transfer XML messages, from a message processing standpoint, the FTP service itself is irrelevant. A message-processing system built on top of FTP must be prepared to monitor a specific directory for incoming files and then process the files in a timely manner. These files could even arrive by other means, such as through an ordinary file share.

Reliability

FTP has been in use for more than two decades. Thousands of files are transferred via FTP every day. When installed and configured properly, an FTP installation should be almost 100% reliable. The major issue affecting reliability is the quality of network connectivity to the server in general. If a large number of simultaneous connections are expected, or if large volumes of messages will need to be processed, the underlying server must be configured accordingly.

Data Integrity

Ensuring that the file sent is the same as the file received is particularly important. One factor to take under consideration is that the FTP protocol provides two distinct file transfer modes: binary and text. FTP servers default to text transfer mode, which means that carriage returns and linefeeds may be replaced by the server to reflect the predilections of the server OS. For instance, Unix systems use a single linefeed (0x0a character) to terminate a line, while Windows-based systems use a carriage return/linefeed combination (0x0d 0x0a).

For portability between machines, XML documents should be transferred in either UTF-8 or UTF-16. Also, file transfers should be done in binary mode, to prevent the server from arbitrarily modifying the incoming files.

Security

FTP servers provide username and password–type authentication. The actual user verification and file security is usually provided by the underlying operating system. Also, unless FTP over Secure Socket Layer (FTPS) is used, all communication between the client and the server is sent in the clear across the Internet. The level and quality of security and encryption depends on the sensitivity of the data being transferred.

Exposing Systems with SOAP

One of the most intriguing applications of XML in the corporate programming world is the Simple Object Access Protocol. SOAP is essentially an XML-based Remote Procedure Call (RPC) protocol that piggybacks on the existing Hypertext Transfer Protocol (HTTP) supported by every existing Web server.

In operation, a SOAP request consists of an XML message that includes an object, a method, and a set of parameters to invoke on the server URL. The HTTP `POST` method is used to transmit this information to the SOAP server. The request is then processed by the server, and the results are sent back to the client in XML format as the body of the HTTP response message.

Compatibility

Tightly coupled technologies (such as COM and CORBA) complicate the process of linking different IT systems. Even platform-independent binary protocols, such as the Interface Definition Language (IDL) defined by the Object Management Group (`www.omg.org`), don't provide the flexibility required to easily combine systems based on different object technologies. Figure 8.3 shows how two companies using different technologies cannot utilize one another's IT systems over the Internet.

SOAP, on the other hand, is a much looser protocol. By leveraging the portability of Unicode and the wide availability of both HTTP servers and XML parsers, new SOAP server implementations are being introduced at a rapid pace. And because most large companies have enabled seamless Internet access throughout their networks, a SOAP client can run almost anywhere within an organization.

Originally, the HTTP protocol was intended only for use by Web browsers and human users. It was designed to be easy for Web browser and server writers to implement. As the Internet and the World Wide Web became more popular, corporate IT departments deployed Web servers and Internet access within the enterprise.

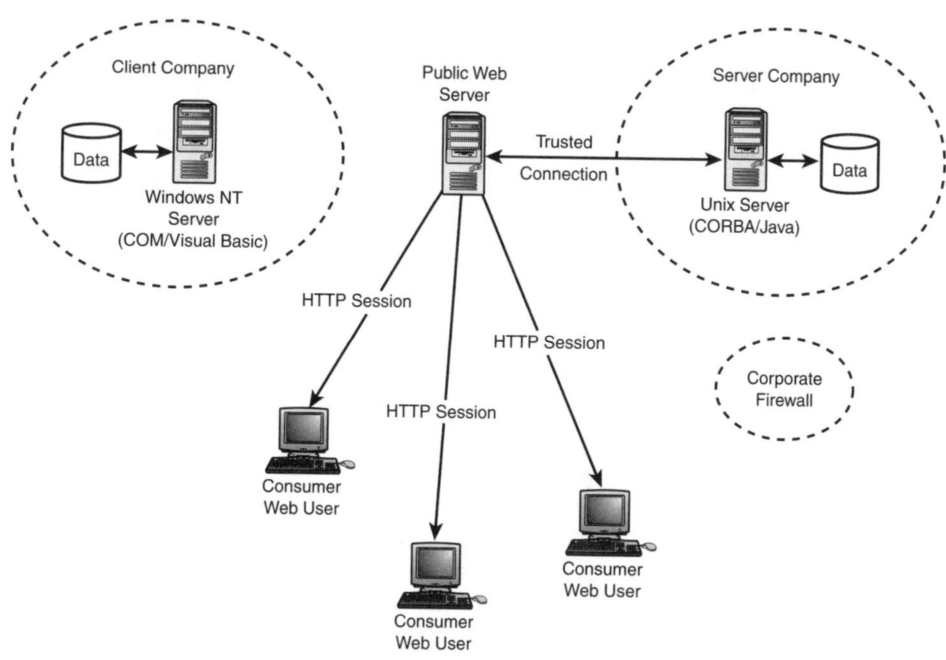

FIGURE 8.3
Back-office systems incapable of communicating because of a technology mismatch.

Most large companies now have production Web servers deployed on the Internet. The required procedures, policies, and network infrastructure for integrating HTTP traffic into corporate IT systems are very mature. As a result, implementing SOAP server functionality requires very little adjustment to existing systems. Figure 8.4 shows how adding a SOAP client and server implementation enables two organizations to link their IT systems. Note that the system based on COM/Visual Basic can now communicate freely with the Unix/Java system. This platform independence functions between any systems that implement SOAP.

Implementation details of the platform (Windows, Unix, Linux, and so on) object broker architecture, and programming language are hidden from consumers by the XML messaging layer. Server processing can occur in any language, using any resources necessary, and the client is never exposed to the internals of the server system.

Reliability

Factors affecting Web server reliability and performance are well understood and documented. The same techniques that are used to improve the reliability and performance of Web sites (clustering, load balancing, and so on) can be applied to SOAP servers.

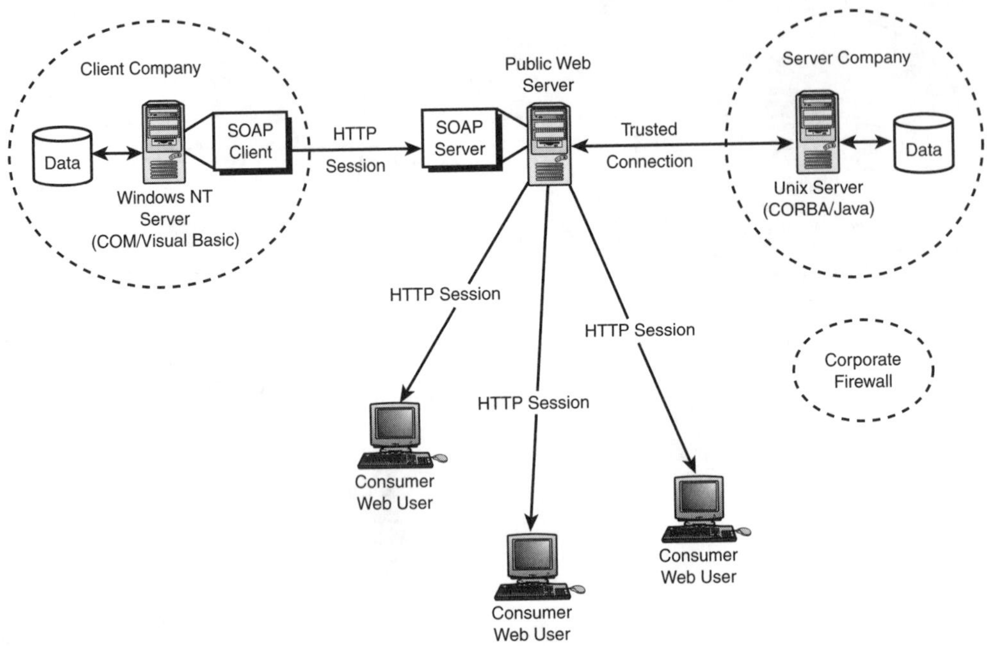

FIGURE 8.4
Back-office systems communicating across the public Internet using SOAP and HTTP sessions.

Data Integrity

SOAP requests are executed as normal object method invocations on the server. Transactional support, if any is required, is provided by the host system, and transaction results are reported as the body of the HTTP/SOAP request.

Security

Secure communications can be provided using normal Web server technologies: HTTPS, basic authentication, client certificates, and even NT challenge/response. SOAP version 1.1 makes no special provisions for message security or encryption, but future releases will address message authentication issues.

The same security techniques used to secure Web-based applications can be used to secure server processing of SOAP requests. On Microsoft Windows NT and 2000–based servers, user security and impersonation can be used to limit access to system resources, files, and database content.

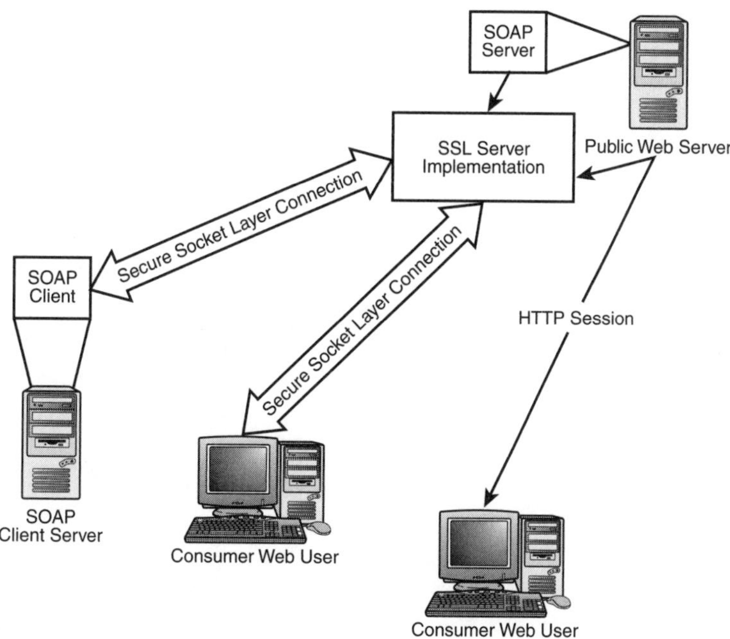

FIGURE 8.5
Secure Socket Layer provides secure communications for both HTTP and SOAP sessions.

Conclusions

Connecting systems within an organization can be difficult enough, but when it comes to connecting systems between different companies, the number of problems seems to increase exponentially. Without trusted networks and common protocols, each connection becomes a custom effort—a full-blown development project in its own right. As XML technologies like SOAP become more widely supported, companies will find that their systems have more in common than ever before. Building new systems to support these standards now will pay dividends in saved effort for years to come.

The Database Zone

CHAPTER

9

No matter what some industry pundits might say, the relational database is in no danger of being replaced by XML database servers anytime soon. Looking at the history of databases, we see that the idea of a hierarchical database is not a new one. The Information Management Systems of the 1950s and 1960s eventually evolved into the tree-oriented hierarchical databases that have been made all but obsolete by relational databases.

The truth is that relational databases can do a fair job of modeling hierarchical data, but hierarchical formats (such as XML documents) do a very poor job of simulating relational operations. But this doesn't mean that XML won't begin to play an integral part in moving information between databases and the systems that use them.

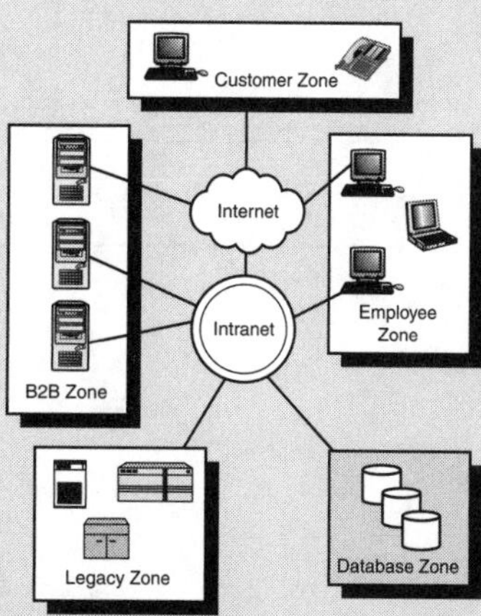

When talking about XML and databases, the questions arise: Where do you draw the line between the client application and the database? Should Microsoft's ActiveX Database Object (ADO) XML support be in the same category as Software AG's Tamino XML database? From the point of view of an application developer, it doesn't really matter where the data comes from. Whether it's stored in an RDBMS and converted to XML on the fly or whether it's served as a complete document from an application server, the only thing that an application developer needs to know is how to use it.

Before getting into the pros and cons of various approaches to integrating XML into back-office solutions, it is useful to have a high-level view of a basic scenario.

Typical Back-Office Application Scenario

Modern operating systems architecture and three-tier design has led to modularization in back-office applications. The same features that made it easy to upgrade business rules and database systems make it easy to modify interfaces between components without affecting the stability of the system as a whole.

Abstract data access methods, such as the Open Database Connectivity (ODBC) interface, have allowed client applications to divorce themselves from the actual database system itself. Figure 9.1 shows a typical modern back-office application involving a relational database and an application server.

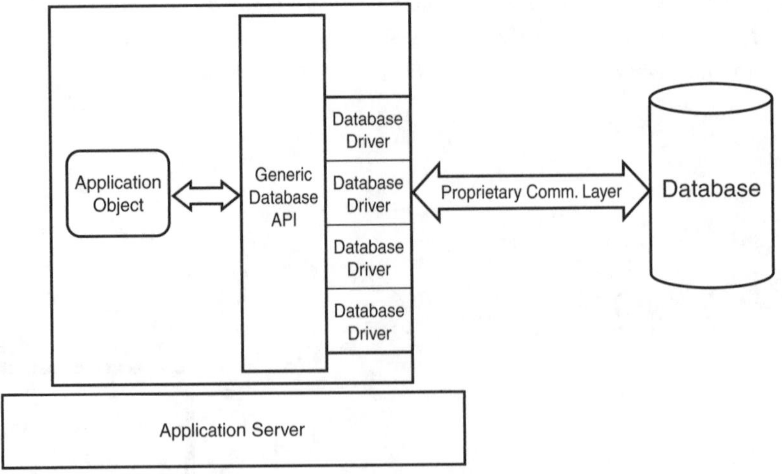

FIGURE 9.1
Typical back-office application.

This modularity provides several points where XML-aware components can be inserted. The following sections outline various ways that XML support can be added to an existing system.

Client-Side Conversion

The most rapid (and least flexible) way to integrate XML into an existing system is through the use of a client-side XML driver. This can be done either by using an XML-enabled database API provider or by inserting an extra component between the client application and the database API provider. Figure 9.2 shows how a relational-data-to-XML mapping layer could be added to an existing system.

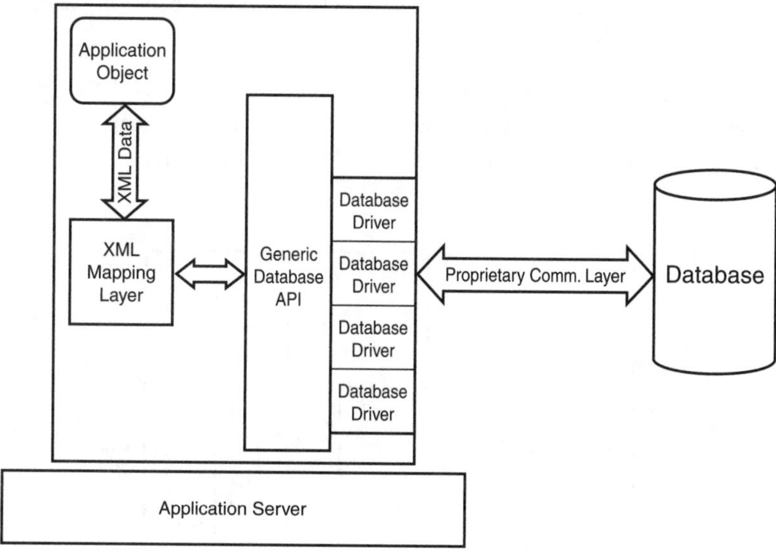

FIGURE 9.2
Adding a client-side conversion layer.

For example, Microsoft's ADO library contains native support for serializing a query's result set into XML. The resulting XML data can then be programmatically manipulated using XML APIs such as the DOM. It can also be transformed using XSLT for display or for input into another XML-based system.

Converting relational database queries into XML using client libraries is the least intrusive approach to implementing XML. In most cases, only the client application itself needs to be modified.

Unfortunately, the types of XML documents that can be constructed from a tabular result set are severely limited. Although more sophisticated commercial products allow nested queries to be executed to construct complex XML documents, for the most part, applications are limited to accessing the same basic tabular data via XML APIs instead of data-access APIs.

Client XML support is, for the most part, read-only. Currently, few client access tools support modifying RDBMS database contents using XML documents.

Middleware and XML Application Servers

Another approach to accessing existing data in XML is through a gateway server or middleware layer. The concept of Message Oriented Middleware (MOM) is not new. Client/server applications were depending on messaging layers long before the first Web-based applications appeared. In this case, a middleware layer or server acts as a bridge between the older, relational model and the new XML model.

One simple way to implement an XML gateway is to configure a normal Web server to retrieve relational data and return it in a predefined XML document format. Figure 9.3 shows how a dedicated application server can be used to hide XML data conversions from client applications.

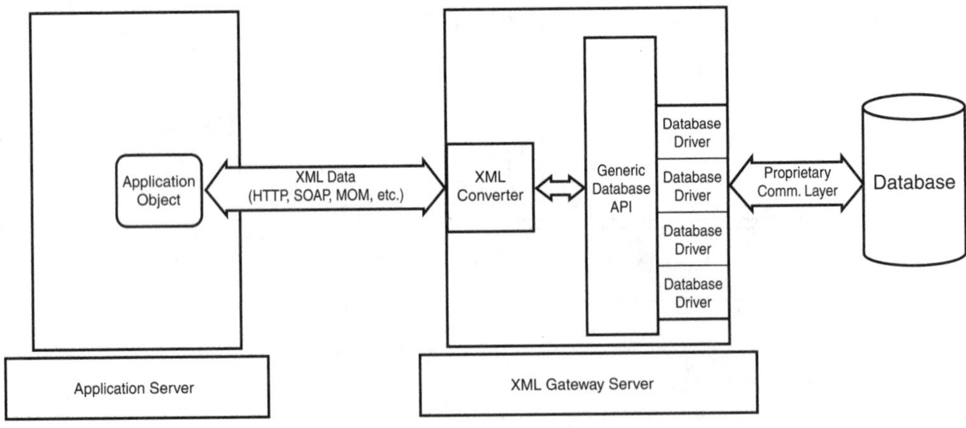

FIGURE 9.3
Adding an XML gateway server.

Using an intermediate server to perform conversions now simplifies the transition to fully XML-aware databases later. If the capabilities of the back-end database change, only the gateway application itself needs to be modified. Abstracting the XML-to-DB linkage isolates client applications from changes in database technology.

XML-Enabled Databases

The latest releases of most popular RDBMS systems include some form of direct XML support. Microsoft's SQL Server 2000 includes features such as the `OpenXML()` function and the `FOR XML` extension to the `SELECT` statement. These two features allow XML data to be incorporated into relational queries in addition to returning query results in XML format. Oracle's 8i and 9i products provide comparable functionality.

Retrieving query results from the database server directly in XML format is the most efficient way to integrate XML into an application. Figure 9.4 illustrates how an application can take advantage of an XML-aware database server.

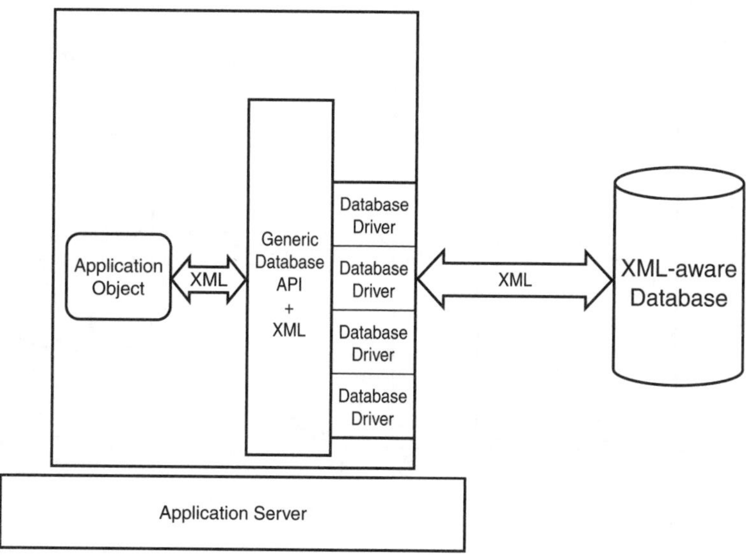

FIGURE 9.4
Application using XML-aware database and drivers.

Currently there is a lack of standardization by database manufacturers when it comes to exposing XML interfaces. This means that applications written to take advantage of a particular database system will be difficult to migrate to other platforms.

Native XML Servers

A new class of emerging database servers markets itself as "native" XML servers. What precisely is meant by *native* varies from product to product, but generally these servers store and retrieve XML data transparently using XML APIs instead of SQL.

Most native XML servers support XML APIs such as DOM and SAX for accessing document data. Queries are generally performed using an XML selection language such as XPath or XQL. In some cases, the actual document contents are stored in a relational database and are retrieved on demand. Other products utilize proprietary hierarchical data-storage facilities. Also, because the domain of the DOM and SAX specifications doesn't address querying multiple documents, this functionality is provided on an ad hoc basis.

Operationally, using a native XML server is similar to using a traditional RDBMS server that supports XML. Unlike the gateway scenario, no additional server is needed. Figure 9.5 shows how the basic back-office application changes to accommodate a native XML server.

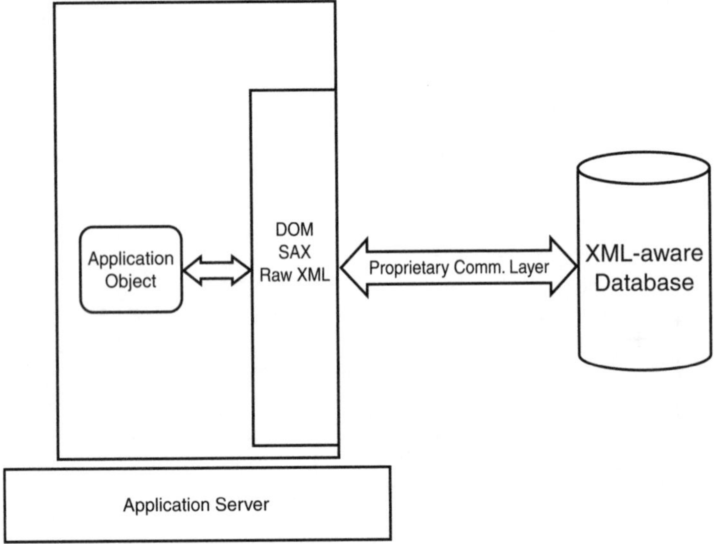

FIGURE 9.5
Application interfacing with native XML server.

Accessing XML data through standard APIs such as SAX and DOM makes application development simpler. The interfaces are well understood and well documented. Most existing applications already use DOM or SAX, so adapting them to work with an XML database requires little effort.

The same application can operate on data stored on an XML server and regular XML documents. This is a useful feature when some documents will reside on the server and others will be processed in remote locations. It also eases the burden on the developer by allowing him to develop applications using simple text files.

Most native XML databases support RDBMS queries poorly or not at all. The unstructured nature of XML data makes it difficult to optimize for typical relational operations, such as joining two sets of information.

The performance of hierarchical databases is inferior to that of relational databases for most operations. Part of the problem is the lack of maturity of XML databases. RDBMS systems have been incrementally improving over a period of decades, while XML systems are typically less than five years old. Another problem is the unpredictability of XML data. A relational database can predict the storage requirements for a given record, but an XML server cannot make many assumptions about the amount and distribution of data within a particular document.

Encoding XML for RDBMSs

It is possible to simulate the operation of a native XML server using a relational database. There are well-established techniques for storing hierarchical data in relational tables. By applying these techniques to the information stored in an XML document, many of the benefits of a native XML server can be achieved without needing to replace or extend existing systems.

Three basic ways exist to encode XML documents in a relational database schema. The next sections examine these.

Raw Document Approach

The simplest approach is to store the XML document as a binary large object (BLOB) or character large object (CLOB) within the database. If the database supports full-text indexing, the stored documents can be searched for particular content. Extracting the document is simply a matter of retrieving the object data and passing it to the client.

The downside of storing documents whole is that no correlations can be made between them. Without extracting individual XML element values, it is impossible to formulate a SQL query to link related records.

XML-Centric Approach

A generic approach to storing XML data is to store each type of data from a source document (element tags, attribute values, character data, and so on) in specialized tables. The relationships among the various document fragments are maintained using database keys. Data can be isolated and correlated between different documents. When it is necessary to reconstruct the document, the stored data is reassembled based on the key relationships.

The strength of this approach is that it can be implemented fairly quickly and will work for virtually any XML document. The disadvantage is that it is very difficult to extract meaningful semantic information from documents encoded this way. Although the character data from a particular element can be associated with the parent tag name, correlating this data with data from other documents requires the construction of sophisticated SQL queries.

Application-Centric Approach

This approach provides the greatest flexibility within the resulting database. Instead of storing XML document pieces in generic database tables, a schema is developed to model the specific information in a given type of document. For example, consider the document shown in Listing 9.1.

LISTING 9.1 Basic Personnel Record

```
<?xml version="1.0" encoding="UTF-8"?>
<!DOCTYPE employee [

<!ELEMENT employee (name, address, absences)>
<!ATTLIST employee
  id CDATA #REQUIRED
>

<!ELEMENT name (first, middle?, last)>

<!ELEMENT first (#PCDATA)>
<!ELEMENT middle (#PCDATA)>
<!ELEMENT last (#PCDATA)>

<!ELEMENT address (street, city, state, zip)>

<!ELEMENT street (#PCDATA)>
<!ELEMENT city (#PCDATA)>
<!ELEMENT state (#PCDATA)>
<!ELEMENT zip (#PCDATA)>

<!ELEMENT absences (vacation | illness | training)+>

<!ELEMENT vacation EMPTY>
<!ATTLIST vacation
  start CDATA #REQUIRED
  end CDATA #REQUIRED
>

<!ELEMENT illness EMPTY>
<!ATTLIST illness
  start CDATA #REQUIRED
  end CDATA #REQUIRED
>
```

LISTING 9.1 Continued

```
<!ELEMENT training EMPTY>
<!ATTLIST training
  start CDATA #REQUIRED
  end CDATA #REQUIRED
>
]>
<employee id="12345">
  <name>
    <first>John</first>
    <middle>Q</middle>
    <last>Public</last>
  </name>
  <address>
    <street>1234 Any Street</street>
    <city>Any Town</city>
    <state>SC</state>
    <zip>29292</zip>
  </address>
  <absences>
    <vacation start="1/1/01" end="2/1/01"/>
  </absences>
</employee>
```

Rather than store the values from each element in a single column of a single table, a normalized database schema would be constructed to encode the data from each document. Figure 9.6 depicts a database schema to contain documents like the one in Listing 9.1.

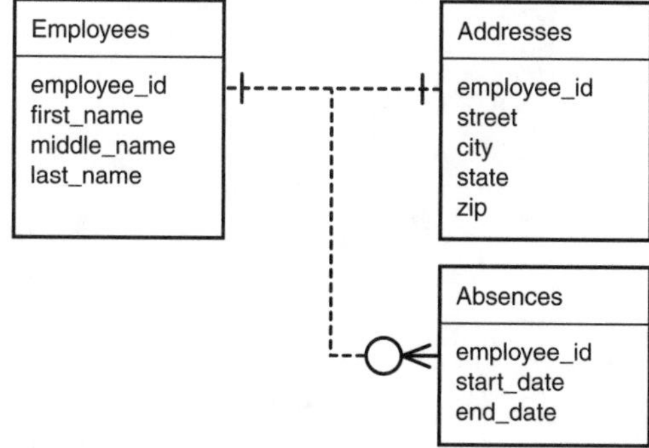

FIGURE 9.6
Simple database schema for storing XML employee data.

By storing the XML data in a schema that precisely reflects its logical structure, meaningful queries can be run against the data being stored. The trade-off is that the formatting information from the original document is lost in the translation. Also, it requires a new database for each class of document that is to be stored.

▶**See** Chapter 15, "Exposing Internal Systems to External Partners" project for an example of a system that implements some of the features described here.

Conclusions

A large number of options exist for incorporating XML data into existing enterprise applications. The final decision about which approach to take depends on the constraints and requirements of the individual project and organization. The volatility and lack of broad standards for implementing XML support within a relational framework dictates that the prudent application developer isolate any dependencies on proprietary APIs as much as possible.

As standards organizations begin to recognize the need to update existing protocols (such as the Structured Query Language) to accommodate XML, the decisions about where and when to incorporate XML into a corporation's database strategy will become easier.

CHAPTER 10

The Legacy Zone

In the late 1990s, I was working for a company as a part of its e-commerce development team. Our job was to build an Internet front end to the data that was generated by the company's COBOL-based legacy systems. After various options were explored, the final solution that was reached between us (the Internet team) and them (the mainframe guys) was that they would export all their data into a SQL server database. Then we would be free to display it however we chose, using normal Web-development techniques.

After the project was launched, I became curious about how they planned to import the data into the SQL database. I met with the tech lead of the back-end system, and he showed me what they were doing. Their solution was to develop a number of brand new COBOL applications that would run on an NT server that would import flat files into the SQL database. When I asked them why they chose COBOL, the answer I received was, "It's the only language my team knows." This drove home the message that the death of the mainframe and the mainframe programmer has been greatly exaggerated.

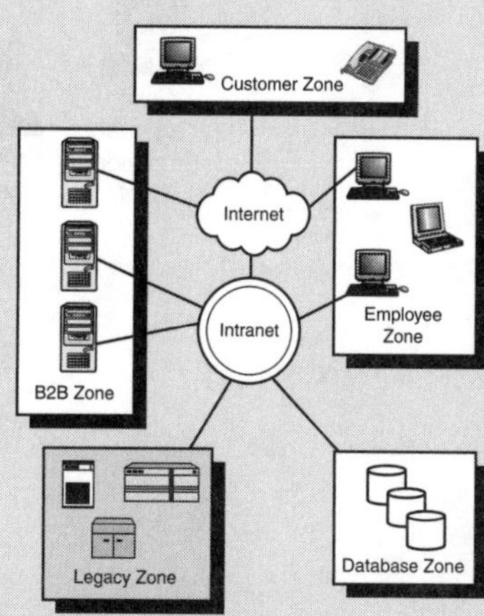

In applications such as banking, stock trading, and utility billing, key transactions are still served by mainframe applications. Despite the high cost of ownership associated with mainframe installations, the immense investment in custom applications and the extremely high reliability of mainframe hardware makes it difficult for large IT departments to justify migrating to a more modern server architecture.

This chapter is written from the point of view of a non-mainframe programmer who needs to interface an application with data stored in a legacy environment. Similar to the old saying about pilots who land with their landing gear retracted, "There are those who have, and those who will." But giving some thought to the proper tools and protocols in advance can make the process much less painful for all concerned.

Bridging the Gap

The great consumer demand for Internet access to real-time information such as account balances and stock transactions means that PC programmers and mainframe programmers must learn to find a common ground. XML is a natural solution to the unique problems encountered by cross-platform applications.

Before understanding how XML can simplify communications between heterogeneous systems, it is useful to take a look at a monolithic mainframe environment. Figure 10.1 shows a typical mainframe system.

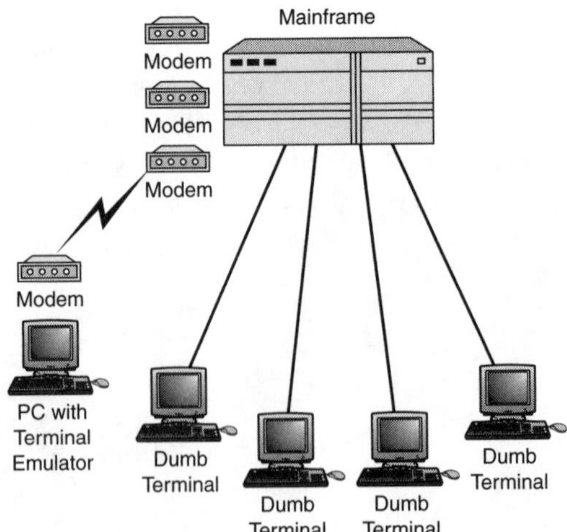

FIGURE 10.1
Typical mainframe system.

The beauty of this system is that all processing and storage functions are owned by the mainframe. No coordination with external servers or applications is required. No data is ever stored by the dumb terminals or dial-up connections, so data integrity is purely a function of the applications running on the mainframe itself.

Extending Closed Systems

But as customers demand more avenues of access to their account information, it becomes necessary to devise ways to share data between mainframe applications and new server-based solutions. One area in which demand has far outstripped IT departments' capability to deliver is in the area of Internet access to legacy data.

Figure 10.2 shows a more complex system configuration that takes into account the presence of Internet users.

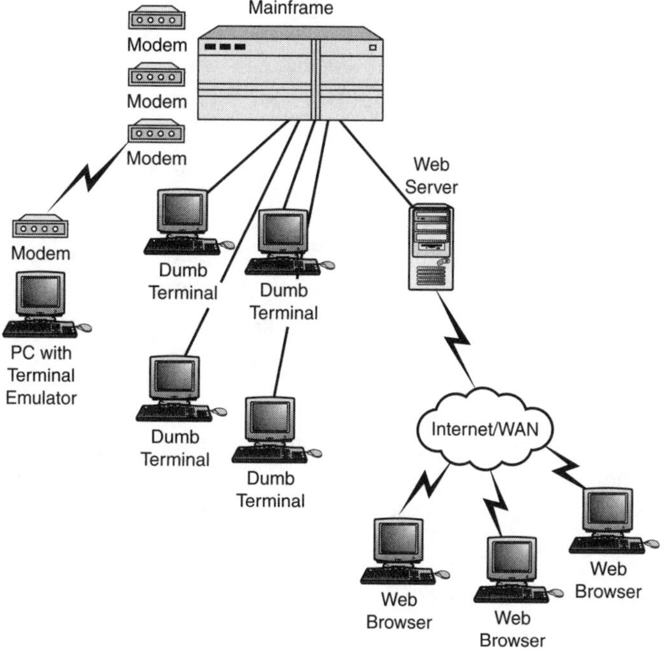

FIGURE 10.2
Mainframe system that incorporates Internet users.

One way to understand the problem of connecting legacy applications with modern, Internet-enabled applications is to view it in terms of the seven-layer Open Systems Interconnection (OSI) networking model. Table 10.1 lists the layers and gives a brief description of each.

TABLE 10.1 OSI Model

Layer	*Description*
Application	Provides access to commonly needed protocols (such as FTP, HTTP, and SMTP)
Presentation	Deals with data-representation issues, such as byte ordering and character sets
Session	Manages flow control and synchronization between connection endpoints
Transport	Provides an abstract, end-to-end connection to the session layer
Network	Handles routing and switching of traffic on a subnet
Data link	Transforms a raw transmission link into a reliable communication channel
Physical	Is the actual physical cabling and electrical characteristics of the connection

Several well-established technologies handle the lower-level connectivity issues. The almost universal adoption of TCP/IP and Ethernet has greatly simplified physical and networking connection issues that previously plagued mainframe operations. Message Oriented Middleware technologies such as Microsoft's MSMQ and IBM's MQ Series provide mechanisms for transmitting arbitrary messages between PCs and mainframes. In addition, relatively new application protocols such as HTTP and SOAP are being introduced in a wide variety of mainframe environments.

Where XML can add value is in the high-level presentation and application layers. Character set issues and byte-ordering problems are answered by the requirement that XML documents be transmitted using Unicode character encoding. At the application layer, XML provides a convenient format for representing complex, hierarchical data structures across different machine architectures.

Moving to an XML messaging format provides numerous benefits to programmers on both sides of the connection. Programmers can focus on the data itself, not necessarily on the operations that need to be performed on it. This data-centric approach can greatly simplify the cross-platform development cycle.

The downside is that many of the benefits of a monolithic, mainframe-based system are lost. Data freshness and consistency become issues. If read and write access to mainframe data is required, some form of basic transaction control must be implemented to make sure that changes made on one platform don't overwrite changes made on another.

A Simple XML Messaging Application

For example, consider the case in which a mainframe is used to manage employee personnel records. To simplify and expand the reach of this personnel system, the IT department is tasked to provide a Web-based interface into the mainframe system. Rather than build a tightly coupled solution using procedural technologies, using a basic messaging facility in conjunction with XML enables a much more powerful and yet simpler system to be rapidly built.

The following list includes the basic information that would be maintained for a single employee:

```
EMPLOYEE_ID
FIRST_NAME
LAST_NAME
SSN
START_DATE
FLEX_DAYS_REMAINING
HOME_PHONE
HOME_STREET_ADDRESS
HOME_CITY
HOME_STATE
HOME_ZIP
```

The Procedural Solution

Before XML, the most obvious solution to this problem would likely be to define a server-based API for manipulating employee records on a field-by-field basis. The problem with this approach is that as the number of fields increases, the complexity of the underlying implementation increases as well. Here's a minimal API in pseudo-code that would be required to support the employee record listed earlier:

```
EMPLOYEE_ID AddEmployeeRecord()
void DeleteEmployeeRecord(EMPLOYEE_ID)
String GetFirstName(EMPLOYEE_ID)
void SetFirstName(EMPLOYEE_ID, NEW_FIRST_NAME)
String GetLastName(EMPLOYEE_ID)
void SetLastName(EMPLOYEE_ID, NEW_LAST_NAME)
String GetSSN(EMPLOYEE_ID)
void SetSSN(EMPLOYEE_ID, SSN)
String GetStartDate(EMPLOYEE_ID)
void SetStartDate(EMPLOYEE_ID, NEW_START_DATE)
String GetFlexDaysRemaining(EMPLOYEE_ID)
void SetFlexDaysRemaining(EMPLOYEE_ID, FLEX_DAYS_REMAINING)
```

```
String GetHomePhone(EMPLOYEE_ID)
void SetHomePhone(EMPLOYEE_ID, NEW_HOME_PHONE)
String GetHomeStreetAddress(EMPLOYEE_ID)
void SetHomeStreetAddress(EMPLOYEE_ID, NEW_STREET_ADDRESS)
String GetHomeCity(EMPLOYEE_ID)
void SetHomeCity(EMPLOYEE_ID, NEW_HOME_CITY)
String GetHomeState(EMPLOYEE_ID)
void SetHomeState(EMPLOYEE_ID, NEW_HOME_STATE)
String GetHomeZip(EMPLOYEE_ID)
void SetHomeZip(EMPLOYEE_ID, NEW_HOME_ZIP)
```

Supplying even this basic level of functionality would require the mainframe team to implement 22 distinct API functions! Additionally, each API call would require a full round-trip to the mainframe. Depending on physical connectivity issues, this could create serious application latency problems. If each API call was routed through a satellite link, the speed-of-light limitation would impose a penalty of 200–600 milliseconds on each call. Creating a new employee record would require 10 separate API calls.

To further complicate matters, an error could occur during any given call. The client application would need to determine what steps to take to correct the problem. And because the API doesn't include any transaction semantics, it is unclear what to do about the partially completed employee record in the meantime.

The XML Messaging Approach

▶**See** the Migrating Legacy Data project (Chapter 17) for an example of a system that implements some of the features described here.

Contrast this approach with an XML message-based approach. The entire API shown previously could be reduced to a single call:

```
String SendMessage(XML_MESSAGE)
```

The actual type of operation and data to be used would be encoded in the XML message body. For example, a message for adding a new employee record could be encoded like this:

```
<message>
  <employee command="add">
    <FIRST_NAME>John</FIRST_NAME>
    <LAST_NAME>Doe</LAST_NAME>
    <SSN>123-45-6578</SSN>
    <START_DATE>01/01/2001</START_DATE>
    <FLEX_DAYS_REMAINING>4</FLEX_DAYS_REMAINING>
    <HOME_PHONE>803.555.1212</HOME_PHONE>
    <HOME_STREET_ADDRESS>123 Any Lane</HOME_STREET_ADDRESS>
    <HOME_CITY>Any Town</HOME_CITY>
```

```
    <HOME_STATE>SC</HOME_STATE>
    <HOME_ZIP>29123</HOME_ZIP>
  </employee>
</message>
```

By encoding the data in the message body, new fields could be added to or removed from the basic personnel record at will. The API itself need never change. Also, because the entire operation can be performed using one API call, network latency ceases to be an issue.

When the message has been received by the mainframe application, it is free to implement the underlying functionality as efficiently as possible. The large number of freely available XML parsers makes the job of extracting information from the message packet relatively simple. The result of the requested operation would be reported to the client in another XML message:

```
<result>
  <employee id="1357911" command="add" result="success"/>
</result>
```

This basic framework can be extended to support other operations, such as deleting employee records:

```
<message>
  <employee id="123456" command="delete"/>
</message>
```

Unlike procedural API calls, incorporating detailed error and diagnostic information into the message reply is extremely simple using XML:

```
<result>
  <employee id="123456" command="delete" result="failure">
    <message xml:lang="en-us">No employee record for ID '123456'
        was found.</message>
    <corrective-action xml:lang="en-us">Verify the employee ID and
        try again.</corrective-action>
  </employee>
</result>
```

Notice the presence of the `xml:lang` attributes to indicate the human language in which the error message is written. This attribute is part of the XML 1.0 standard and can be used to support rich internationalized applications that return language-appropriate responses to users. When this response is received by the client application, the application can parse it and return the appropriate error message to the end user.

Although the add and delete operations are fairly straightforward, performing record updates requires more complicated logic. In most cases, the current record data will be presented to the user, probably via a Web page. This creates a window where the original data can be modified by another user before the first user submits his updates. One possible solution to this problem is to include a time stamp or serial number in the data record on the mainframe. For example, consider the following query request:

```
<message>
  <employee id="1357911" command="query"/>
</message>
```

The mainframe would read this request, access the corresponding record, and return the record to the caller:

```
<result>
  <employee id="1357911" serial="10">
    <FIRST_NAME>John</FIRST_NAME>
    <LAST_NAME>Doe</LAST_NAME>
    <SSN>123-45-6578</SSN>
    <START_DATE>01/01/2001</START_DATE>
    <FLEX_DAYS_REMAINING>4</FLEX_DAYS_REMAINING>
    <HOME_PHONE>803.555.1212</HOME_PHONE>
    <HOME_STREET_ADDRESS>123 Any Lane</HOME_STREET_ADDRESS>
    <HOME_CITY>Any Town</HOME_CITY>
    <HOME_STATE>SC</HOME_STATE>
    <HOME_ZIP>29123</HOME_ZIP>
  </employee>
</result>
```

The `serial` attribute is a simple numeric counter that is incremented each time this particular employee record is modified. This serial number can be used by the host to detect when changes have been made to an out-of-date copy of the employee's record. Consider the case in which a Web user has viewed the record and made a modification to a field (for instance, the `FLEX_DAYS_REMAINING` field). The Web server could submit a change request message to the mainframe using the same basic message format as before:

```
<message>
  <employee id="1357911" serial="10" command="update">
    <FLEX_DAYS_REMAINING>3</FLEX_DAYS_REMAINING>
  </employee>
</message>
```

By sending the serial number that was previously retrieved from the mainframe, it is possible to detect whether the employee record has been changed in the meantime by another process. If the serial number in the request doesn't match the serial number in the actual record, an error could be generated.

Conclusions

The sheer variety of legacy systems and applications in use by large corporations makes it impossible to provide a single approach that will work in every case. But one of the common factors that can be found in every successful legacy integration project is simplicity. Using XML to transmit data between different, incompatible platforms removes many layers of application complexity for programmers on both sides.

Applying the Technology

PART III

IN THIS PART

About the Applications

CHAPTER 11

One of my consulting clients has two favorite phrases that I hear over and over:

> *"That wouldn't be a problem, would it?"*
>
> *"That shouldn't take too long, should it?"*

Whenever I hear one of these phrases, I get a cold chill down my spine. Even if you're not a freelance consultant, you probably don't like to hear either of these from your "customer" (or your boss). The following project chapters are meant to give you a good solid foundation on which to build a very wide range of XML-based solutions, and this chapter is meant to help you use them effectively.

One of the primary objectives of this book has been to remain as technology-neutral as possible. The software development world has become somewhat polarized between those developers who favor Microsoft technologies and those who favor open source. One of the greatest properties of XML is the fact that it is not tied to a particular platform or architecture. It can bridge an entire organization's IT department, from mainframes to handheld devices. The following projects have been built using technologies and tools from both sides of the fence, preferably together.

Using the Samples

Each of the following chapters in this section completely describes a real application of XML. Each describes the problem to be solved, the requirements of the solution, and the design and implementation of the resulting system. These applications are not meant to be "toy" projects, and are actually fully functional solutions to problems that professional enterprise developers encounter every day.

The full source code as well as a working demonstration of the solution are available on this book's Web site (`www.strategicxml.com`). These applications were designed and built with the idea that they would be taken and used to accelerate the development of real-world solutions. Although it is tempting to simply download the example and immediately begin tweaking it, reading the associated project chapter first will save time in the long run.

Sample Chapter Organization

To minimize the learning curve, each sample chapter follows the same format. The format moves sequentially from a particular problem through the design, development, and deployment of the solution.

Each sample application chapter is organized to mirror a classic project development cycle:

- *Problem Description* Explains the business problem that is to be solved by the application.
- *Requirements* Outlines the parameters of the solution. Any special restrictions or features would be mentioned here.
- *System Design* Explains the various components of the final deliverable product and how they will work together.
- *Implementation Notes* Gives a step-by-step narration of the development process, including tips, tricks, and traps of the trade.
- *Deployment* Covers the practical details of how to set up the solution in a real-life environment.
- *Conclusions* Summarizes how the techniques used for the project could be applied to other problems.

Tools and Technologies

The rapid acceptance of XML has resulted in an explosion of new standards, applications, and tools that use, implement, or depend on it. The projects in this book were selected to provide the broadest possible coverage of the most popular XML-related standards, and their most popular implementations. Table 11.1 lists the standards used within the projects and the version that was used. This table, along with up-to-date links to the related specifications, is available on the book's Web site.

TABLE 11.1 Standards Used in the Examples

Standard	*Version*
XML	1.0
XSLT	1.0
Namespaces in XML	14-January-1999
WSDL	1.0
SOAP	1.0
Java	1.2.2
ADO	2.5
SAX	2.0
COBOL	ANSI-85

There are many products on the market today that implement these standards, with varying degrees of accuracy and reliability. The tools selected to implement the samples were the most widely used and stable that were available at the time. New XML tools are being introduced every day, and good programming practices dictate that dependencies on a particular tool be minimized.

In the early days of XML, many implementations of XSLT and DOM (most notoriously, Microsoft's MSXML parser) included vendor-specific enhancements to the core specifications. Although these enhancements met real needs in the marketplace, as the standards matured, these products were forced to support their own proprietary extensions as well as the new "official" versions of the same functionality. Application developers who took advantage of these extensions were forced to either continue using the same tool or modify their applications to comply with the standard.

Microsoft Versus Open Source

That being said, the two most pervasive development camps today are those that use Microsoft products and those that gravitate toward open-source solutions. Unfortunately, in many cases frontline programmers don't have the luxury of working in a completely homogeneous environment. XML provides the universal language that can help bind these two worlds together, at least well enough to get a particular job done.

All the samples were designed to minimize their dependence on a particular tool or platform. For the most part, this means strict adherence to the core XML standards. In some cases, choosing one approach over another might make the sample slightly clumsier, but allows the same source files to be used with as many different tools as possible.

The following sections give a brief introduction to platforms and tools that are used throughout the following chapters.

MSXML and Microsoft Internet Information Server (IIS)

The foundation of Microsoft's XML strategy is its MSXML parser. It is a COM-based XML parser that includes support for XSLT transformations, SAX, and DOM applications. It is also used by Internet Explorer to provide client-side XML services, such as Microsoft's XML data island mechanism.

IIS is Microsoft's Web server product, and beginning with Windows 2000 it is built-in to the operating system. Together with MSXML, IIS is the core for building a Microsoft-centric server-side XML application. There are also facilities for automatically applying stylesheet transformations based on different client capabilities, through the XSL ISAPI Filter plug-in.

Xalan and Apache HTTP Server

Xalan is an open-source XSLT stylesheet processor that is part of the Apache XML Project. It depends on a DOM- or SAX-enabled XML parser, and by default it uses the Apache Xerces parser to perform transformations.

The Apache HTTP Server is currently the most popular Web server on the Internet. It is an open-source product that is managed under the auspices of the Apache Software Foundation. Together with Xalan, Apache provides the open-source platform for building server-side XML applications.

Saxon

Saxon is an XSLT stylesheet processor developed by Michael Kay, originally based on the Ælfred parser from Microstar. It fully supports the XSLT 1.0 recommendation, and the

6.1 version includes support for the <xsl:document> element, which greatly simplifies the generation of multiple output documents from a single source file.

Java 2 SDK

All of the Java applications in this book were developed using the 1.2.2 version of the Java 2 SDK. This is the version of Java installed with Borland's JBuilder version 3.0 (which can be downloaded from Borland's web site at `www.borland.com`).

Microsoft SOAP Toolkit 2.0

This is Microsoft's implementation of the Simple Object Access Protocol (SOAP) version 1.1 recommendation. It provides a set of client- and server-side objects that implement the SOAP messaging protocol. The server side objects can be configured to be called from IIS as either ISAPI plug-ins or from ASP code. There is also a utility that will generate the necessary configuration files to expose a COM object via a SOAP connection.

Fujitsu COBOL v3

The COBOL applications were developed using an early release of the Fujitsu COBOL compiler. This compiler supports the COBOL85 standard.

Apache Formatting Object Processor (FOP)

The Fop program transforms XSL-FO documents into Adobe's PDF format. It also can be linked with Saxon to produce a streamlined transformation and publishing system using XSLT.

Web Content Publishing

CHAPTER

12

Before XML started gaining traction with enterprise Internet developers, one company I worked for wanted a user-friendly Web-based newsletter publishing application. It took two ASP programmers a couple of months to build the database, the display screens, the administrative tools, and such to make the thing work. When the application was done, it was so popular that other groups wanted a customized version to meet their needs. The resulting development effort easily added another six man-months to the entire project.

Because certain features were added for one group whereas other groups had different requirements, the code driving this publishing site turned into a quagmire. Making even the smallest change in one place had unforeseen consequences in other places. Not a bad design per se, just too programmer-intensive to be practical in the long term. The happy ending to the story is that the entire publishing application/database combo was replaced by a much simpler XML-driven solution that can be extended ad infinitum without any programmer involvement at all. As users demand more direct control over Web-site content, XML will become the de facto platform for Web publishing.

Technologies Used:

- **XML**
- **XSL Transformations (XSLT)**
- **XPath**
- **HTML**

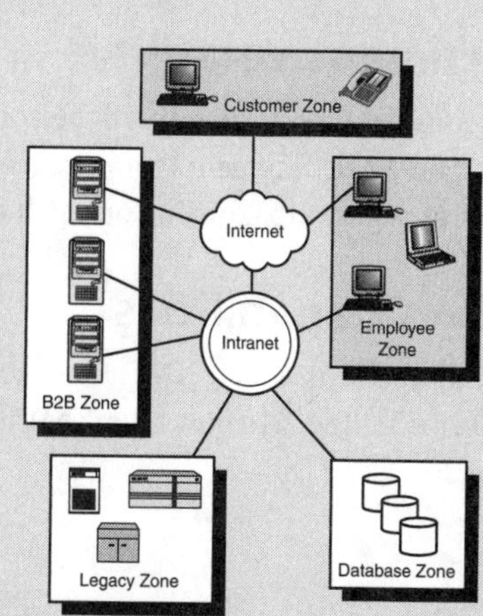

Problem Description

A company is moving to XML as the primary format for creating all product documentation. The contents of any product manual XML document need to be formatted for display on the Internet. The particular document instance used in this example is an XML representation of a complete product manual for a videocassette player. See Chapter 18, "Unifying Product Documentation," for more information about how the document was constructed.

The document will change frequently during production, but after the associated product has been shipped, it will change rarely if at all.

This is the desired output of this project:

- An XSLT stylesheet that will convert any document conforming to the product manual DTD into a basic HTML document.

Requirements

This system must meet the following requirements:

- The resulting HTML document should be viewable by the greatest possible variety of Web browsers. This requirement will dictate which version of HTML will be generated, and which HTML/browser features will be available for use in the final document.
- The final solution must be compatible with the company's existing Web server infrastructure. If real-time transformations are to be done, they must be compatible with available tools for the current Web server platform. For the purposes of illustration, this example will work with either Microsoft's Internet Information Server or the Apache Web server.

System Design

The process of transforming XML to HTML is fairly straightforward, but a few factors must be considered.

Document Volatility

One consideration is how often the source document will change. Is it really a static document, or is it an XML fragment that is generated on-the-fly by a script or database server? If the document changes often, offline or batch conversion solutions will not be responsive enough.

Server Capabilities

Another factor is which XML transformation capabilities are supported by your Web server platform. Table 12.1 shows the XML transformation capabilities of the most popular Web servers.

TABLE 12.1 Web Server XML Transformation Capabilities

Web Server	*XML Transformation Support*
Apache	The Apache XML Project's Cocoon server uses Xerces and Xalan to provide on-the-fly XSLT transformations as part of its 100% pure Java publishing framework.
Microsoft Internet Information Server (IIS)	Microsoft provides a little-known ISAPI extension that will use the MSXML parser to perform real-time XSLT transformations on static XML documents as well as XML that is generated using ASP logic.
iPlanet	iPlanet's Java-based 4GL environment (Forte) includes support for performing XSLT transformations on XML messages and documents.

Client Capabilities

Very few Web browsers support client-side XSL transformations. Microsoft's Internet Explorer began supporting XSLT in version 5.0, but the final XSLT specification had significant differences from the version implemented by Microsoft. Besides a general lack of support, the variations among different browsers make it impractical to rely on client-side transformation.

Besides transformation, some browser clients support applying Cascading Style Sheets (CSS) to XML documents. Although CSS support for HTML pages is fairly mature, the extensions that allow them to be used with XML documents are still not widely supported. Also, unlike XSLT, CSS has very little support for massaging the underlying structure of the XML document. This limitation prevents most data-centric documents from being displayed in a human-readable format.

Application Requirements

You also need to consider whether the application in question requires real-time transformations. Is the data being served generated on demand, or is it simply a static file that is stored on the server? Does the data need to be transformed differently depending on the client viewing it?

In some cases, such as displaying personal account information to a user, offline transformation will be impossible. The data must be prepared on demand for each user. Also, if the data must be transformed differently depending on the capabilities of the client (older Web browsers, text-only browsers, PDAs, cell phones, people with disabilities, and so on), the Web server must perform transformations on demand.

Conclusions

Client-side transformations allow for greater flexibility and more dynamic content, but too few browsers currently support them. Although new versions of the most popular browsers either already support XML or have plans to, users are not upgrading to newer browser versions very quickly. Client-side applications are really practical only when the audience is known and minimal configurations can be dictated (such as employees or partners).

Server-side transformations are safer but may incur unnecessary performance penalties for static XML documents. Transforming on demand ensures that the client receives only the most up-to-date data from the source document. However, invoking an XSLT transformation each time a client requests a static document wastes server processing power and reduces overall site response time. Although most Web servers provide for caching of transformed document images, if the underlying data changes infrequently, static transformation is a more viable option.

Based on the stable nature of the underlying documents for this particular application, static transformation is the most efficient and straightforward way to implement this application.

Implementation Notes

The process of static transformation is similar to the process of compiling program source code into executable format. An initial version of the XSLT stylesheet is developed. It is then applied to the source document to produce the transformed output. This output is then checked for errors and display quality, and the stylesheet is modified accordingly.

Because presentation logic is encoded in the stylesheet, a single XML document can be transformed into multiple target formats. This separation enables rapid deployment of fresh content via a large number of delivery channels. Figure 12.1 shows how a single XML document can be rendered in multiple formats using different stylesheets.

For the sake of simplicity, we will transform the source document into a single monolithic output file.

Page Development Process

The process of developing an XSLT stylesheet is similar to that of developing a program using a language compiler, as shown in Figure 12.2.

The tool used to develop this example is the Saxon processor, which was developed by Michael Kay. See this book's Web site for instructions about where to download this tool and how to configure it on your system.

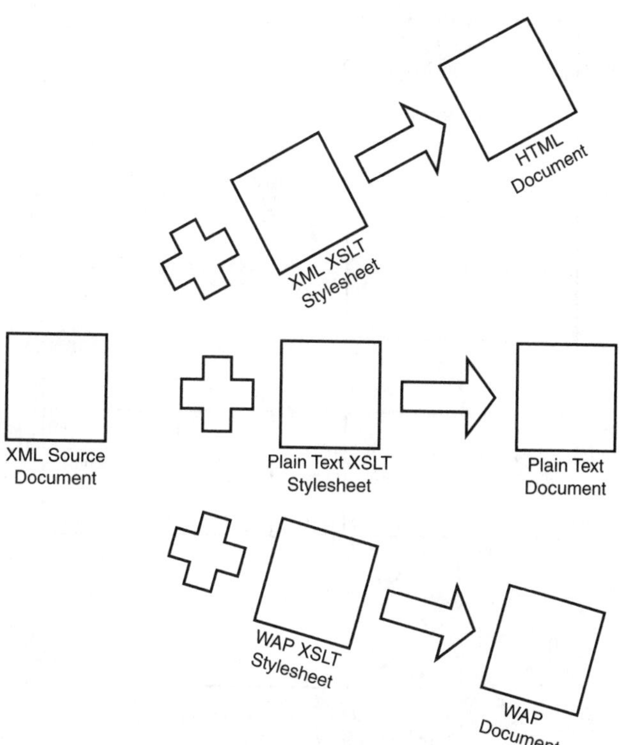

FIGURE 12.1

A single XML document can be transformed into multiple output formats.

Basic Stylesheet Usage

Here's a very simple XSLT stylesheet:

```
<?xml version="1.0" encoding="UTF-8"?>
<xsl:stylesheet version="1.1" xmlns:xsl="http://www.w3.org/1999/XSL/Transform">
  <xsl:template match="/">
    <xsl:apply-templates/>
  </xsl:template>
</xsl:stylesheet>
```

Because every XSLT stylesheet is a valid XML document, it must have a single top-level element. The top-level element of an XSLT stylesheet must be the `<xsl:stylesheet>` element. This element is a good place to declare any namespaces needed within the body of the stylesheet.

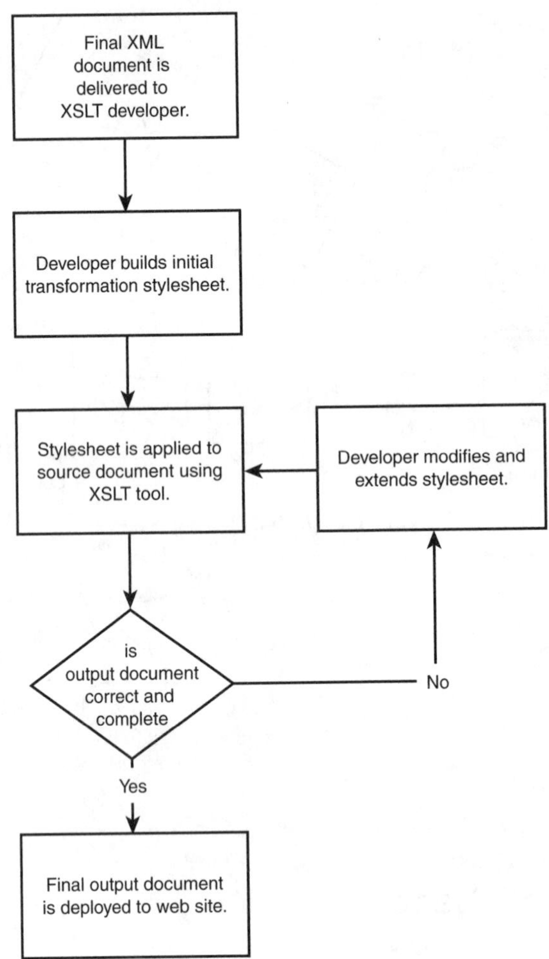

FIGURE 12.2
Stylesheet development cycle.

Although it is not required, the stylesheet should include an XML declaration. The XML declaration can be used by an XML parser on a foreign system to automatically detect the character encoding that was used to create the document. Also, it is conceivable (although unlikely) that a new version of XML may be released. These concerns may not seem important now, but in the real world, systems frequently spread far beyond their initial environments.

When a stylesheet is applied to a source document, any character data or element tag that isn't interpreted by the XSLT processor will be echoed verbatim to the output stream. Depending on which type of output is being generated (XML, HTML, or plain text), the XSLT processor will slightly modify how it outputs certain elements. For instance, in the stylesheet the HTML `<br>` tag must obey XML well-formedness rules (for example, `<br/>` or `<br></br>`). However, many HTML browsers don't recognize this syntax, so the XSLT processor will emit a regular HTML `<br>` tag.

The top-level `<xsl:stylesheet>` element includes a single `<xsl:template>` element. Templates are used to match elements in the source document and emit the desired transformed text into the output document. Think of templates as subroutines that are executed when an element from the source document matches the XPath expression in its `match="..."` attribute.

In this particular template, the `/` string indicates that this template matches the special root element in the XML source file. The root element is officially the parent of the single top-most element, which is called *the XML document element.*

The `<xsl:apply-templates/>` tag inside the `template` tag instructs the processor to recursively invoke any other matching templates on the current element's children, including the built-in templates. Using `apply-templates` without any attributes causes every child element to be emitted. It is also possible to limit which elements will be processed by using the `select` attribute with an XPath test expression.

An XSLT processor will apply one of several built-in templates if no explicit rule applies. These templates basically dictate that all character data and attribute values will be echoed to the output document. The contents of comment, processing instruction, and namespace nodes will not be echoed.

Basic XPath Usage

XSLT is heavily dependent on the XPath specification for selecting nodes, retrieving values, and matching elements. Most XSLT elements define at least one attribute that accepts an XPath expression. XPath expressions are used in two distinct capacities: for filtering and for locating document nodes.

The full XPath specification is very involved, and it permits sophisticated selection of any part of a source document from any position within the document. Elements, attributes, comments, and processing instructions are all node types that can be accessed through the full XPath syntax. For a complete reference to XPath expressions, see the Saxon documentation and other resources 🔗 available on this book's Web site.

The abbreviated syntax is much simpler to use, and it closely resembles the path/file syntax of operating systems such as UNIX or the hierarchical syntax of URLs. Element tags are the "directories" that are separated by the `/` character. Special names such as `.` and `..` allow relative references to be used. Table 12.2 shows the most frequently used XPath syntax elements.

TABLE 12.2 XPath Syntax Elements

XPath Element	*Meaning*
Name	Any XML name token matches any element with the same local name and namespace URI. This means that the prefix between the XPath expression and the target element may be different, as long as the xmlns attributes of each contain the same identical URI.
.	This represents the current context node. Used within an XSLT template, it refers to the current element.
..	This represents the parent node of the context node.
/	This is used to separate parent and child elements. Paths that begin with the / are absolute and are matched starting with the document root. Paths that do not begin with a / are relative to the current node.
//name	This special separator tells XPath to find every element below the current one with the name given.

Making a Quick-and-Dirty Stylesheet

To produce a high-quality output document, it will be necessary to exercise a fine level of control over the output of the stylesheet processor. Whenever possible, the default rules should be used to emit text into the output document. But because the default rules don't deal properly with attribute values, for instance, it is necessary to provide template rules for most of the elements that are found in the source document.

Rather than identify every element tag name in the source document and manually create a template rule, you can use an automated tool to do a faster (and better) job. To generate the basic skeleton stylesheet for this project, I developed the MakeXSLT tool. There are also commercial XML editors (such as XMetal and XMLSpy) that provide some XSLT authoring support. Sites such as `xml.com` contain very comprehensive lists of currently available tools and products.

This tool is written in Java. It parses an XML document, then emits a basic `<xsl:template>` rule for each tag type encountered in the source document. The simple rule that is generated by the tool for each element simply invokes the `<xsl:apply-templates/>` directive. This allows templates to be implemented one at a time while still displaying some reasonable default output.

Sharing Stylesheet Templates

Because XSLT stylesheets are actually XML documents, the normal external parsed entity facilities are available to share templates between stylesheets. The insertion of tags into the stylesheet happens transparently to the XSLT processor, and any conflicts between included elements and elements in the main document are resolved as if the included elements were in the original document all along.

There is another, XSLT-only option for including templates from an external source: the `<xsl:import>` element. This element expects a single attribute, `href`, that sets the URI of the external stylesheet to be imported. Unlike including an external parsed entity, the external stylesheet must be a well-formed standalone XML document. It must have a top-level `<xsl:stylsheet>` element. When it encounters an `import` element, the XSLT processor parses the external stylesheet and adds its template rules to the current set of active templates.

If an external stylesheet includes a template that conflicts with a template in the main stylesheet, the main template will be used. This behavior can be overridden by using the special variation of the `<xsl:apply-templates>` element, `<xsl:apply-imports>`. When this element is used, only rules from imported stylesheets are applied.

Output Document Structure

Before you begin to populate the stylesheet, it is important to determine what the final HTML document will look like. HTML page design is beyond the scope of this discussion, but in most cases the output document will resemble the structure of the input document.

Unless you are well versed in writing raw HTML, in most cases it is easier to build a mock-up of a portion of the desired output page using a WYSIWYG Web page editor. Tools like DreamWeaver and Microsoft FrontPage are useful for developing the desired look and layout of the final HTML document. Then the underlying HTML code can be grafted onto the XSLT stylesheet as necessary.

The source document represents a single product manual that is broken down into separate sections. To simplify navigation, the HTML version should consist of a table of contents with hyperlinks to the start of each individual section. It would also be desirable to create next and previous links between adjacent sections. These links will use the bookmark capabilities of the HTML `<a>` tag.

One of the primary tenets of XML design is that a document does not contain redundant information. Rather than containing a hard-coded list of sections in the document itself, it is assumed that the transformation script will generate any summary information (such as the table of contents) dynamically. To do this, you will need to use two new XSLT features: modes and iteration.

Template Modes

Ordinarily, the entire tree structure of the source document is traversed a single time by the XSLT processor, and each matching template is evaluated in turn. If an element would match more than one template, the last one appearing in the stylesheet would be used. However, in some cases it is useful to have the same element match different templates at different times. This is accomplished by use of the mode attribute.

Besides the match="..." attribute, the <xsl:template> tag also supports the mode attribute. The mode attribute can be used to distinguish between two templates with the same match value. The following XSLT fragment illustrates how one template can cause a different template to be executed based on the provided mode attribute:

```
<xsl:template match="manual">
. . .
  <xsl:apply-templates select="." mode="TOC"/>
. . .
</xsl:template>

<xsl:template match="manual" mode="TOC">
. . .
</xsl:template>
```

Whenever a <manual> element is encountered in the source document, the first rule is evaluated. During the evaluation of the first rule, the <xsl:apply-templates...> tag with a select attribute of . and mode of TOC causes the XSLT processor to locate another rule with match="manual" and mode="TOC". The second rule is evaluated, and then control returns to the first rule. Using modes, the same source element can be processed differently at different times.

Iteration

The rule that creates the table of contents also shows off another interesting XSLT feature: iteration. The following fragment uses iteration to generate the table of contents for the source document:

```
<ul>
  <xsl:for-each select="//section">
    <li><a href="#{@id}"><xsl:value-of select="title"/></a></li>
  </xsl:for-each>
</ul>
```

The <xsl:for-each> tag creates a list of every element that matches the expression in the select attribute ("//section"). Then it processes the nested tags in order once for each element in the list. Any XPath expressions inside the for-each element is relative to the current element being processed.

Notice that several elements in this fragment do not belong to the xsl: namespace. These elements are the actual output elements that will be written to the newly generated document. The default XSLT rule is to echo any non-XSL elements directly to the output file. In this case, the `<ul>` and `<li>` elements are HTML tags that will create an unordered list in the resulting HTML page.

Working with Attribute Values

The line that emits a single `<li>` tag also illustrates how attribute values are referenced:

```
<li><a href="#{@id}"><xsl:value-of select="title"/></a></li>
```

Attribute values are retrieved by prefixing the desired attribute name with the `@` character. This syntax is valid anywhere an XPath expression is accepted (in this case, the `select` attribute of an `xsl:value-of` element). Figure 12.3 shows the HTML page resulting from the table of contents template.

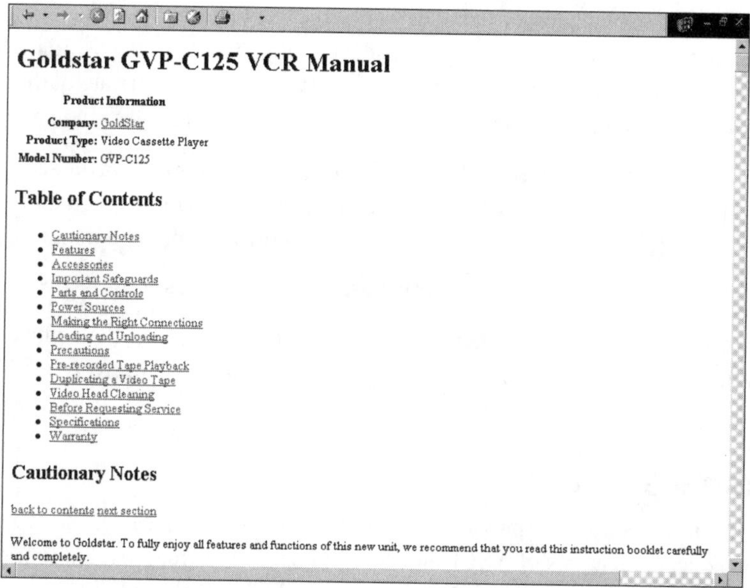

FIGURE 12.3
Table of contents as generated by XSLT iteration.

Notice that in the output document, the `<a>` tag's `href` attribute contains a bookmark with the value of the current element's `id` attribute rather than the string `"#{@id}"`. The `{}` characters have a special meaning whenever they appear in an attribute value in XSLT. The expression inside the curly braces is evaluated, and the resulting value is inserted in the output document.

Automatic Numbering

There are several ways to automatically number elements in an output document. The easiest technique is to use the <xsl:number> element, as in the following example:

```
<xsl:template match="safeguard">
  <tr>
    <td valign="top" rowspan="2"><b><xsl:number/>)</b></td>
    <td><font size="+2"><b><xsl:value-of select="@desc"/></b></font></td>
  </tr>
  <tr>
    <td><blockquote><xsl:apply-templates/></blockquote></td>
  </tr>
</xsl:template>
```

The <xsl:number> element generates sequential numbers. The Saxon documentation provides a very good explanation of the behavior of the <xsl:number> element and its parameters. This instance numbers each <safeguard> sequentially, based on its position relative to its immediate siblings. The <xsl:number> element can also be used to generate outline numbers, figure numbers, roman numerals, and even numbering in other languages (such as Japanese).

An alternative method for numbering elements involves using the <xsl:value-of> tag and the position() XPath function. This method is much less flexible and not as reliable as the <xsl:number> tag. The following code fragment shows how this could be done:

```
<td valign="top" rowspan="2"><b><xsl:value-of select="position()"/>)</b></td>
```

The problem with this approach is that the position() function returns the context node's position "in the context node set." The value returned is not always intuitively obvious, because whitespace nodes such as carriage returns may be counted.

Conditional Sections

To generate the next-section and previous-section hyperlinks, it is necessary to tap some of the more sophisticated features of XSLT and XPath. For obvious reasons, the first section shouldn't have a previous link, and the last section shouldn't have a next link.

In many cases, portions of an output document need to be included only when certain conditions are met. XSLT provides two basic mechanisms for conditional inclusion: <xsl:choose> and <xsl:if>. The first problem we need to solve is this: how do we include a previous section link for every section after the first section?

The <xsl:if> element evaluates the XPath expression provided in its test attribute. If the expression is true, the template code contained in the <xsl:if> element will be included. Now the only thing that remains is to build an XPath Boolean expression that returns true for every

<section> element in the source document except for the first one. Table 12.3 lists the Boolean operators that are provided by XPath.

TABLE 12.3 XPath Boolean Operators

XPath Operator	*Test Performed*
`=`	Compares the left- and right-side expressions for either string or numeric equality.
`!=`	Compares the left- and right-side expressions for inequality.
`<`	Evaluates to true if the left-side expression is lexically or numerically less than the right-side expression.
`<=`	Same as the < operator, but also evaluates to true if the left- and right-side expressions are identical.
`>`	Evaluates to true if the left-side expression is greater than the right-side expression.
`>=`	Same as the > operator, but also evaluates to true if the left- and right-side expressions are identical.
`and`	Performs a Boolean `and` operation on the Boolean values of the left- and right-side expressions. If both expressions are true, the entire expression is true.
`or`	Performs a Boolean `or` operation on the left- and right-side expressions. If either one is true, the entire expression is true.

The following template emits a previous-section hyperlink only if the position of the current section is greater than one:

```
<xsl:if test="position() > 1">
  <xsl:text disable-output-escaping="yes">&amp;nbsp;</xsl:text>
  <a href="#{preceding-sibling::*[position()=1]/@id}">previous section</a>
</xsl:if>
```

The output of one instance of this template in the resulting HTML document looks like this:

```
 <a href="#SEC1">previous section</a>
```

Outputting Raw Markup

Note the usage of the <xsl:text> element to emit the HTML ` ` entity. Emitting entity references into the output document is complicated by the fact that the XSLT stylesheet itself is an XML document. If the raw entity reference ` ` was included directly in the template, the XML parser used by the XSLT processor would try to expand it just like any other XML entity. We could try to escape the ampersand, using the built in & entity reference, like so:

```
&amp;nbsp;
```

Unfortunately, this doesn't produce the desired result in the output document. When the stylesheet itself is parsed, the string " " is passed to the XSLT processor. The XSLT processor then automatically escapes the & character in the output document. The resulting HTML code would look like this:

```
&amp;nbsp;
```

This would cause the string " " to be displayed in the user's Web browser, which was not the desired effect at all. To prevent this automatic character-escaping functionality, XSLT provides the <xsl:text> element. Logically, this element behaves like the XML CDATA tag. It treats its contents as nothing more than text to be echoed to the output document. The crucial feature for producing the   entity required by our application is the disable-output-escaping attribute.

When disable-output-escaping is set to yes, the character data inside the <xsl:text> element is reproduced verbatim in the output document. Therefore, the markup

```
<xsl:text disable-output-escaping="yes">&amp;nbsp;</xsl:text>
```

instructs the XSLT processor to emit the string " " directly into the output document. Note that it is still necessary to escape the initial ampersand character in the " " string. Otherwise, the XML parser used to parse the stylesheet would treat it as a live entity reference.

Referencing Other Nodes

The markup that actually generates the hyperlink uses some advanced features of the XPath language. The value of the <a> tag's href attribute includes the following XPath expression:

```
preceding-sibling::*[position()=1]/@id
```

This is an example of a full XPath expression, one that includes an XPath axis and node test. The term *axis* comes from the tree-oriented nature of XPath. The entire XML document that is referenced by an XPath expression is treated as a tree, and the various types of XML content are encoded as different XPath node types. The axis indicates in which direction to search for the node to be located, and the node test portion determines which nodes are to be included in the result set. The following very simple XML document can be used to better understand the various node axes available:

```
<?xml version="1.0" encoding="UTF-8"?>
<A>
  <B>
    <C/>
    <D>
      <F/>
      <G>
        <I>
          <J/>
        </I>
      </G>
      <H/>
    </D>
    <E/>
  </B>
</A>
```


Figure 12.4 visually displays the relationships between the various document elements.

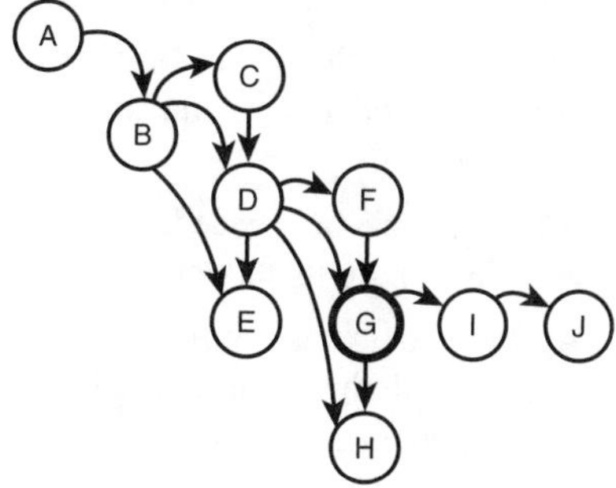

FIGURE 12.4
A simple tree structure to illustrate node axes.

The highlighted node (labeled G) is the current context node. Table 12.4 lists the axes available in an unabbreviated location path, a brief explanation, and the node set that would be returned in each case given the tree in Figure 12.4. Note that the sequence of the nodes in the set matches the order in which they would be visited by an inorder traversal of the document tree.

TABLE 12.4 Axes in an Unabbreviated Location Path

Axis	*Explanation*	*Nodes Returned*
`child`	All the direct child nodes of the context node.	[I]

TABLE 12.4 Continued

Axis	*Explanation*	*Nodes Returned*
`descendant`	All nodes contained in the context node (child nodes, their children, and so on).	[IJ]
`descendant-or-self`	The same node set as the `descendant` axis, including the context node itself.	[GIJ]
`parent`	The direct parent of the context node. This set would be empty for the root node.	[D]
`ancestor`	The parent of the context node and each of its parents, in reverse order (nearest parent first).	[ABD]
`ancestor-or-self`	The same node set as the `ancestor` axis, plus the context node itself.	[ABDG]
`following-sibling`	All the nodes that follow the context node in the document and share its parent.	[H]
`preceding-sibling`	All the nodes that precede the context node and share its parent.	[F]
`following`	All the nodes that begin after the context node in document order. This can include elements at the context element's level and higher.	[HE]
`preceding`	All the nodes that end before the context node begins. This can include elements at the context element's level and higher.	[CF]

NOTE

The XML document and stylesheet that produced the node sets in Table 12.4 are available on the book's Web site as `Listing12-2.xml` and `ShowAxis.xsl`.

The concept of the result set can be somewhat confusing at first. Unlike a directory and file-name string, an XPath expression can actually point to more than one node at the same time. Whenever a single node is called for, XPath silently returns the first node in the result set to the application. When the first node in the set is not the correct node, it becomes necessary to make the XPath expression more precise through the use of XPath predicates. In this respect, an XPath expression is somewhat like a SQL query.

An XPath predicate is nothing more than a Boolean expression that further qualifies which nodes will be returned as a result of an XPath selection path. In the expression used to generate the preceding-section hyperlink, the base path `preceding-sibling::*` would return a set containing all preceding-section elements. To make sure that only the section that immediately precedes the current section is selected, it is necessary to append the predicate `[position()=1]`. This will include only the first element in the preceding sibling's set. Then the `/@id` path selects the value of the `id` attribute from the selected `<section>` tag.

Deployment

Because the HTML page is created through static transformation, deployment involves copying the generated page to the Web server.

Conclusions

Although some applications do not lend themselves to static transformation (such as real-time XML stock quotes, weather reports, and so on), in cases where the underlying XML data rarely changes it is by far the simplest and most efficient solution available. By providing static HTML pages, your content can be deployed on any web server in the world. As one of my favorite bumper-stickers says: eschew obfuscation.

Automating Internal Processes with XML

CHAPTER

13

In the late 1980s, just after I'd started working as a full-time Software Design Engineer (SDE) at Microsoft, I started subscribing to the weekly update that was produced by the Microsoft technical library. At that time, it consisted of about 100 photocopied magazine covers and journal-article abstracts that were stapled together and sent out to interested parties within the company. To facilitate finding the corresponding article or magazine, each page was laboriously hand-numbered by one of the librarians before the update was duplicated and sent out.

Offended at the inefficiency of hand-numbering all those pages (and, to be honest, my regular duties at the time weren't particularly demanding), I set out to come up with a way to automate the process. After doing some research and experimentation with one of our postscript laser printers, I determined that it was possible to run the photocopied sheets through and print a nice, neat page number on each one. Although I didn't get a reward for all of this extra effort, I did make a new friend of the librarian, who no longer had to take an hour out of her day to hand-number these pages. In many business situations, more than friendship can be earned by automating time-consuming and error-prone processes.

Technologies Used:

- **XML**
- **ASP**
- **XSLT**
- **HTML**
- **ADO**

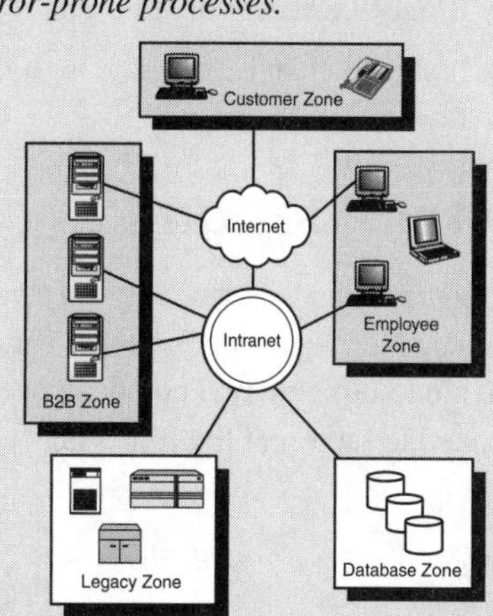

As distasteful as procedures and processes sometimes are, they are a necessary part of modern life. And when they become cumbersome to manage manually, computers tend to get involved. The open-ended nature of an XML document provides a natural basis for encoding business logic that would otherwise have to be described in software.

This project shows how a simple Internet-based workflow system can be built using XML to describe and track the movement of documents through the system.

Problem Description

After a few expensive and embarrassing missteps, a medium-sized advertising agency has decided that it needs a formal workflow system to prevent documents and projects from falling through the cracks in their organization. This system must allow documents to be routed between authors, reviewers, account executives, customers, and even external service providers such as printers and publishers. The particular people involved and even the basic routing process will vary from client to client, so the system needs to be flexible enough to accommodate present and future needs.

Requirements

This system must meet the following requirements:

- It must be robust and fault-tolerant.
- It must incorporate security that prevents documents for one client from being viewed by another client.
- It must support different workflows for each customer, based on the customer's own preferences and needs.
- It should be simple enough for nontechnical users to quickly master.
- It must work across the public Internet. Customers, remote workers, and traveling employees must be able to use the system remotely.
- It must be accessible to users of any operating system.
- It should cleanly integrate with the existing informal Windows NT directory–based workflow.

System Design

The requirements describe a system in which a single company (the ad agency) needs to route documents through different users for approval in a predefined sequence. The system must be available to both internal company users and external users on the public Internet. The system will need to represent the following types of objects:

- Clients
- Projects
- Project files
- Workflows
- Roles
- Users

One important requirement of the system is that files belonging to one client or project be safe from unauthorized viewing. The company's existing system uses Windows NT security and access control lists (ACLs) to limit access to sensitive files. The solution we provide should leverage the processes that they already have in place for tracking files and projects using file-system directories.

Clients and Projects

An example of the existing NT file-system structure used by the company to track client files is shown in Figure 13.1. Each client is given a subdirectory. Each client project with the client subdirectory is given a single subdirectory, which is where all the documents and files related to the project are stored.

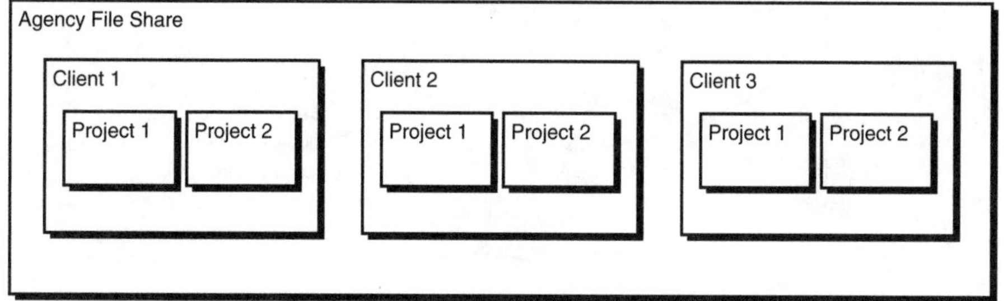

FIGURE 13.1
A sample of the existing file-server directory structure.

Because the resulting workflow system must be accessible from the Internet, the most straightforward way to extend the company's existing system is to run a Web server on its file server. With the existing directory structure used as the framework, internal users can continue to work and save files normally while external users can access the workflow system and view their changes using a Web browser.

Because the system will be running on a Windows NT server, Microsoft IIS is a natural choice for the Web server. The application will be written in VBScript for the ASP platform. For parsing and working with XML files, the COM-based MSXML parser will be used.

Modeling Workflows

Now that the basic platform issue has been resolved, it is necessary to determine how the workflow itself will be represented by the system.

A workflow involves moving a file or group of files through a predetermined sequence of steps. At each step, a single user of the system is designated as the *owner*. Upon receiving ownership, the user will perform some actions (make changes, make comments, reject changes, and so on) and pass the files on to another owner.

As a concrete example, Figure 13.2 shows a simple workflow that would be used in the development of a new magazine ad.

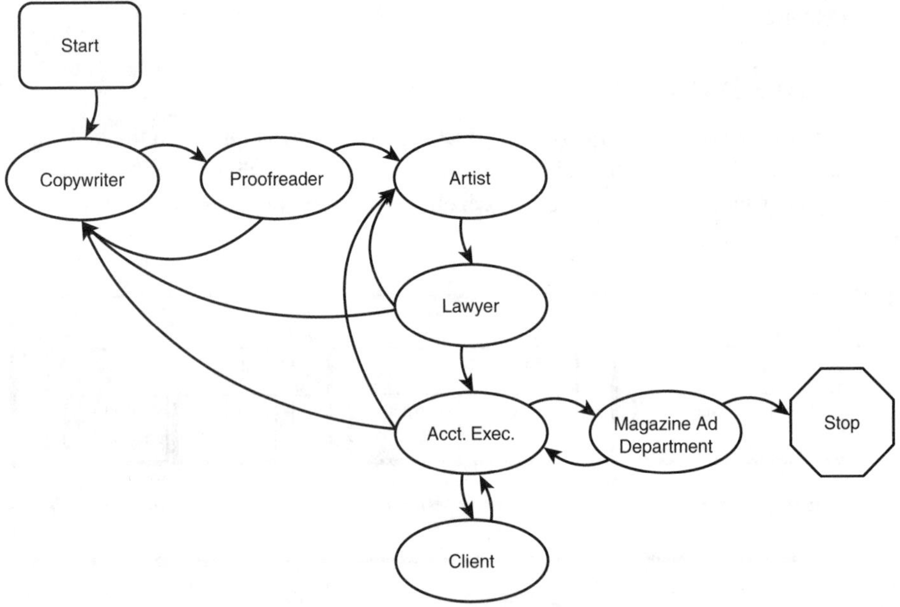

FIGURE 13.2
The basic workflow for creating a new magazine ad.

The circles represent the abstract users who need to modify or review the document at each point in the process. The arrows represent the various paths a document can take from one user to another. The system must be able to model these interconnections, then track the progress of documents as they move through the system. A single abstract workflow might be used by half a dozen projects at the same time, using different users for each role. The system must allow for this workflow reuse.

Besides modeling the abstract workflow, the system must be able to assign concrete users to the various roles in the process. The same basic workflow might be used by three different clients, with different ad-agency personnel fulfilling the duties of writer, proofreader, account executive, and so forth.

A single large client company may also have multiple projects running simultaneously. The system will need to support the concept of a project. A project will consist of a single workflow, the users who will participate in the workflow, and all the documents that make up that project.

To support this functionality, the system will use a single XML document for each project that will contain the following elements:

- Basic project information (for example, the name of the project)
- Status information about the project, such as the current workflow step
- The workflow instructions to be used for the project
- A list of concrete users who will be participating in this project
- A mapping from abstract workflow roles to the concrete users
- A project history log that captures the sequence of steps the project has gone through, along with any user comments that were submitted along the way

Managing Roles and Users

The application will be relying on Windows NT to perform authentication and limit access to project directories. This means that each project document will need to provide a simple lookup table that maps NT usernames to workflow-specific roles.

Also, the agency currently has a simple Access database of users that contains additional information (such as email addresses). To simplify ongoing maintenance and management, it would be optimal if the workflow system could extract this additional information from the database instead of referencing a static document. Next, in the "Implementation Notes" section of this chapter, we will explore how to exploit the features of IIS and ASP to integrate dynamic content like this with static XML documents.

Implementation Notes

To minimize the impact on the existing file structure, the application will be implemented as a set of ASP pages that will be interspersed with the existing project directories and files. The root directory will be shared as an IIS virtual directory, and home pages within the root, client, and project subdirectories will provide navigation links to the workflow system users.

Combining Online and Offline Users

By mixing a Web application with data from a regular file share, we expose ourselves to various problems. To users of the file share, the client and project directories look like a normal hard drive. The IIS Web server, on the other hand, will interpret some types of files (such as ASP scripts) differently. In particular, we have these concerns:

- File-share users accidentally damage the Web application.
- Data files being inadvertently executed by the Web server.
- Web application files being mistaken for data files by file-share users.

To prevent the file-share users from inadvertently damaging the workflow application, Windows NT (or 2000) file access permissions should be used. This will prevent local users from accidentally overwriting Web application files with other files with the same name. Application development users should be added to a single group, and only that group should be given write access to application source files. Another simple step that can be taken to prevent name collisions is to prepend an underscore (_) character to all of our application's filenames (for example, `utilities.inc` becomes `_utilities.inc`).

The second problem is a bit more difficult. By default, various file extensions are associated with Microsoft IIS script processing DLLs. This means that if a file-share user should happen to create a project file with a recognized extension (such as `.ida`, `.shtml`, or `.asp`), IIS would attempt to execute it rather than deliver it to the Web-site user.

One solution to this problem is to remove these file-extension associations from the workflow application virtual directory. This can be done using the Internet Services Manager. The installation instructions, which can be found on this book's Web site, show how the Internet Services Manager can be used to modify the default file-extension associations to minimize the chance that unintended code will be executed. For this application, all ASP pages will have the extension `.aspx`.

The simplest answer to the last issue (application files being mistaken for data) is to mark all the Web application files as hidden. They will still be interpreted properly by IIS, and most file-share users will not see them. Only advanced users (who enable viewing hidden files) will see them.

Security Considerations

On the Internet, security is always a primary concern. For this application, it is important to ensure that only authorized users can view the project contents over the Web. Also, user security is required so that the current owner of the project can be identified.

Combining NTFS file access control lists with the various directory security options available through IIS, the workflow application can force Internet users to log in using either Basic Authentication (supported by most Web browsers, but not very secure) or Windows NT Authentication (which is supported only by Microsoft Internet Explorer 5.0 and above). The workflow application can then use the contents of the `Request.ServerVariables("AUTH_USER")` variable as a trusted user ID within the application. This will be the same as the NT logon name (either `user` or `domain\user`). Later, when we dissect the `_project.xml` file, we will see how this name is used to control application flow.

Application Structure

Basically three types of users must be accommodated by the system: agency employees, clients, and third-party vendors. Although it is beyond the scope of this application, the NT file permissions would be configured to allow these different types of users different levels of access to the directory tree. Agency employees would be given full access to all clients and files, whereas clients would be able only to view the contents of their own client folder. And third-party vendors (such as printers or publishers) would be limited to viewing only those projects and files that were necessary to do their job.

Based on these user types, Figure 13.3 shows the site navigation map for the application. **See** page 137 for an example of online workflow application Web-site navigation.

Root Directory and Client Home Pages

The physical directory structure of the application actually mirrors the logical organization of the Web site, so the obvious solution is to create a home page for the root directory and each client directory that displays a list of its subdirectories as hyperlinks. Then, as client and project directories are added and removed, the Web site will automatically reflect the changes. Listing 13.1 shows the VBScript code for the `ShowDirMenu()` subroutine. This subroutine is used by the client and project home pages to display a list of hyperlinks to their child directories.

LISTING 13.1 The `ShowDirMenu` Subroutine

```
<OBJECT RUNAT="Server" SCOPE="Page" ID=fso PROGID="Scripting.FileSystemObject">
</OBJECT>
<OBJECT RUNAT="Server" SCOPE="Page" ID=pc PROGID=
➥"MSWC.PermissionChecker">
</OBJECT>


<%
  Sub ShowDirMenu(strParentDir)
%>
  <ul>
```

LISTING 13.1 Continued

```
<%
  Dim dir
  Set dir = fso.GetFolder(Server.MapPath(strParentDir))

  Dim fld

  For Each fld In dir.SubFolders
    If (fld.Attributes And 2) = 0 And pc.HasAccess(fld.Path + "\_default.aspx")
➥Then
%>
  <li><a href="<%=strParentDir & "/" & fld.Name%>"><%=fld.Name%>
➥</a></li>
<%
    End If
  Next
%>
  </ul>
<%
  End Sub
%>
```

This code uses the ASP `Scripting.FileSystemObject` object to enumerate the physical subdirectories of the directory given (which may be "." for the current directory). The single `If` statement performs a test to see whether the directory is hidden (the 2-bit is set) and whether the current user is permitted to see it. To perform the access check, it uses the `MSWC.PermissionChecker` object that ships with IIS.

> **NOTE**
>
> For some reason, the `HasAccess()` method of the `PermissionChecker` object does not work correctly when given a directory path. The code therefore has to check for a file that is known to exist (`_default.aspx`) in the target directory.

The ASP code for each client home page is identical. Rather than copying the code for the entire page to each client directory, a simple stub file that uses the `#include` ASP directive to include the actual page is used. Then any changes that are made to the master document (`_clienthome.aspx`) will be automatically propagated to all the client directories.

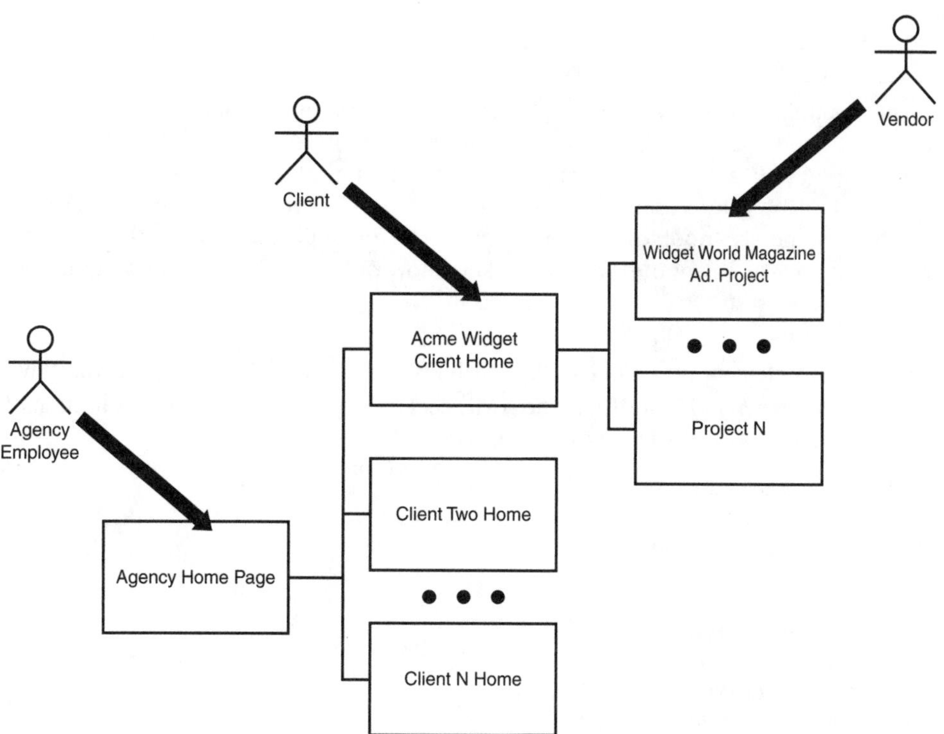

FIGURE 13.3
Online workflow application Web-site navigation.

Project Document DTD

The details about the project (list of participating users, which type of workflow is being used, current workflow state, user role assignments, and project history) are stored in a file called `_project.xml`. Each project has its own distinct XML document so that different workflows and groups of users can be easily supported. Before you examine a specific document instance, it is useful to look at the project document type definition. The complete DTD can be found in the `_workflowproject.dtd` file.

The document element type for a project document is `<project>`, which is declared like this:

```
<!ELEMENT project (name, current_state, workflow, users, roles,
➥history)>
```

The first two element types (`<name>` and `<current_state>`) are leaf nodes that contain global information about the project. The name is a simple string. The text of the `<current_state>` element is actually a reference to one of the `<state>` elements of the document's workflow.

NOTE

If you're familiar with XML, you might wonder why this application doesn't use the ID and IDREF attribute type mechanism to create the link between the <current_state> and <state> elements. The major limitation of the ID/IDREf framework is that the values used must match the XML Name production. In this application, the state name also doubles as a descriptive label for UI purposes. XML names must begin with a letter, cannot have spaces, and allow only limited punctuation (_ or :).

The <workflow> element type provides the capability to fully describe a complex workflow, such as the one shown in Figure 13.2. The XML declaration of a workflow is a collection of <state> and <action> elements, declared like so:

```
<!ELEMENT workflow (state+)>
<!ATTLIST workflow
  start_state CDATA #REQUIRED
>

<!ELEMENT state (action*)>
<!ATTLIST state
  name CDATA #REQUIRED
  owner CDATA #IMPLIED
>

<!ELEMENT action EMPTY>
<!ATTLIST action
  target CDATA #REQUIRED
  desc CDATA #IMPLIED
>
```

What this means is that a workflow is composed of one or more states, and a state has zero or more actions. A state must have a name and an owner attribute. To allow workflows to be easily reused, the owner attribute is an abstract role name that points to a <role> element within the document. Later, we'll see how this extra level of abstraction allows new projects to be quickly defined.

A <workflow> element must have a start_state attribute that is used as the starting point for a new workflow. The application uses this attribute when a project document has an empty <current_state> element (such as when it is first created).

The collection of <action> elements for a particular state defines how the project can advance from one state to another. Within the application, the current project owner is shown these options as part of the project home page. When the project owner selects a particular action, the application updates the <current_state> element of the document.

The <users> element contains a directory of all the actual system users that will fill roles in the workflow. It is a simple list of <user> elements, declared as shown here:

```
<!ELEMENT users (user*)>
```

Each <user> element represents a system user ID (which the ASP application gets from the Request.ServerVariables("AUTH_USER") value). By mapping system user IDs to <user> elements, the ASP application can access additional user information (such as the user's real name and email address). The following XML declarations define the contents of the <user> element:

```
<!ELEMENT user (name, title, company, email)>
<!ATTLIST user
  userid ID #REQUIRED
>

<!ELEMENT title (#PCDATA)>

<!ELEMENT company (#PCDATA)>

<!ELEMENT email (#PCDATA)>

<!ELEMENT name (#PCDATA)>
```


The <roles> element serves as a map between system users and workflow role names. Each <state> element within a <workflow> has an owner attribute, which is a role name. The ASP application uses the list of roles to map this owner role name to an actual system user ID. The contents of the <roles> element is declared to be

```
<!ELEMENT roles (role+)>

<!ELEMENT role EMPTY>
<!ATTLIST role
  name CDATA #REQUIRED
  userid CDATA #REQUIRED
>
```

This two-step lookup process allows the same workflow to be used in multiple projects. If user IDs were hard-coded into the workflow specification, the workflow itself would need to be copied and modified for each project. In the next section, the operational aspects of XML content reuse are addressed in more detail.

The final top-level element in a <project> document is the <history> element. Whenever the current project owner advances the project to a new workflow state, the ASP application inserts a new <state-change> element into the history. This state-change record includes information about the old project owner, the previous workflow state, the new state, the date and time the change occurred, and a user comment. This history is later displayed to all project users on the project home page. These are the declarations for the `<history>` element:

```
<!ELEMENT history (state-change*)>

<!ELEMENT state-change (owner, old-state, new-state, timestamp, comment)>

<!ELEMENT owner (#PCDATA)>
<!ATTLIST owner
  role CDATA #REQUIRED
  userid CDATA #REQUIRED
>

<!ELEMENT old-state (#PCDATA)>
<!ELEMENT new-state (#PCDATA)>
<!ELEMENT timestamp (#PCDATA)>
<!ELEMENT comment (#PCDATA)>
```

Implementing a `_project.xml` Document

To gain access to information about a project, the ASP application simply causes MSXML to parse the appropriate `_project.xml` document file on the server. This is a normal XML document, and it is subject to the normal rules of well-formedness and validity of any XML 1.0 document. How a project document is created is beyond the scope of this project, but for the ASP application to interpret it properly, it must conform to the document type definition in `_workflowproject.dtd`.

Although all the content for the project document could be contained in a single file, XML provides support for including external content through the external parsed entity facility. Listing 13.2 shows a sample project document that uses external entities to include document content.

LISTING 13.2 A Sample Project Document

```
<?xml version="1.0" encoding="utf-8"?>
<!DOCTYPE project SYSTEM "../../_workflowproject.dtd" [

<!--
  This entity reads a list of current system users from
  the database in XML format.
-->
<!ENTITY system_users SYSTEM
    "http://www.strategicxml.com/examples/workflow/demo/_system-users.xml">
```

LISTING 13.2 Continued

```
<!--
  The next entity links to the workflow that will be used for this project.
-->
<!ENTITY new-magazine-ad-workflow SYSTEM
    "../../_workflows/_new-magazine-ad.ent">
]>
<project>
  <name>Widget World Magazine Ad.</name>
  <current_state>copy proofing</current_state>
  &new-magazine-ad-workflow;
  <users>
    &system_users;
  </users>
  <roles>
    <role name="copywriter" userid="aalpha"/>
    <role name="proofreader" userid="bbravo"/>
    <role name="graphic_designer" userid="ccharlie"/>
    <role name="lawyer" userid="ddelta"/>
    <role name="account_exec" userid="eecho"/>
    <role name="client_rep" userid="ffoxtrot"/>
    <role name="ad_sales_rep" userid="ggolf"/>
  </roles>
  <history>
    <state-change>
      <owner role="copywriter" userid="aalpha">Alex Alpha</owner>
      <old-state>copy development</old-state>
      <new-state>copy proofing</new-state>
      <timestamp>5/19/2001 11:26:42 PM</timestamp>
      <comment>Ready for artwork.</comment>
    </state-change>
  </history>
</project>
```


Two external entities are declared in this document: system_users and new-magazine-ad-workflow. The first one is used to include a list of <user> elements that will participate in the workflow. The second entity includes a predefined magazine ad–creation workflow from the _new-magazine-ad.ent file. There are important differences between how the files containing the two entities are referenced and how the actual file contents are generated.

The SYSTEM keyword in each entity declaration indicates that the entity should be loaded using the URL given. In this case, the URL for the system_users entity is a fully qualified HTTP

URL that points to an entity on this book's Web site (`www.strategicxml.com`). No matter where this project document is located, the user list will always be loaded using that particular URL.

The `new-magazine-ad-workflow` entity, however, is a relative URL that points to a subdirectory somewhere above the directory where the document is located. Notice that there is no protocol (for example, `http:`) given in the URL itself. This indicates to the XML parser that it should use the same protocol as was used to load the original XML document. For example, if the `_project.xml` file were loaded using a URL, such as

```
http://localhost/workflow/Acme%20Widgets/
➥Widget%20World%20Project/_project.xml
```

the XML parser would attempt to load the `new-magazine-ad-workflow` entity using the following URL:

```
http://localhost/workflow/_workflows/_new-magazine-ad.ent
```

But if the XML parser loaded the project document using a file path, such as

```
file://c:/workflow/Acme%20Widgets/Widget%20World%20Project/_project.xml
```

then the parser would use a file URL to find the entity:

```
file://c:/workflow/_workflows/_new-magazine-ad.ent
```

The choice between absolute and relative URLs should be made on a case-by-case basis, depending on the requirements of the document. For instance, encoding a fully qualified URL to a Web server is convenient if the document will be parsed only on Internet-connected computers. Relative URLs enable documents to be freely relocated, as long as their surrounding directory structure is intact.

Another convenient feature of loading portions of the document via external entities is that the source of the external content can vary. In this case, the content for the `system_users` entity is loaded from a URL on the Strategic XML Web site. The XML parser doesn't need to be aware of how the content is generated by the Web server, any more than a user's Web browser needs to be concerned about how a Web page is written.

In this case, the information about the system users is stored in an Access database that is updated by the agency personnel. This database has a table named `Users` that contains a row for every NT user that will use the workflow system. The `strUserName` column gives the login name that needs to be used in the `userid` attribute of each `<user>` element. There are several options for generating the requisite `<user>` elements from the data in the database:

- Have a user manually generate the external entity file from the data in the database, and host the document on the Web site.

- Write a batch program to generate the entity file on demand, and store the generated file on the Web server.
- Generate the entity file dynamically, using server-side scripting.

Although the first two options might be acceptable (depending on the frequency and scope of the changes made to the database), the last option is remarkably simple to implement using the power of IIS's ASP scripting engine. Although by default only files ending in `.asp` are interpreted by the ASP scripting engine, modifying the file-extension associations through the Internet Services Manager can cause any text file (such as an XML document) to be interpreted as an ASP script.

Although there will be some performance consequences for documents of the same type that are completely static, creating this association is a low-impact operation. Unless the `<%%>` ASP delimiters appear in a document, the ASP processor will simply echo the entire document to the HTTP client verbatim. Figure 13.4 shows the Application Configuration dialog after the `.xml` extension has been associated with the ASP script processor.

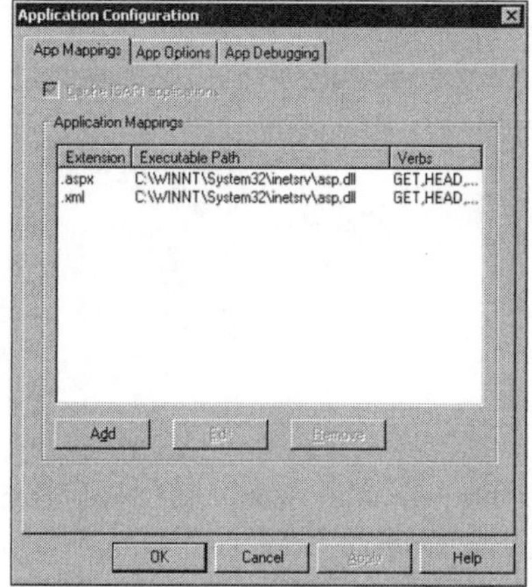

FIGURE 13.4
Enabling dynamic XML scripting on IIS.

For the most part, generating an XML document for use by an XML parser is not much different from generating an HTML document for use by a Web browser. Listing 13.3 shows the source code for the `_system-users.xml` script that generates a list of `<user>` elements using the `FirstVirtualAgency.mdb` sample database.

LISTING 13.3 _system-users.xml Source Code

```
<%@ language="vbscript" %>
<% Option Explicit %>
<!--#include file="_utilities.inc"-->
<%
  Response.ContentType = "text/xml"
  Dim cn
  Set cn = Server.CreateObject("ADODB.Connection")
  cn.Open "SXML-FVADemo"

  Dim rs
  Set rs = Server.CreateObject("ADODB.Recordset")

  rs.Open "select * from UserCompanyView", cn

  If Not rs.BOF Then
    While Not rs.EOF
%>
    <user userid="<%=XMLEscape(rs("strUserName"))%>">
      <name><%=XMLEscape(rs("strName"))%></name>
      <title><%=XMLEscape(rs("strTitle"))%></title>
      <company><%=XMLEscape(rs("strCompanyName"))%></company>
      <email><%=XMLEscape(rs("strEmailAddr"))%></email>
    </user>
<%
      rs.MoveNext
    Wend
  End If
%>
```

The basic code flow should be very familiar to any ASP programmer who has worked with databases using ActiveX Database Objects (ADO). First an ADO `Connection` is opened to the database, and then a `Recordset` is created and opened. The SQL statement used to open the recordset returns all the rows from an Access view called `UserCompanyView`. Then the script loops through each row, emitting a single `<user>` element for each.

Each of the values to be included in the XML documents is passed through the `XMLEscape()` function. This function is located in the `_utilities.inc` ASP include file. Because certain characters cannot appear within parsed character data (most importantly <, >, and `&`), this function escapes them using the predefined `>`, `<`, and `&` entities.

The only line of code that might be somewhat unfamiliar to an ASP programmer is this:

```
Response.ContentType = "text/xml"
```

This is not absolutely necessary for our application, but it is a good idea. By explicitly setting the content type, a Web browser will be able to properly format and display the content of the page if it is requested directly. Unlike Windows, in most cases the Web browser will ignore the extension of the file and honor the MIME type sent through this mechanism. In this case, the stream will be read directly by an XML parser, and the MIME type will not be significant.

NOTE

Although this feature allows browsers to display XML documents, in this particular case the `_system-users.xml` page is not a well-formed XML document. Well-formed documents have only one top-level element, and this script generates a list of `<user>` elements without an enclosing document element. This is not a problem when it is included as an entity, but it cannot be parsed by itself.

The other entity (`new-magazine-ad-workflow`) simply links to a static file that contains the new magazine ad workflow. Storing these workflows separately enables them to be reused for different projects.

The Project Home Page

Although some users might actually prefer to read the raw XML source for a project, most would prefer a more user-friendly HTML version. Also, the application logic for moving from one workflow state to another must be implemented somewhere. Each project directory has a home page that performs the following functions:

- Displays global project information.
- Shows a list of hyperlinks to the project data files.
- Gives the current workflow status and owner of the project. Provides options for moving to another workflow state to the owner of the project.
- Lists the complete project history, including user comments, status changes, and timestamps.

All of this information resides in the `_project.xml` document that is in each project directory. The project home page parses this document, then constructs the appropriate HTML view of the data for the current user. The HTML is generated using a combination of ASP and XSLT techniques. Figure 13.5 shows an example of the project home page as it might appear to the current project owner.

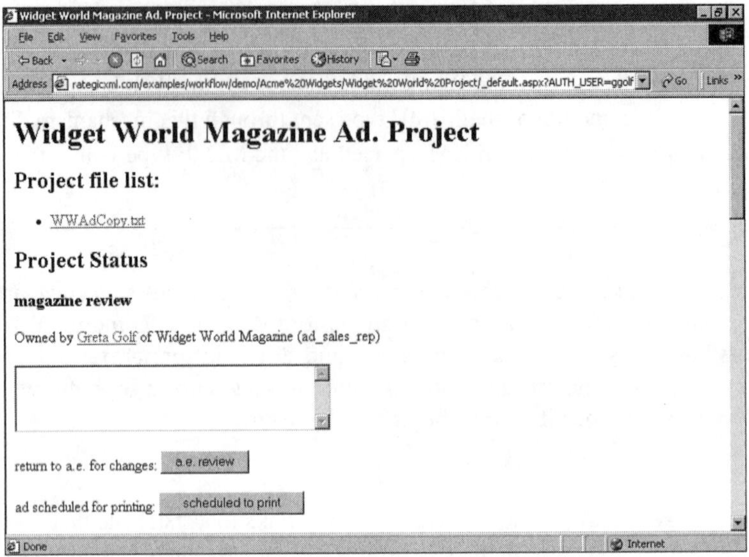

FIGURE 13.5
The project home page for the current project owner example.

The ASP code for displaying this page is located in `_projecthome.inc` and `_utilities.inc`. See the source-file comments for more detailed information about how the page is generated. There are a few peculiarities about server-side XML parsing using MSXML that need to be addressed both within the application source code and on the Web server itself. See the the installation notes for more information about server-side XML parsing.

Deployment

These are the steps to deploy this example:

1. Unpack the sample files onto a server that has Microsoft IIS installed.
2. Create a new virtual directory in the Internet Services Manager for the `/examples/workflow/demo` subdirectory of the unpacked source.
3. In the IIS GUI, open the properties for the new virtual directory, and make the following changes:

    - On the Virtual Directory tab, click the Configuration button. In the App Mappings tab of the configuration dialog, remove all the Application Mappings except the one for `.asp`. Change the extension in `.asp` to `.aspx`. Then add a new mapping that is identical to the `.aspx` mapping, except that the extension is `.xml`. (See Figure 13.4).

- On the Documents tab, remove all the default document names and then add `_default.aspx` to the list.
- In a real-live application, the Directory Security tab should be used to configure the application to force users to log in using Basic or Windows NT authentication. There is a comment in `_utilities.inc` about enabling security within the workflow application.

4. Create a new ODBC data source called `SXML-FVADemo` that points to the `FirstVirtualAgency.mdb` database located in the `/examples/workflow/source` subdirectory.

The site should now be functional.

Conclusion

The primary purpose of this application is to show how XML can be used to greatly simplify tasks that would have previously required more elaborate and less flexible technologies. Before XML, a workflow application like this would probably have been written using RDBMS technology to store and track project changes. This approach is not inherently bad, but it does require more rigorous engineering and additional layers of application logic. XML provides an attractive alternative to database technology for certain types of applications in which no additional value can be gained from performing relational analysis on the application data.

Offline Order Processing Using Store-and-Forward

CHAPTER 14

In the always-on post-Internet world, instant worldwide connectivity is often taken for granted. This was brought home to me rather abruptly when my ISDN connection through my local telephone company went down one sunny Friday afternoon, and stayed down for 11 days. Sure, it would occasionally come up for 10 minutes here, a couple of hours there. But the fact was that most of the time my little home network was on its own, adrift. For a programmer, writer, and e-mail junkie, this was a far-from-acceptable situation.

Ten years ago, incomplete and unreliable networks were the rule, not the exception. Systems had to be built to accommodate these little unexpected outages, and take advantage when connectivity was available. Even though my new cable modem service has been down only a handful of times (and never for more than an hour), building reliable systems will never go out of style.

Technologies Used:

- **Java**
- **JDOM**
- **SMTP**
- **POP3**

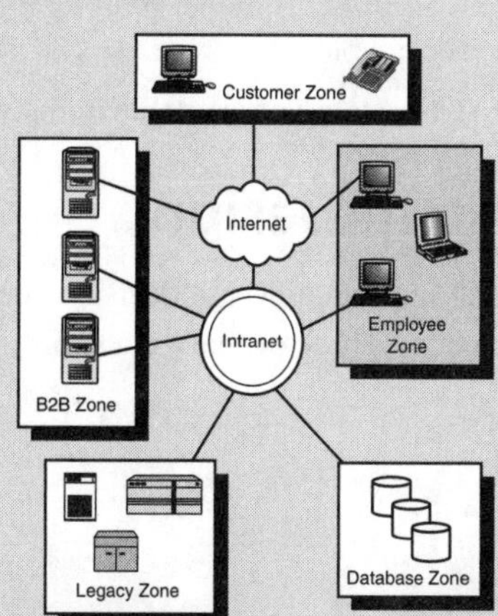

Despite the appealing vision of an always-on wireless Internet connection, there are still many situations in which connectivity just won't be available. Even if perfect wireless access were an option (which it isn't), rural areas, airplanes, and shielded buildings would still require solutions that don't depend on continuous connectivity. This chapter shows how XML can be used as a data format for an asynchronous messaging application.

Problem Description

A large consumer electronics company needs to equip its sales force with a very reliable, portable order-entry system. The order-entry client application will run on the sales rep's laptop, and the central order processing system will reside on the corporate network at the home office.

The sales force is highly mobile. It must be possible for them to enter new orders at any time. Figure 14.1 shows a conceptual view of the system.

Requirements

This system has the following requirements:

- It must be possible to enter new orders at any time, even when the sales person's laptop isn't connected to the Internet.
- Orders should be forwarded to the central order processing service whenever network connectivity is restored.
- Users should not have to change their behavior based on whether the system is in online or offline mode.
- The order client application should be platform independent, allowing the sales force the freedom to change operating systems in the future.
- Due to schedule and budget constraints, the system should be built using off-the-shelf or freely available components.
- Real-time inventory control is not a priority. Collecting orders for batch processing is acceptable.
- The catalog of available items will not change frequently.

System Design

Several important design decisions need to be made that will affect the overall architecture of the system. Three primary questions need to be answered:

- What technology will we use to store and forward orders to the central system?
- What language and/or design tool will we use to build the client application?
- What language or technology will we use to implement the order processing service?

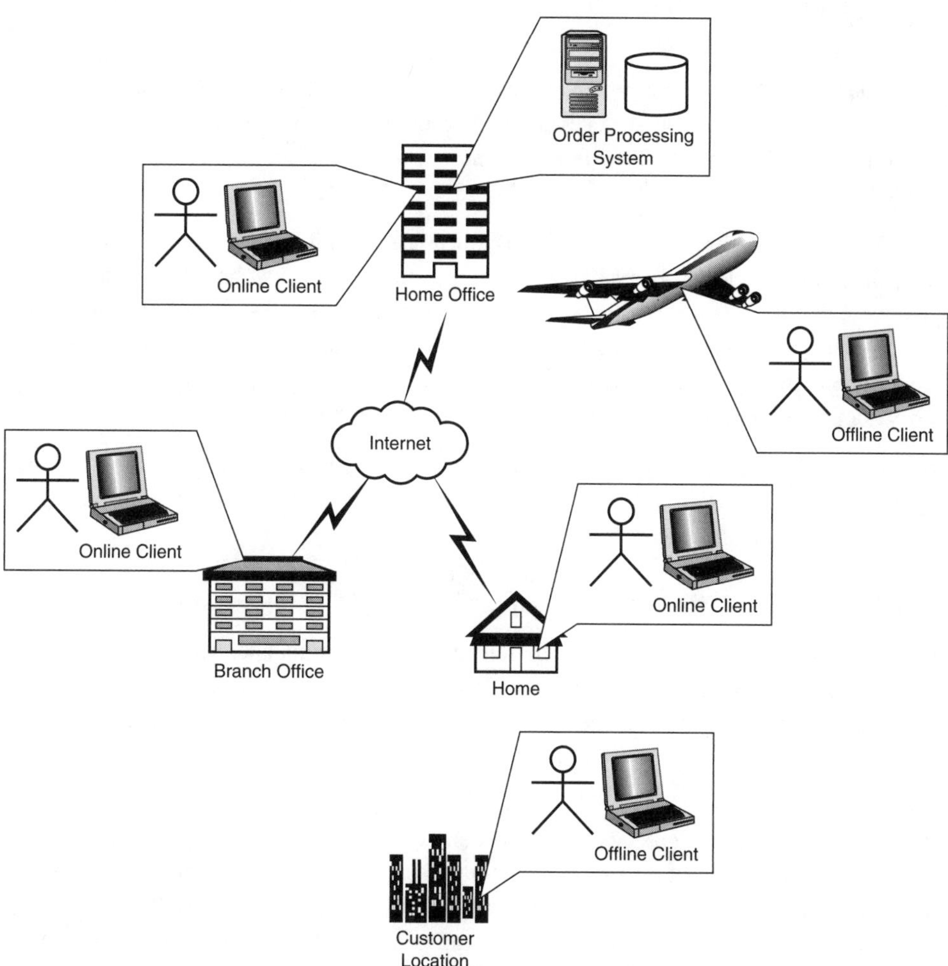

FIGURE 14.1
A conceptual view of the required order processing system.

Store-and-Forward Technology

There are several possible answers to the first system-design question, but time and budget constraints dictate that a custom developed solution is impractical. Although several commercial message queuing technologies are available, one of the oldest and most reliable messaging platforms is the Simple Mail Transfer Protocol (SMTP).

In this application, the order processing service will have a well-known e-mail address to which the clients will send messages containing order information. The order processing service will periodically poll its inbox, retrieving new orders and deleting them as they are processed.

Using SMTP as the underlying message transport offers several benefits. It is well understood. Various open-source and freely available SMTP implementations can be incorporated into our system without cost. Because virtually every major company already has some sort of e-mail system in place, the only real configuration necessary is to add a new public e-mail account for the order processing system. In most cases, this is much easier than convincing the network security administrator to open a new public TCP/IP port in the corporate firewall.

Another incidental benefit of selecting a mature and open standard such as SMTP is the flexibility it gives us in choosing the client and server technologies. Many commercial and open-source SMTP interface packages are available.

Client Application Design Tool

As for the second design question, the requirement for platform independence makes Java a natural choice for building the client application. Because the client will make heavy use of XML data, the large number of open-source XML parsing packages also weighs heavily in its favor.

Server Implementation

As for the final system-design question, almost any operating system or platform can be used to build the server portion of the order processing system. Every major operating system and programming language in use today contains support for interfacing with TCP/IP sockets. Also, because the order processing system will run on a protected corporate network in a controlled environment, the underlying system can be changed at any time without impacting clients in the field.

With this in mind, the order processing system for this example will be written in Java as well. Incoming orders will be queued in an XML file for subsequent processing (presumably by an order-fulfillment system).

System Architecture

Figure 14.2 illustrates the basic architecture of this system and shows how the parts will fit together.

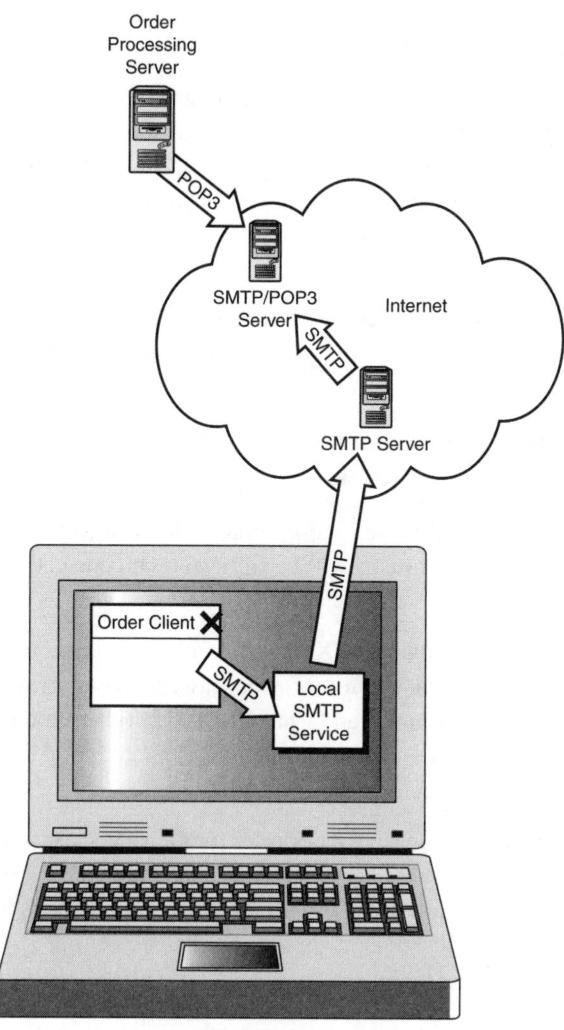

FIGURE 14.2
Architectural diagram of order processing system.

The local SMTP service running on the sales rep's laptop will queue outgoing order messages, and continually try to forward them to the order processing system's e-mail box at the home office. Whenever the sales person connects to the Internet, any queued messages will be transmitted automatically, without the need for user intervention.

Implementation Notes

The completed system will consist of two distinct programs: the GUI order-entry client and the non-interactive order processing service. Although an SMTP service plays a vital part in the overall system, it will be treated as a black-box component. The "Deployment" section later in this chapter explains the role of the SMTP server and its use.

Business Analysis

Before examining the nuts-and-bolts details of the client and server applications, we must spend some time gathering the business requirements behind the system. Before proceeding, it is necessary to answer the following two questions:

- Where will the list of items that can be ordered come from?
- Exactly what information needs to be collected to complete an order?

Because it is known in advance that the catalog of items for sale will change infrequently, a simple text file containing a list of items will be sufficient. Of course, this file will be written in XML.

To help tie together the ideas surrounding XML and unified business processes, our hypothetical salesman will be selling accessories for the videocassette player used for the examples in Chapter 12, "Web Content Publishing," and Chapter 18, "Unifying Product Documentation." Figure 14.3 shows the various publications that can be generated from the authoritative information in the product manual document.

Within the product manual itself, several accessories for the videocassette player are mentioned. If our business processes dictate that the product manual is the canonical source of information about the product, it is possible to generate a definitive list of accessories from the manual.

Building the Catalog

Because the information about the items to be included in the catalog is already stored in an XML document, constructing the catalog dynamically using XSLT is an obvious solution. Before we can construct the XSLT script, however, we need to know what needs to be included in the final document.

The information included in the catalog will fall into three main areas: product information, item information, and order application configuration information.

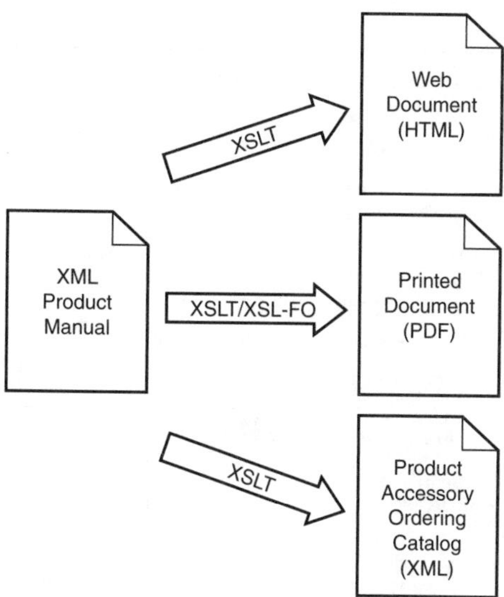

FIGURE 14.3
Generating multiple views of the base XML document.

The product information will be identical to the product information included in the product manual XML document. The XSLT stylesheet will be able to copy it verbatim from the source document.

The item information is scattered throughout the source document in `<accessory>` nodes, so the catalog generation stylesheet will need to extract them.

The following information needs to be included in the catalog about each item:

- A part number
- A description
- The item manufacturer's name

Listing 14.1 shows the document type definition for the simple catalog file that is read by the order client application.

LISTING 14.1 DTD for Simple Item Catalog Document (`OrderCatalog.dtd`)

```
<!--
  OrderCatalog.dtd

  DTD for the simple distributed ordering application example
  included in the book Strategic XML.
-->
```

LISTING 14.1 Continued

```
<!ELEMENT catalog ( product_info, order_info, items ) >

<!ELEMENT company_name ( #PCDATA ) >

<!ELEMENT desc ( #PCDATA ) >

<!ELEMENT item ( desc, manufacturer ) >
<!ATTLIST item part_num NMTOKEN #REQUIRED >

<!ELEMENT items ( item+ ) >

<!ELEMENT manufacturer ( #PCDATA | company_name | web_site )* >

<!ELEMENT model_num ( #PCDATA ) >

<!ELEMENT order_info EMPTY >
<!ATTLIST order_info address CDATA #REQUIRED >
<!ATTLIST order_info method NMTOKEN #REQUIRED >

<!ELEMENT product_info ( manufacturer, product_type, model_num ) >

<!ELEMENT product_type ( #PCDATA ) >

<!ELEMENT web_site ( #PCDATA ) >
```

Any catalog conforming to this document type definition could be used by the order client application. In this case, the catalog will be generated from the product manual document using a simple XSLT transform. The stylesheet that performs this transformation is `build_catalog.xsl`. This same stylesheet could be used to create catalogs from other product manuals in the future.

Contents of an Order

Now that the contents of the order catalog have been defined, it is necessary to determine what information must be collected as part of a given order.

A real-world order processing system would need to collect a great deal of information about the purchaser, delivery instructions, billing requirements, and so forth. Because the purpose of this application is only to illustrate the principles involved, an order will include the following information:

- The customer's name
- The customer's credit-card number
- A list of item numbers to order, with a quantity for each

This information will be encoded as an XML document that will be sent as the body of an e-mail message by the `OrderClient` application. The document will conform to the document type definition shown in Listing 14.2.

LISTING 14.2 DTD for a Simple Order Message (`OrderMessage.dtd`)

```
<!ELEMENT order (customer_name, credit_card_num, items)>

<!ELEMENT customer_name (#PCDATA)>

<!ELEMENT credit_card_num (#PCDATA)>

<!ELEMENT items (item+)>

<!ELEMENT item EMPTY>

<!ATTLIST item
  part_num CDATA #REQUIRED
  quantity CDATA #REQUIRED
```

The `OrderClient` Application

The client application that is used to transmit orders is written in Java. It provides a very simple GUI for selecting which items to order, the quantities for each, and the customer's name and credit-card number. Figure 14.4 shows the client application in action.

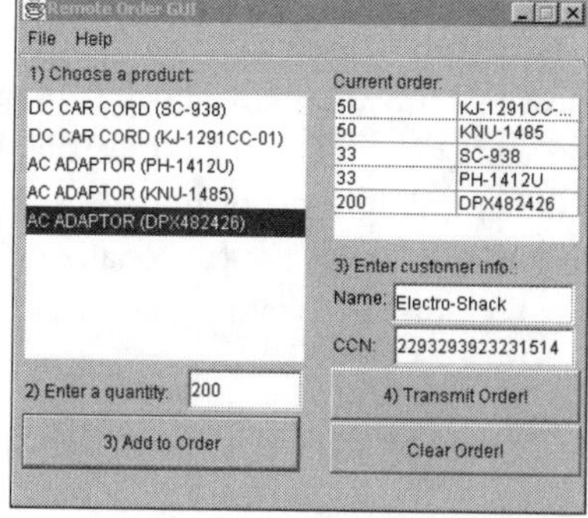

FIGURE 14.4
The GUI client.

This application was built using Borland's JBuilder 3.0 IDE. The controls were created and laid out using the JBuilder designer.

The main program entry point is located in `OrderClient.java`. The `OrderClient` class creates a new instance of the `OrderFrame` class and passes the command-line arguments on to it. All the real work is done by the `OrderFrame` class.

The constructor of the `OrderFrame` class performs several important functions:

- Initializes AWT and runs the control creation code that was generated by JBuilder
- Loads the client configuration file
- Locates and loads the catalog
- Initializes the window controls and current order document to prepare for a new order to be placed

After the application window has been created and prepared for a new order, the user adds new items to his order by selecting an item from the product list, entering a quantity, and then clicking the Add to Order button. This causes a new `<item>` element to be added to the current order document. When the user is done selecting items, he clicks the Transmit Order button to send it to the order server's e-mail inbox.

Several different APIs and implementations of those APIs are available for working with XML in a Java application. This particular application uses the relatively new JDOM library. JDOM is an open-source project that was created by Jason Hunter and Brett McLaughlin and is maintained by a community of developers through the project Web site, `www.jdom.org`. In February 2002, JDOM was accepted by the Java Community Process (JCP) as Java Specification Request 102. This is the first step toward making JDOM part of the official Sun core Java platform.

JDOM provides a lightweight, Java-specific API for creating in-memory document trees. These trees can be created either by parsing an XML source document or by programmatically creating document, element, and attribute objects. The JDOM distribution includes different classes for creating JDOM trees using either a W3C Document Object Model parser or a Simple API for XML parser. It also includes a rich output class for serializing a document to a Java stream. The order client application uses both of these features, because it needs to both read existing documents and write new documents.

Two types of XML documents are read by the order client: the client configuration file and the product catalog.

The Client Configuration File

Most applications have various parameters and settings that need to be preserved between program invocations. Most operating systems provide some facilities for this task (such as the Windows Registry), but this solution is not appropriate for a cross-platform application.

In the past, most application developers chose to formulate their own proprietary configuration file formats. They would then write code to read and write these files. Fortunately, XML has relieved the developer from the burden of developing new and inventive file formats to solve a relatively mundane problem. XML is a good format for storing arbitrary hierarchical information in a flexible text format. The file is human-readable, so in case of corruption or misconfiguration, it is actually possible for a user to fix his settings using a text editor.

Listing 14.3 shows a sample configuration file. It is parsed when the main application frame window is created, and the resulting JDOM `Document` object is kept as an instance member throughout the life of the application.

LISTING 14.3 A Sample Order Client Configuration File

```
<?xml version="1.0" encoding="utf-8"?>
<order_client_config>
  <salesman>
    <name>Scott Means</name>
    <email>smeans@strategicxml.com</email>
  </salesman>
  <catalog_url>file:c:/OrderClient/VCPCatalog.xml</catalog_url>
  <smtp_server>localhost</smtp_server>
</order_client_config>
```

Before it is possible to use the JDOM library to parse an XML document, it is necessary to create either a `SAXBuilder` or a `DOMBuilder` object instance. JDOM includes no XML parser of its own. Instead, it allows the registration of standard parsers that conform to one of the two major XML parsing APIs, which it then uses to create its in-memory document images. The following code appears in the `OrderFrame()` constructor:

```
m_bBuilder = new SAXBuilder(DEFAULT_SAX_DRIVER_CLASS);
```

The single parameter is a Java classname for the SAX parser that will be used by the builder to parse new documents. For this application, the `DEFAULT_SAX_DRIVER_CLASS` member is a `final String` that gives the fully qualified classname of the Apache XML Project's Xerces SAX parser.

The configuration document includes the current user's name and e-mail address (which is used when an order e-mail message is sent), the URL for the product catalog to display, and the hostname of the SMTP server to use. In this case, it indicates that there is an SMTP server running on the local machine.

The order client sample doesn't include any support for modifying these settings. Modifications can be made using any text editor or dedicated XML editor.

The Product Catalog

As discussed earlier in this chapter, the particular catalog used by this application is for a videocassette player that is described in Chapter 18. This catalog could just as well be for a barbecue grill or a 777 aircraft. As long as the catalog conforms to the DTD in OrderCatalog.dtd, the order client application will be able to use it to submit orders.

One of the most important parts of the order catalog is the <order_info> element:

```
<order_info method="email" address="demo-orders@strategicxml.com"/>
```

This element includes two required attributes. The first attribute (method) indicates the method to use to submit new orders. The only method understood by this sample application is e-mail. The second attribute (address) gives the e-mail address where orders are to be submitted. Later, we'll see how the order processing service monitors this mailbox for new orders.

The rest of the product catalog includes basic information about the product in question and a list of items that can be ordered. The loadCatalog() method (shown in Listing 14.4) parses the product catalog document and populates the items list box using the elements found in the <items> element.

LISTING 14.4 The loadCatalog() Method

```
public void loadCatalog(String strCatalogURL) throws Exception
{
  // parse the product catalog
  m_docCatalog = m_bBuilder.build(strCatalogURL);

  // init UI with catalog info

  // first, get a list of all of the item elements in the catalog
  Element elCat = m_docCatalog.getRootElement();
  Element elItems = elCat.getChild("items");

  java.util.List lstItems = elItems.getChildren("item");

  // now, populate a Vector with text descriptions of each item
  Vector vItems = new Vector();
  Iterator i = lstItems.iterator();
  Element e;

  while (i.hasNext()) {
    e = (Element)i.next();
```

LISTING 14.4 Continued

```
    vItems.add(e.getChildText("desc") + " ("
        + e.getAttributeValue("part_num") + ")");
  }

  // now initialize the list box with the list of items
  lstCatalog.setListData(vItems);
}
```

The `loadCatalog()` method is a good example of basic JDOM usage. The first call, to the `build()` method of the `SAXBuilder` class member, invokes the registered SAX parser to parse the catalog document. The resulting `Document` object will be kept in the `m_docCatalog` member, where it can be referenced later.

After the document has been parsed, the `getRootElement()`, `getChild()`, and `getChildren()` methods are used to get a list of all the `<item>` elements in the catalog. The list is then used to construct text descriptions of each item, which are added to a Java `Vector` object. This vector is used to initialize the `JList` control.

Using the Application

After the application has been initialized, the user is free to select items from the catalog list, enter a quantity to purchase, and add them to the current order table. The items and quantities to be ordered are actually stored in a JDOM XML document in real-time. The XML order document is displayed using a `JTable` and a custom table model class, `OrderTableModel`.

The current order document is created and initialized in the `resetOrder()` method, shown in Listing 14.5.

LISTING 14.5 The `resetOrder()` Method

```
public void resetOrder()
{
  // create a new order document object
  Element elRoot = new Element("order");
  m_docOrder = new Document(elRoot);

  // create the empty structure of the order document
  elRoot.addContent(new Element("customer_name"));
  elRoot.addContent(new Element("credit_card_num"));
  elRoot.addContent(new Element("items"));

  // set up the on-screen order table with a new table model
  OrderTableModel otm = new OrderTableModel(m_docOrder);
```

LISTING 14.5 Continued

```
    tabOrder.setModel(otm);

    // reset the other text controls
    txtCustName.setText("");
    txtCreditCardNum.setText("");
    txtQuantity.setText("1");
}
```

First, the empty root <order> element is created. Then, the new JDOM Document object is created using the new root element. The addContent() method of the Element interface is used to create the basic structure of the order document. As the user adds new items to the order, new <item> children will be added to the <items> element. To ensure that the order display is always current, the application uses a custom table model class that returns data from the XML document to the JTable control.

Within the OrderTableModel class, the getValueAt() method translates row and column references from the table control into elements within the attached order document. For example, take the sample order document shown in Listing 14.6.

LISTING 14.6 A Sample Order Document

```
<?xml version="1.0" encoding="UTF-8" ?>
<order>
  <customer_name>Electro-Shack</customer_name>
  <credit_card_num>2293293923231514</credit_card_num>
  <items>
    <item part_num="KJ-1291CC-01" quantity="50" />
    <item part_num="KNU-1485" quantity="50" />
    <item part_num="SC-938" quantity="33" />
    <item part_num="PH-1412U" quantity="33" />
    <item part_num="DPX482426" quantity="200" />
  </items>
</order>
```

The OrderTableModel class interprets the contents of the <items> element as a table. The getRowCount() method returns the number of <item> elements in the list. The two attributes (part_num and quantity) are interpreted as columns in the table. The getValueAt() method shows how row and column references can be converted into XML document references when the underlying data is regular in structure:

```
public Object getValueAt(int parm1, int parm2) {
  Element elItems = m_docOrder.getRootElement().getChild("items");
```

First, the row number is used to find the proper <item> element:

```
Element elRow = (Element)elItems.getChildren().get(parm1);
```

Then, the column number indicates which attribute value needs to be returned:

```
  switch (parm2) {
  case 0: {
    return elRow.getAttributeValue("quantity");
  }

  case 1: {
    return elRow.getAttributeValue("part_num");
  }

  default: {
    return "";
  }
  }
}
```

After the order is complete, the user clicks the Transmit Order button. This fires the `btnXmit_actionPerformed()` event handler, which populates the current in-memory order document with the customer name and credit-card number from the text box controls. Then, if the requested transmission method is e-mail (others could be added in the future), it calls the `sendEmailOrder()` method.

The `sendEmailOrder()` method uses a simple open-source SMTP helper class from `www.gjt.org` (see the `Smtp.java` source file for more information about usage and licensing of this object). The bulk of the method initiates an SMTP session with the server given in the application configuration document. First it sets the sender's e-mail address, and then it sets the destination address using the address from the order catalog document. Finally, the actual body of the message is transmitted using JDOM's `XMLOutputter` class:

```
XMLOutputter xo = new XMLOutputter();

xo.output(m_docOrder, pwOut);
```

After the `smtp.sendMessage()` method is called, the message is on its way to the order server for processing.

The OrderServer Service

The order processing server is a command-line Java program that periodically checks a given e-mail box for new order messages from the order client. The service continues to run until the user terminates it by pressing Enter.

This is the basic flow of the order processing service:

1. The `main()` method creates a new `OrderServer` object instance.
2. The service reads configuration information from the XML configuration file.
3. The service initializes the various server settings from the values contained in the configuration file.
4. The service listener thread starts.
5. The listener thread checks the POP box for new messages.
6. The service parses new messages and appends the order information to the global order database document.
7. After waiting for a predetermined amount of time, execution continues with step 5.

The workhorse routine of the service is the `processMessage()` method. Given an array of strings that contain single lines from the incoming message, it reconstructs the order document that was created by the order client. It then saves various bits and pieces of information from the e-mail message itself into the new order document. After the order document is complete, it appends the new order to the master order database:

```
Document docDB;

try {
  docDB = m_sb.build(new FileInputStream(m_fileOrderDB));
} catch (Exception e) {
  // either the order database document doesn't exist, or
  // there was an error while parsing it
  docDB = null;
}
```

If there is no order database document, or an error occurred while parsing, the service creates a new empty document:

```
if (docDB == null) {
  docDB = new Document(new Element("order_database"));

  docDB.getRootElement().addContent(new Element("orders"));
}
```

All `<order>` elements are children of the `<orders>` element. The following code fragment detaches the root element from the order document that was just constructed and appends it to the `<orders>` element of the order database:

```
Element elOrders = docDB.getRootElement().getChild("orders");

Element elRoot = docOrder.getRootElement();
```

```
docOrder.setRootElement(new Element("temp")); // set a placeholder

elOrders.addContent(elRoot);
```

Now it is necessary to write the order database document back to the disk. This occurs after each order is read, but before the corresponding order e-mail is deleted from the POP mailbox. This provides a primitive type of transaction safety. Here's the necessary code:

```
try {
  XMLOutputter xo = new XMLOutputter();

  FileOutputStream fos = new FileOutputStream(m_fileOrderDB);
  xo.output(docDB, fos);
  fos.close();
} catch (IOException ioe) {
  System.err.println(ioe);
}
```

The rest of the code in the `OrderServer` object deals with creating and stopping the listener thread, interfacing with the POP server, and reading the server configuration.

Deployment

The steps to deploy this application's order server are as listed here:

1. Create a mailbox that the order server will be able to check for incoming messages.
2. Install the order server class binaries on your system and make sure that they are listed on the Java classpath system variable.
3. Modify the server configuration file (`OrderServerConfig.xml`) to contain the correct POP3 server, username, and password. Also set the `<order_db_file>` element to point to a valid directory and filename. The file need not exist, but the directory must.
4. Start the server and watch the program output to make sure that the mailbox is being checked.

To deploy each order client, follow these steps:

1. Install an SMTP server on the client, if orders will be taken while the machine is offline.
2. Install the order client class files and update the Java classpath appropriately.
3. Modify the client configuration file (`OrderClientConfig.xml`) to contain the correct values for the salesman name and e-mail, catalog URL, and SMTP server hostname.
4. Run the client, giving the full URL to the configuration file on the command line if it isn't in the current directory.
5. Enter a sample order, and check the server to see that the message is received.

Conclusion

The order processing system presented in this chapter is very primitive, but before XML tools were available it would have taken much longer to implement. There are still several issues that would need to be addressed in a real production system (such as message authentication/ encryption, more sophisticated order entry processes, and catalog updates), but this sample system does illustrate how much value an XML library (such as JDOM) can add to a project.

Exposing Internal Systems to External Partners

CHAPTER 15

The adoption of new technologies into the mainstream retail world is not always as rapid as one would think it should be. A glaring case of this came to my attention one day when I went into a popular mega-bookstore looking for a book about improving your eyesight without glasses.

I went to the service counter and asked the clerk to search for the book by title. No luck. Then I asked him to look by author. Still no listing. Obviously chagrined, the clerk then told me that I might try going to the chain's online store and searching there. Apparently the in-store inventory system didn't have every title that is available on the .com site, and although the clerks have access to a proprietary stock and ordering system, they do not have access to the company's retail Web site. Although this is a case of failing to expose external systems to internal partners, the logical benefits of doing so remain the same.

Technologies Used:

- **WSC**
- **SOAP**
- **WSDL**
- **WSML**
- **VBScript**
- **ADO**

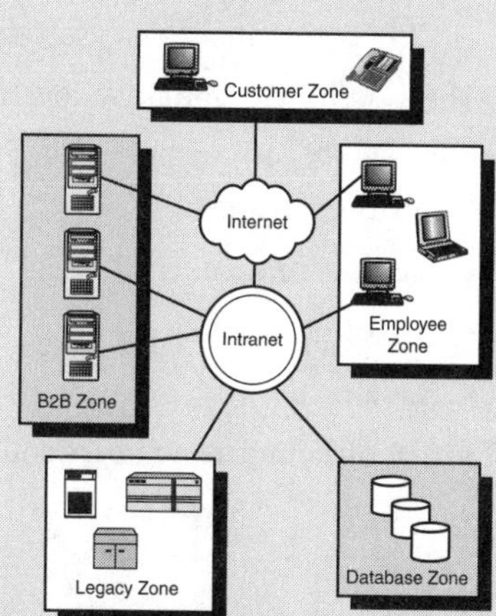

Safely sharing internal systems with external entities is something that should never be taken lightly. Careful thought must be given to how to protect the application from unauthorized users. Also, the scope of the application must be carefully defined, to ensure that the capabilities granted to legitimate users are carefully constrained.

The Simple Object Access Protocol (SOAP) and the Web Services Description Language (WSDL) enable IS departments to formally expose APIs with at least the same level of protection and isolation at which they can publish Web sites for human consumption.

Problem Description

A manufacturing company would like to enable its distributors to link their ordering systems directly into its order processing system.

At this stage, the system need only allow external vendors to submit new orders. No functionality for querying order status or updating customer information is necessary at the present time.

The company already has a public Web site with ordering capabilities based on Microsoft COM and IIS technologies.

Requirements

This system must meet the following requirements:

- The resulting system must be secure, allowing only pre-approved partners to submit orders.
- The system must be available over the public Internet, without requiring any special VPN or dedicated leased lines.
- The system should run on the existing public IIS servers.
- The system should merge seamlessly with the existing Web-based order processing system.
- The published API should be simple enough that partners will be able to implement it quickly within their own systems.
- The system will initially allow new orders to be submitted, containing the following information:
    - Customer name
    - Credit-card number
    - E-mail source address
    - E-mail date
    - List of item part numbers and quantities

System Design

Based on the requirements, SOAP is an obvious choice as base technology for the exposed API. Figure 15.1 shows the high-level structure of the application in relation to potential external clients.

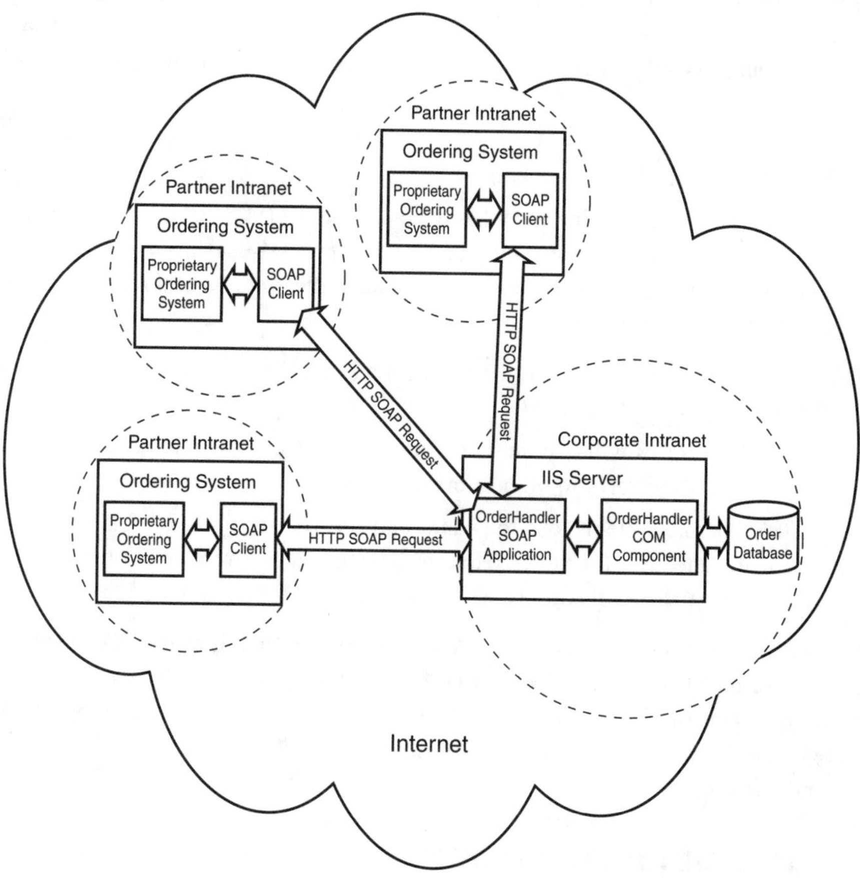

FIGURE 15.1
Public order processing system high-level overview.

SOAP Considerations

SOAP is an XML-based Remote Procedure Call protocol that was originally intended to be served via HTTP requests. Each SOAP request is logically mapped to a method invocation on a server object. The object processes the arguments that were passed in by the SOAP client, then sends a result that the client reads as an HTTP response.

Like HTTP, SOAP calls are inherently stateless. Each SOAP request is intended to stand on its own, with any transactional support being built into the object on the server.

Because SOAP messages are conveyed as HTTP requests, all the IIS security features (IP restriction, SSL, and so on) may be employed to protect the integrity of system transactions.

Microsoft's implementation of SOAP is distributed as the Microsoft SOAP Toolkit, currently at version 2.0. The toolkit uses the Web Services Description Language (WSDL) and Web Services Meta Language (WSML) to expose and link SOAP requests to the methods of COM objects.

COM Development

In a real-world scenario there would most likely be existing COM interfaces into the order processing system. Although simply publishing these existing COM interfaces might seem to be a viable and efficient way to rapidly implement the system, there are several reasons to create a brand-new SOAP-specific object:

- The existing interfaces will most likely not support the connectionless requests presented by SOAP requests.
- The internal interfaces will expose more functionality (for example, modifying customer records) than it is desirable to offer to outside clients.
- Proprietary internal systems tend to change and evolve over time. Even if the internal API is already adequate for SOAP requests, having external vendors write to an intermediate interface allows flexibility when redesigning internal systems.

After the decision has been made to use the Microsoft SOAP Toolkit as the SOAP server platform and to develop a new SOAP-specific COM object to implement order processing, a COM development platform must be selected. A few common languages used to develop COM objects are Visual Basic, C++, and Borland's Delphi. Each of these languages has its own strengths and weaknesses.

Windows Scripting Components

However, one of the lesser-known (but very useful) COM development tools is the Microsoft Windows Scripting Component (WSC) platform. A WSC is an XML document that describes the registration information, properties, and methods of a COM object using XML. The code for the object is written in one of the scripting languages supported on your platform (such as VBScript, JScript, or even ActiveState's Perl scripting language). The WSC document may then be registered using `regsvr32.exe` like a regular COM object.

Support for WSCs is built into the latest Windows Scripting Host package, which can be downloaded from the Microsoft Web site. No special development environment (beyond a text editor) is needed. The `OrderHandler` component will be developed as a WSC component, written in VBScript.

Component Design

When designing a COM interface that will be called via SOAP, a few factors need to be taken into consideration.

Because each SOAP request is stateless, either the entire transaction must take place in one method call or the object must implement its own transactional support.

SOAP supports marshalling arguments of most basic types, but some consideration needs to be given to how much of a burden the marshalling will place on the SOAP client.

To keep the overall application and interface simple, the `OrderHandler` object will expose a single method, `ProcessOrder()`. `ProcessOrder()` will accept all the information for an order (per the "Requirements" section) and return a unique order ID if the transaction is successful.

Final Order Disposition

In a real-world application, the SOAP object would submit orders to the actual corporate order-processing system. For this example, the orders will be written to a Microsoft Access database using ActiveX Database Objects (ADO).

Implementation Notes

These are the major items that must be completed for this project:

1. Design and implement the order database.
2. Develop the `OrderHandler` WSC component.
3. Install and configure the Microsoft SOAP Toolkit.
4. Create the required support files to expose the `OrderHandler` object as a SOAP service.
5. Round-trip test the entire system using a SOAP client.

The tools that will be required to complete these steps include the following:

- A text editor (or XML editor)
- The Microsoft SOAP Toolkit
- Microsoft Access (or another tool capable of designing an Access database)

Before anything else can be done, the database that will capture orders must be designed.

Designing the Order Database

In a real-world situation, there would most likely be some type of order-processing system already in use, and this step would not be required. However, the techniques for interfacing with a simple Access database do not differ greatly from those for accessing a larger production database. Figure 15.2 shows an Entity Relationship Diagram (ERD) for the database that can be found in `OrderDatabase.mdb`.

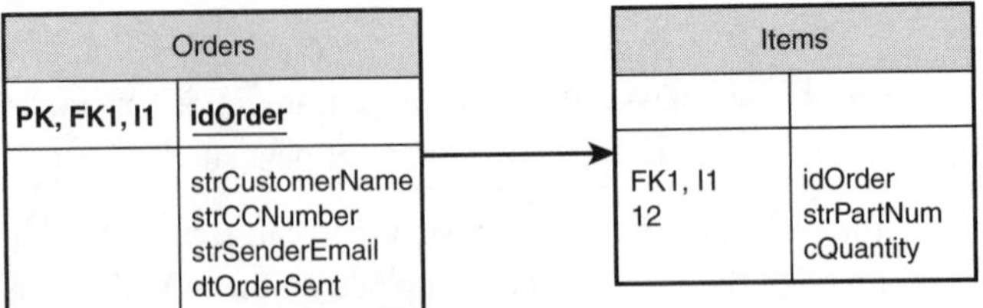

FIGURE 15.2
An entity relationship diagram for `OrderDatabase.mdb`.

NOTE

The cryptic abbreviations in the ERD in Figure 15.2 refer to the various database roles that a particular column plays:

- PK—Primary Key
- FK—Foreign Key
- I—Index

The structure is very simple. Each order will occupy a single row in the `Orders` table. The list of items and quantities associated with a particular order will be inserted into the `Items` table, using the order ID (`idOrder`) to relate them back to an order record.

Writing the `OrderHandler` Component

Before tackling the implementation of the `OrderHandler` object, a quick introduction to Windows Scripting Components is in order.

Most Web developers working in a Microsoft environment have had some contact with the Microsoft Scripting Runtime, most likely from developing Active Server Page (ASP) applications. In an ASP application, script fragments are embedded within static content (such as HTML). These script fragments can then deliver dynamically generated content to the Web browser client. ASP scripts can also create and reference COM objects, allowing for almost unlimited extensibility.

WSC Development

The WSC framework is a feature of the Microsoft Scripting Runtime that allows COM objects to be developed using the same scripting engine that drives ASP pages. The structure of the COM object (registration information, methods, properties, events, and so on) is encoded in a simple XML format. The resulting XML document may then be registered using the standard COM object registration procedure (`regsvr32.exe`).

WSC files may be created using nothing more than a text or XML editor. Also, if you download the Microsoft Windows Script toolkit, you also get the Script Component Wizard. This tool automates the process of creating a WSC file, creating a GUID, and so forth. For more information about the Microsoft Windows Script toolkit, see the Web site.

Listing 15.1 shows the bare XML skeleton of the `OrderHandler` object, before the actual code has been written. The entire working component is available on the Web site as `OrderHandler.wsc`.

LISTING 15.1 The XML skeleton of the `OrderHandler` component.

```
<?xml version="1.0"?>
<package>
  <?component error="true" debug="true"?>

  <component>

    <registration
        description="Order Handler Object"
        progid="SXML.OrderHandler"
        version="1.00"
        classid="{ad1afddc-73c8-468e-9700-371eff4a1156}">
    </registration>

    <reference object="ADODB.Recordset"/>

    <public>
        <method name="ProcessOrder">
            <parameter name="strCustomerName"/>
            <parameter name="strCCNum"/>
            <parameter name="strEmailName"/>
            <parameter name="strEmailDate"/>
```

LISTING 15.1 Continued

```
            <parameter name="astrPartNums"/>
            <parameter name="astrQuantities"/>
        </method>
    </public>

    <implements type="ASP" id="ASP"/>

    <script language="VBScript">
    <![CDATA[
Option Explicit

' !!!LATER!!! object implementation goes here
    ]]>
    </script>

  </component>
</package>
```

WSC Document Structure

The following sections discuss the components of a WSC file in more detail.

<package> Element

In this example, the top-level `<package>` element is technically unnecessary. If only one COM object is being declared (only one `<component>` element is present), the `<component>` element itself may be the top-level element. If more than one component will be declared in a single document, they all must be contained by a top-level `<package>` element. On the other hand, it costs nothing to include the `<package>` element, and it will simplify life if we choose to declare additional components in the future.

<component> Element

This element is the one used to actually declare a COM object that can be instantiated by other programs. Everything related to that object will be contained in an element within the top-level `<component>` element. Multiple `<component>` elements may be included in a single top-level `<package>` element, simplifying deployment of complex COM framework packages. All declared components are registered or unregistered simultaneously whenever the WSC file is passed to `regsvr32.exe`.

<?component?> Processing Instruction

The `<?component?>` processing instruction is used to tell the scripting runtime how to handle runtime errors and debugging requests. In this case, both the `error` and `debug` attributes are set to `true`, indicating that runtime errors should be reported, and the script debugger should be invoked to debug errors as they occur. Debugging WSC components is somewhat of a black art, because errors can occur due to malformed XML, syntax errors in the underlying scripting code, mismatches between the object property and method declarations, or runtime programming errors.

Debugging works differently depending on whether the object was created by an interactive process (such as a `.vbs` script file) or in a background context (such as from an ASP page). It is generally preferable to do any debugging and troubleshooting using an interactive test script before attempting to deploy the object using IIS. See the Web site for a short description of the problems with debugging Windows Scripting Components in a non-interactive environment.

`<registration>` Element

This element contains all the information that will be used to register the COM object in the Windows registry. The element supports several attributes that control how the object is instantiated and used:

- `description`—A human-readable description of the component. Some development tools will make this string available to the programmer. This attribute is optional.
- `progid`—A friendly name (instead of the somewhat less-than-friendly class ID) that can be used to instantiate this COM object using a call such as `Server.CreateObject()`. This attribute is optional, if a `classid` attribute is present.
- `version`—A version number for this component. Although this attribute is optional, it is a good idea to set it and update it regularly as your object evolves. It simplifies debugging if you know which version of your object is actually being created.
- `classid`—This attribute may contain a Globally Unique Identifier (GUID) that positively identifies your component as distinct from any other component. If you created the component with the Microsoft Script Component Wizard, your object was automatically assigned a GUID. Another way to generate a GUID is by using the Microsoft `UUIDGEN.EXE` tool (shipped with most MS development tools).

There are additional attributes and features of the `<registration>` tag, which you can find in the documentation that ships with the Microsoft Windows Script toolkit.

`<reference>` Element

This element imports the type information from a COM type library. This allows your script code to use symbolic constants when calling methods of COM objects associated with the imported type library. In this case, the component is importing the type information associated with the Microsoft ADO Recordset object.

<public> Element

This element is used to expose the component's public properties, methods, and events. The `OrderHandler` object has only one method, the `ProcessOrder()`method. The method is exposed using the `<method>` element, which contains multiple `<parameter>` elements that expose the arguments to the method.

After a method has been exposed using the `<method>` element, a corresponding script subroutine or function must be written in a `<script>` block within the `<component>` element. Exposing a method without providing an implementation will cause the scripting library to generate a runtime error, even if that method is never called by client code.

Besides the `<method>` element, the `<public>` element may also contain `<property>` and `<event>` elements.

<implements> Element

This specialized element indicates that your component will support one of the nonstandard COM interfaces predefined by the WSC framework. In this case, the component is marked as supporting the Active Server Pages interface. This means that the scripting code for this component may reference ASP-specific global objects (`Response`, `Server`, and so on). Although it is not explicitly used in this example, this is a useful feature of WSCs that should be noted.

<script> Element

Similar to `<script>` elements found in normal ASP and HTML pages, the script blocks in a WSC contain scripting code that implements the various methods, properties, and events that are exposed through the `<public>` element. The `<script>` tag supports a single attribute: the `language` attribute. This attribute determines which scripting processor will be used to interpret the script within the tag.

Because the WSC file is itself a valid XML document, the entire contents of the `<script>` block are normally enclosed in a `CDATA` block. Without the `CDATA` block, each occurrence of special XML characters (such as <, >, and &) would need to be escaped. Within a `CDATA` block, this is not necessary.

Implementing the `ProcessOrder()` Method

After the WSC framework has been built, validated, and successfully registered (either by right-clicking from the Windows shell or using `regsvr32.exe`), it is time to develop the scripting code for the component. This version of the component will be developed in VBScript; however, it could just as easily be written using JScript, Perl, or any other language available for the Windows Scripting Host.

The scripting code that makes up the implementation of the object will be written in the `<script>` block of Listing 15.1. The first line of the script (`Option Explict`) indicates that all variable names must be declared.

Based on the declared parameter list, and the fact that the `ProcessOrder()` method will return an order number, this will be the VBScript function signature:

```
Function ProcessOrder(strCustomerName, strCCNum, strEmailName,_
    strEmailDate, astrPartNums, astrQuantities)
```

The last two parameters are intended to contain arrays: the first an array of part numbers, the second an array of quantities. Because the scripts in a WSC are typeless, all parameters and variables are of the type `Variant`. No explicit restrictions are placed on what type of variable may be passed for any given argument. However, if a type mismatch occurs in the method code, a runtime error will be thrown.

The logic of the application will be familiar to most programmers who have written ADO applications in VBScript. First, an ADO `Connection` object will be created and used to open the ODBC data source for the order database:

```
Dim cn
Set cn = CreateObject("ADODB.Connection")
cn.Open "SXML-OrderDatabase"
```

After the connection has been opened, a SQL statement is constructed to insert incoming information into the `Orders` table in the database:

```
Dim strSQL
strSQL = "insert into Orders (strCustomerName, strCCNumber,"
strSQL = strSQL & " strSenderEmail, dtOrderSent) values ("
strSQL = strSQL & "'" & strCustomerName & "', '" & strCCNum & "'"
strSQL = strSQL & ", '" & strEmailName & "', '" & strEmailDate & "')"
```

This SQL statement is then executed (using the open ADO connection), and the unique ID of the new row is retrieved using the special `@@identity` variable that is associated with the connection:

```
cn.Execute strSQL

Dim idOrder
idOrder = cn.Execute("select @@identity")(0).Value
```

Now that the order ID is known, it is possible to insert each item that was passed in using the `astrPartNums` and `astrQuantities` arguments:

```
Dim i

For i = 0 To UBound(astrPartNums)
```

```
    strSQL = "insert into Items values (" & idOrder & ", '" & astrPartNums(i) & "'"
    strSQL = strSQL & ", " & astrQuantities(i) & ")"

    cn.Execute strSQL
Next
```

Finally, the connection can be closed, the return value of the method can be set, and the function ends:

```
    cn.Close
    Set cn = Nothing

    ProcessOrder = idOrder
End Function
```

Standalone Component Testing

Now that the component has been written and registered, it is a good idea to test and debug it in an isolated environment before attempting to execute it through the SOAP framework. The easiest way to do this is to create a simple script that can be executed using the Windows Scripting Host. Listing 15.2 shows the contents of `StandaloneOrderHandlerTest.vbs`, which is a simple script that instantiates an `OrderHandler` object and calls the `ProcessOrder()` method with some test arguments.

LISTING 15.2 A standalone test script for an `OrderHandler` object.

```
Dim oh

Set oh = CreateObject("SXML.OrderHandler")
Dim idOrder
idOrder = oh.ProcessOrder("Customer One", "223234234",_
  "customer@strategicxml.com", "2/2/01", Array("Q123", "B234"), Array(2, 5))
MsgBox "Order ID: " & idOrder
```

After the WSC file has been successfully registered (using `regsvr32.exe`, for example), this script may be executed either by double-clicking on it from the Windows shell, or from the command line by typing its name (in the directory where it is located):

```
c:\Sams\StrategicXML\Chapter15Project>StandaloneOrderHandlerTest.vbs
```

After the order has been successfully added to the database, a Windows message box will appear with the new order ID in it.

Setting Up a SOAP Service

Now that the component has been developed and verified in a simple environment, it is time to make it available to SOAP clients. The first step is to install the Microsoft SOAP Toolkit on the Windows server that will host the SOAP application.

Installing the Microsoft SOAP Toolkit

The Microsoft SOAP Toolkit is available for download from the Microsoft Developer Network (MSDN) Web site. Before installing the toolkit, be sure to check the prerequisites and minimum system configuration to ensure that your system is compliant. SOAP runs as either an ISAPI plug-in or an ASP page. Either method provides the same functionality to SOAP clients.

After the SOAP toolkit has been installed, it is time to configure an IIS virtual directory that will contain the SOAP application files.

Creating a Virtual Directory

SOAP clients specify which SOAP service they want to invoke by connecting to a specific URL that is hosted on a SOAP-compliant server. Although it is possible to co-mingle SOAP and non-SOAP content in a single virtual directory, this application will isolate all SOAP-related content in a single IIS virtual directory called `OrderHandler`.

The examples and test scripts for this application assume that IIS is running on the local machine (that is, all URLs begin with `http://localhost/`). Create an empty subdirectory that will contain the SOAP-related gateway files, and share it using IIS as the `OrderHandler` subdirectory of the IIS `Default Web Site`. This directory will contain the WSML and WSDL files that are used by the SOAP ISAPI plug-in to serve SOAP client requests.

NOTE

It is not necessary (and in fact quite insecure) to place the WSC component file (`OrderHandler.wsc`) in the `OrderHandler` virtual directory. The SOAP server will instantiate the object using the component's progid (`SXML.OrderHandler`). The COM framework deals with mapping that progid to a physical path, which means that the component may be located anywhere on the system. Also, security permissions must be considered when placing the component. The identity of the incoming SOAP request will be determined by the settings in the Directory Security tab of the IIS virtual directory properties dialog. If anonymous browsing is used to link to the SOAP directory, the anonymous user must have file-system permissions to read the WSC component file.

After the virtual directory has been set up, it is time to create the WSML and WSDL files that will be used by the SOAP server (and some SOAP clients) to call the `OrderHandler` object.

Using WSML and WSDL

To expose a COM object using the SOAP toolkit, it is necessary to provide two different XML documents that describe the SOAP service to be provided, as well as the concrete COM object methods that must be invoked. The close relationship between the WSML and WSDL files can be confusing at times, but the basic purpose of each is easy to understand.

The WSDL document exposes a set of generic SOAP services, bindings, ports, and messages for use by any SOAP client. It is a W3C-endorsed standard that is being promoted by Microsoft and other vendors as a standard way to expose programmatic services on the Web. It does not contain any Microsoft- or COM-specific information.

However, these generic declarations do not provide sufficient information for the SOAP server to actually process a request. To do this in a Windows framework, there must be some way to associate an actual COM object and specific method with each inbound SOAP message. This is the purpose of the WSML file. It defines which COM objects will service which incoming messages. It links the message elements from a SOAP request to specific methods in the requested COM object. Together, the WSDL and WSML files allow end-to-end processing of SOAP requests.

Writing the WSML File

In most of the literature associated with the Microsoft SOAP Toolkit, the WSDL file is explained before the WSML. Basically, the WSDL file lists the various abstract services and messages that the SOAP server supports, whereas the WSML file explains how to link these abstract requests to physical COM object instances and methods.

NOTE

Although the SOAP toolkit provides the WSDL/WSML Generator tool that can automatically generate these files for most COM objects, it will not work for our WSC-generated COM object. Because the `ProcessOrder()` method uses variants for all of its arguments, it is necessary to explicitly define the expected argument types for the SOAP framework.

The complete contents of `OrderHandler.wsml` are shown in Listing 15.3.

LISTING 15.3 The WSML file for the `OrderHandler` SOAP service.

```
<servicemapping name='OrderHandler'>
  <service name='OrderHandler'>
    <using PROGID='SXML.OrderHandler' cachable='0'
      ID='OrderHandlerObject'/>
    <port name='OrderHandlerSoapPort'>
      <operation name='ProcessOrder'>
        <execute uses='OrderHandlerObject' method='ProcessOrder'>
          <parameter callIndex='1' name='strCustomerName'
              elementName='strCustomerName'/>
          <parameter callIndex='2' name='strCCNum'
              elementName='strCCNum'/>
          <parameter callIndex='3' name='strEmailName'
              elementName='strEmailName'/>
          <parameter callIndex='4' name='strEmailDate'
              elementName='strEmailDate'/>
          <parameter callIndex='5' name='astrPartNums'
              elementName='astrPartNums'/>
          <parameter callIndex='6' name='astrQuantities'
              elementName='astrQuantities'/>
          <parameter callIndex='-1' name='retval'
              elementName='Result'/>
        </execute>
      </operation>
    </port>
  </service>
</servicemapping>
```

The three major entities exposed in this file are service, ports, and operations. A service is linked to a public SOAP service that is exposed in a WSDL file using the `name` attribute of the `<servicemapping>` element. Within the `<servicemapping>` element, a `<service>` element contains all the information required to link the abstract SOAP messages declared in the WSDL file to concrete COM object instances and methods.

Within a `<service>` element, one or more `<using>` elements declare the COM objects that will be exposed and give hints about how they may be used. These are the three attributes used in this example:

- `PROGID`—This is the COM progid of the object that must be instantiated.
- `cachable`—This is a Boolean value that indicates whether the object instance may be cached by the SOAP service for use to serve multiple SOAP requests.
- `ID`—This is the XML ID that will be used by subsequent `<execute>` elements to indicate which object their methods apply to.

The <port> element contains one or more <operation> elements that define specific COM methods that can be invoked by the SOAP server. The port name is a linkage between the SOAP port declared in the WSDL <portType> element and the COM object operations defined in the WSML file. There is a one-to-one mapping between operations declared in the WSML <port> element and operations declared in the WSDL <portType> element.

An operation contains an <execute> element that defines precisely which COM object and method should serve a particular request. The execute element must include a `uses` attribute that references a particular COM object through a <using> element that is declared within the current <service> element. The `method` attribute gives the method name within the object that should be invoked. The <execute> element must contain <parameter> elements that map between the COM method parameters and the SOAP message elements that are declared in the corresponding <message> element of the WSDL document.

Each <parameter> element links a particular element from a SOAP request to a parameter position in a COM object method invocation. The `callIndex` attribute is a one-based index that indicates which position the current parameter occupies in the parameter list. If it is –1, it represents the return value of the method. The `name` attribute is not actually used by SOAP at the present time, but for documentation and consistency purposes it should be set to the COM method parameter name. The `elementName` attribute maps to a <part> declaration of a <message> element defined in the WSDL file.

Now, having defined the concrete linkages in the WSML file, we need to define the abstract SOAP interfaces in the WSDL file.

Writing the WSDL File

A WSDL document enables a SOAP client to retrieve complete information about the services, operations, and message types that are supported by a particular SOAP server. The full details of the WSDL file format would require an entire chapter (if not another book), but by examining a concrete example it is possible to become productive rather quickly.

A WSDL document serves as a contract between the client and server so that each understands what is expected of the other. The types of SOAP entities that are exposed by the WSDL file are shown in Table 15.1.

TABLE 15.1 SOAP entities exposed in a WSDL document.

Entity	*Explanation*
Service	Is a named collection of related SOAP ports.
Port	Defines the binding, port type, and physical URL that the client will use to transmit and receive SOAP requests for this service.

TABLE 15.1 Continued

Entity	*Explanation*
Binding	Specifies the concrete encoding details (preferred character encoding, message element names, and so on) for a given SOAP port.
Port type	Enumerates the various operations that can be performed over a particular SOAP port. An operation is equivalent to a single method call on an object.
Message	Describes the logical structure of the content being transferred back and forth in a given SOAP request. Messages are composed of parts, which map an XML element name to a specific data type.
Types	Is the section where application-specific types may be declared for use in message declarations. Types are declared using XML Schema notation.

To help clarify the linkages between the various parts of the WSDL and WSML documents, Figure 15.3 is a graphical representation of the contents of the two XML documents that shows the relationships between them.

The complete WSDL file for the `OrderHandler` service is located in `OrderHandler.wsdl`. It provides the declarations necessary to allow the Microsoft SOAP server to receive and process SOAP requests for the `OrderHandler` service. To complete the application setup, the WSDL and WSML files must be copied to the IIS virtual directory that was created previously. Then, it is time to test the SOAP connection to make sure that the system is properly configured from end to end.

Testing the SOAP Connection

To test the connection, a simple VBScript file will be used. It will use the Microsoft SOAP client object to open a connection to the server and call the `ProcessOrder()` method on the `OrderHandler` object. Listing 15.4 shows the contents of the SOAP test script in `OrderHandlerSOAPTest.vbs`.

LISTING 15.4 The SOAP server test script.

```
Option Explicit

Dim soapClient
Set soapClient = CreateObject("MSSOAP.soapClient")

On Error Resume Next
soapClient.mssoapinit "http://localhost/OrderHandler/OrderHandler.wsdl",_
  "OrderHandler", "OrderHandlerSoapPort"

If Err <> 0 Then
```

LISTING 15.4 Continued

```
  wscript.echo "initialization failed " + Err.description
End If

wscript.echo  soapClient.ProcessOrder("Customer One", "223234234",_
  "customer@strategicxml.com", "2/2/01", Array("Q123", "B234"), Array(2, 5))
If err <> 0 Then
  wscript.echo   Err.description
  wscript.echo   "faultcode=" + soapClient.faultcode
  wscript.echo   "faultstring=" + soapClient.faultstring
  wscript.echo   "faultactor=" + soapClient.faultactor
  wscript.echo   "detail=" + soapClient.detail
End If
```

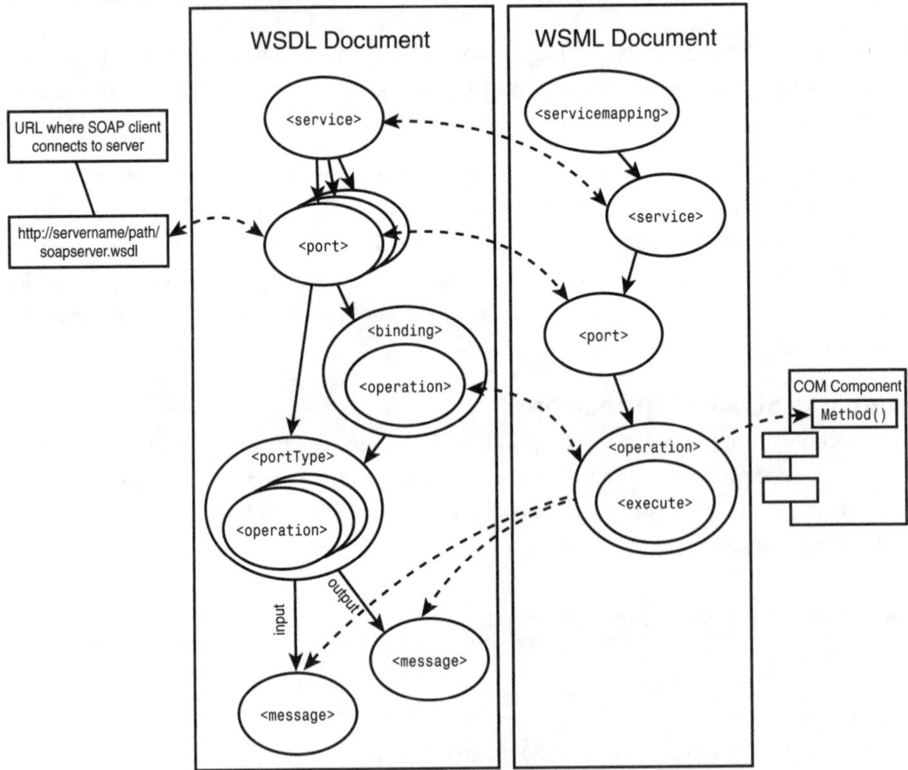

FIGURE 15.3
WSDL and WSML document relationships.

This script creates and initializes an instance of the Microsoft `soapClient` object. The URL location of the WSDL file is set to the local host, in the `OrderHandler` virtual directory. Besides specifying the location of the WSDL file, the `mssoapinit()` method also takes the name of the SOAP service requested as well as the port name (both items are declared in the WSDL file).

After the SOAP connection is successfully initialized, the `ProcessOrder()` operation is invoked with a set of test parameters. Notice that the `Array()` VBScript function is used to create the temporary arrays that contain the part numbers and quantities for the order. If an error occurs during the request, the script uses the `wscript.echo()` method to report it to the console. To run this script, either double-click it from the Windows shell or run it from the command line:

```
c:\Sams\StrategicXML\Chapter15Project>cscript OrderHandlerSOAPTest.vbs
```

The `cscript` executable runs the script as a console script, which causes output to be echoed to standard output. If the script is run through the shell, the `wscript.echo()` method output will be displayed using a Windows message box.

Deployment

These are the steps to deploy this application:

1. Download and install the Microsoft SOAP Toolkit from `http://msdn.microsoft.com/SOAP` on your system. Be sure to read the prerequisites before installation.
2. Download and unzip the sample files to a subdirectory on your local system.
3. Create the `SXML-OrderDatabase` ODBC System data source using the ODBC applet of the Control Panel. The data source should point to the `OrderDatabase.mdb` database that is included with the sample files.
4. Register the `OrderHandler.wsc` component either by right-clicking and selecting Register from the shell, or by using `regsvr32.exe` from the command line:

   ```
   c:\Sams\StrategicXML\Chapter15Project>regsvr32 OrderHandler.wsc
   ```
5. Share the `OrderHandlerIIS` sample subdirectory as the `OrderHandler` virtual directory of the default Web site, either by using the Internet Services Manager or by right-clicking on the subdirectory and going through the Web Sharing tab of the Properties dialog using the Windows shell.
6. Test the installation using the `StandaloneOrderHandlerTest.vbs` and `OrderHandlerSOAPTest.vbs` scripts.

Conclusion

As companies begin to see the bottom-line value of sharing pieces and parts of their IT infrastructure with partners and customers, technologies like SOAP will become much more crucial. Learning the ins and outs of creating and configuring SOAP services now will help make the transition to Web-based programming services that much more seamless.

Accessing Remote Systems with SOAP

CHAPTER

16

When I was still working at Microsoft, I went in to visit one of my friends and see what he was working on at the time. This was in the early 1990s, and dial-up Internet connections were still ubiquitous. My friend was an expert in signal compression technologies, and he proceeded to explain to me what he was doing.

The gist of his explanation was this: "Now, with superior compression technology, we are able to make a computer digitize a human voice, compress it, and transmit it over a telephone line to another computer, which can then decompress it and play it back." He also told me that they were getting "near-telephone quality." I told him that that was great, and that pretty soon it looked like we might be able to transmit telephone-quality conversations over a simple telephone line.

When you put it like that, it does sound a little bit silly. When I tell programmers that now we are able to marshal object method invocations into a very verbose, text-based format and transmit them over a TCP/IP socket connection to a remote server, I get the exact same feeling. But that being said, SOAP is going to be one of the fundamental building blocks of the future software-as-a-service models that are appearing on the horizon.

Technologies Used:

- **XSLT**
- **Java**
- **SAX**
- **SOAP**

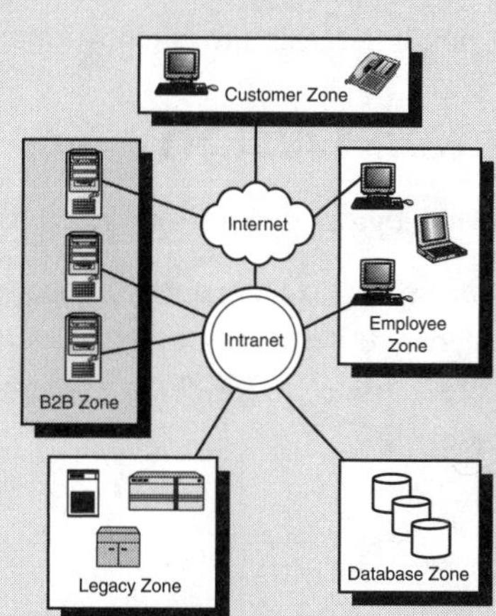

This chapter is intended to tie together the offline order store-and-forward system that was built in Chapter 14, "Offline Order Processing Using Store-and-Forward," and the SOAP-based order server that was built in Chapter 15, "Exposing Internal Systems to External Partners." It takes an XML list of orders and submits them to the SOAP order server using a solution that combines XSLT and Java.

NOTE

Although this example may be reviewed and studied on its own, it requires a SOAP server that provides the services described in Chapter 15 to function fully.

Problem Description

An electronic parts wholesaler previously implemented their own order processing system that collects order requests from the field into a monolithic XML data file. Now, the parts manufacturer has informed them that they must begin submitting orders via a new Internet-based SOAP service that they have recently implemented.

What is needed is a batch-oriented system that will submit the orders that have been collected in an order document to the newly implemented SOAP service.

Requirements

The system must meet the following requirements:

- The system must not require any modification of the existing order collection system.
- It must conform to the SOAP interface that has been published by the manufacturer.
- Batch type error handling is acceptable; simply logging the results of each order submission to a log file will be sufficient.
- The resulting process should be machine and operating system independent. It should be possible to run the batch from any server connected to the Internet.

System Design

The basic logical flow of the system is depicted in Figure 16.1.

One very straightforward way to accomplish this task would be to parse the order database document and iterate through each order element using an API such as DOM or SAX. Then for each order, use a SOAP client implementation to invoke the required SOAP operation on the target server.

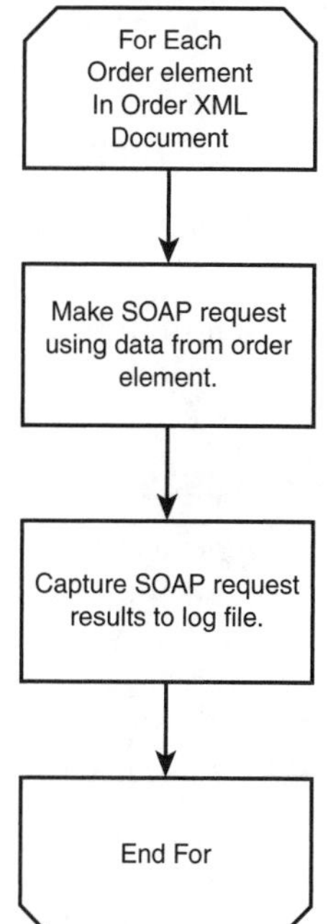

FIGURE 16.1
The SOAP order submission system's application logic.

This solution would meet the requirements but would require a relatively large amount of custom coding to carry it out. It would also lack flexibility when it comes time to extend or modify either the order collection process or the supplier's SOAP application.

Code Versus Data

One of the most interesting side effects of the adoption of XML as the foundation for an RPC mechanism (such as SOAP) is the blurring of the line between code and data. On one side of our application, we have a data file that contains XML elements with order information. On the other side, we have a SOAP server that is expecting another type of XML document that represents an object method invocation. Wouldn't it be nice if we could transform the static XML-as-data file into the dynamic XML-as-RPC-request messages for the SOAP server?

The good news is that we can. It will require a bit of plumbing code to make the system hang together, but using XSLT to transform our proprietary XML data into well-formed SOAP requests is no more difficult than transforming it into HTML for display to a human being.

The other obstacle that must be overcome is determining how to submit the request to the server. The server requires that the SOAP message be transmitted over a TCP/IP socket using the HTTP protocol. It also expects to be able to return the results of the call as an HTTP response to the client.

To implement this approach, we will need to develop the following:

- A transformation script that converts the proprietary order records into SOAP client requests.
- A utility that can "play back" these transformed requests to a SOAP server, and capture the results in a log file.

Roll-Your-Own SOAP Requests

Writing an XSLT script to transform a proprietary order element into a valid SOAP request is not much different from transforming it for presentation as an HTML document. The two pieces of information we need are the structure and content of the source and target document formats.

Listing 16.1 is a sample of an order database document (`OrderDB.xml`) that needs to be processed.

LISTING 16.1 A Sample Order Database Document

```
<?xml version="1.0" encoding="UTF-8" ?>
<order_database>
 <orders>
  <order>
   <customer_name>Scott</customer_name>
   <credit_card_num>2234 2344 2233 2234</credit_card_num>
   <items>
    <item part_num="SC-938" quantity="1" />
    <item part_num="SC-938" quantity="1" />
    <item part_num="SC-938" quantity="1" />
   </items>
   <email_info>
    <from><smeans@strategicxml.com></from>
    <date>Sat, 14 Jul 2001 16:40:48 -0400</date>
   </email_info>
  </order>
 </orders>
</order_database>
```

Although this database contains only a single `<order>` element, in a production environment there will most likely be several orders in a single batch. Based on the `ProcessOrder` operation that is exposed by the SOAP server built in Chapter 15, each `<order>` element will need to be transformed into a single SOAP request. Creating the structure for the outbound SOAP request requires a basic understanding of how a SOAP client works.

SOAP Mechanics

Although with the latest incarnation of the SOAP specification HTTP is no longer the sole transport mechanism available to a SOAP client, it is still the most popular. Virtually every SOAP client and server implementation supports transmitting a SOAP request via a HTTP `POST` operation. The body of the `POST` request consists of a SOAP *envelope* that contains the types, meta-information, and arguments necessary to perform the SOAP action on the server. The server then transmits the results of the operation as the body of the HTTP response. Figure 16.2 shows the steps in a typical SOAP request that use a SOAP client library.

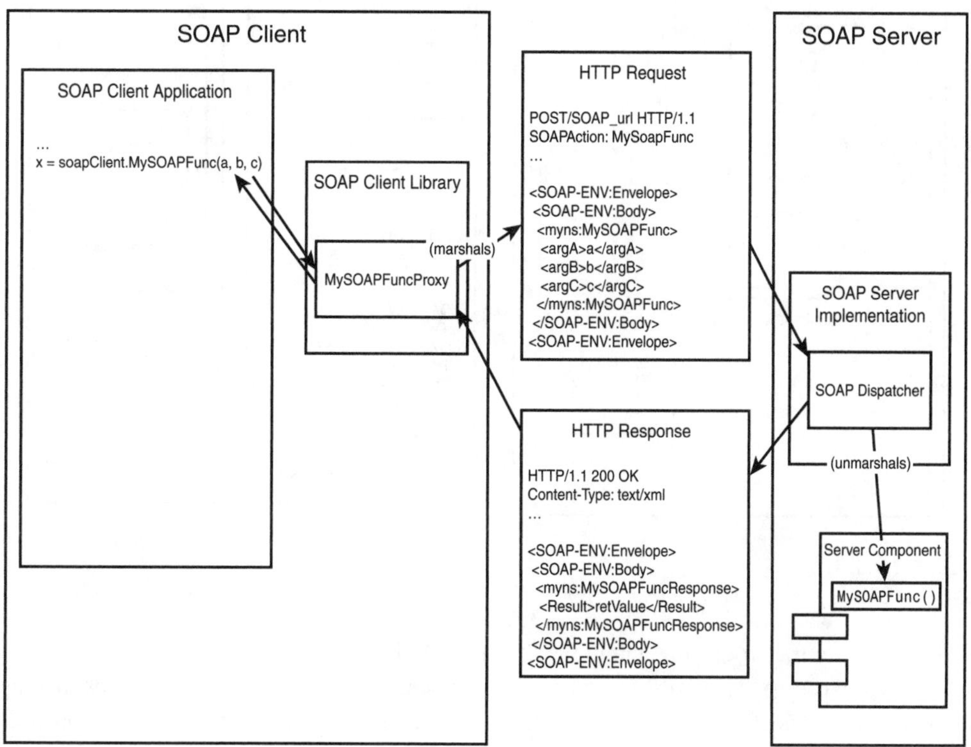

FIGURE 16.2
A typical SOAP exchange using a SOAP client library.

Notice that the SOAP client library insulates the client application from the complexity of constructing the SOAP XML message, performing the HTTP request, reading the response, and parsing out the return value. From the client's perspective, it did a normal object method invocation and received a return value.

Compare this flow with Figure 16.3, which shows how our XSLT-based SOAP client will function.

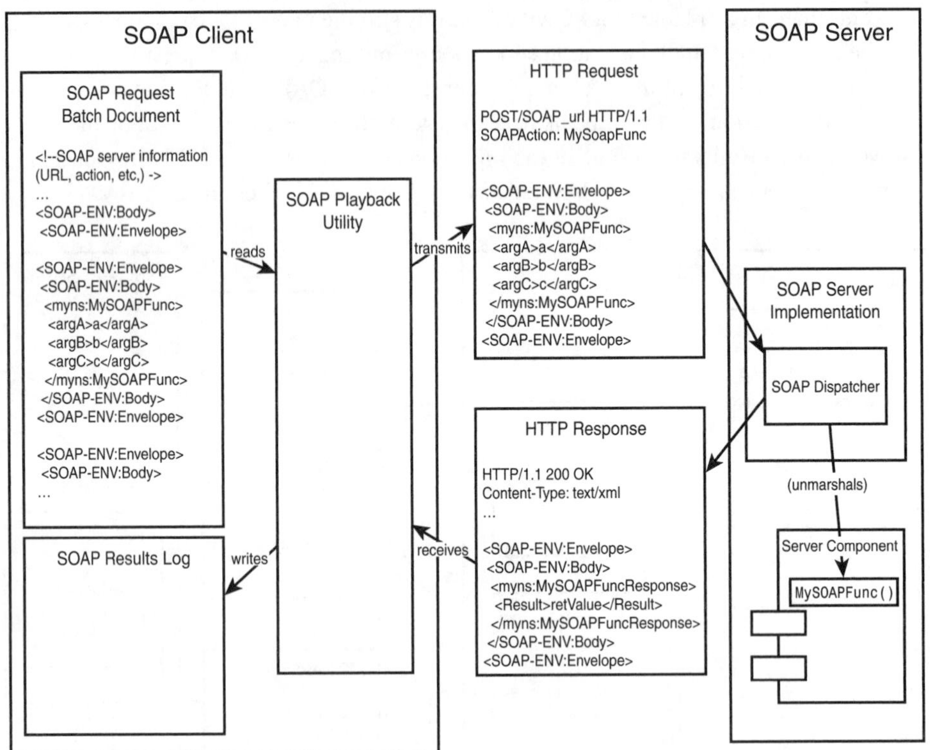

FIGURE 16.3
A SOAP exchange using a SOAP "playback" client.

Notice that only the processing within the SOAP client has changed. To the SOAP server, requests appear to be exactly the same as they were when the SOAP client library was making the requests. In this case, the SOAP client has no actual understanding of the SOAP protocol. It simply reads a particular XML element from a document, transmits it to an HTTP server, and then records the results in a separate log file. The logic for constructing the SOAP envelope exists outside of the SOAP client, presumably in an XSLT stylesheet.

The SOAP Envelope

SOAP requests and responses both use the SOAP envelope as the top-level container for transmitting messages back and forth. Listing 16.2 shows a skeleton SOAP request, consisting of an `Envelope` and a `Body` element.

LISTING 16.2 A Skeleton SOAP Message

```
<SOAP-ENV:Envelope xmlns:sxml="http://namespaces.strategicxml.com/message/"
        xmlns:xsi="http://www.w3.org/2001/XMLSchema-instance"
        xmlns:xsd="http://www.w3.org/2001/XMLSchema"
        SOAP-ENV:encodingStyle="http://schemas.xmlsoap.org/soap/encoding/">
    <SOAP-ENV:Body>
        <application-specific-message/>
    </SOAP-ENV:Body>
 </SOAP-ENV:Envelope>
```

The contents of the `Body` element depend on the specific action being requested from the SOAP server. These are the three pieces of information that determine what SOAP operation will be performed:

- The URL where the request is sent (determines the SOAP server configuration that will process the request)
- The contents of the `SOAPAction` custom HTTP header
- The contents of the SOAP message itself

Defining the SOAP Batch Format

To convey this information, we will define our own XML document format that allows multiple SOAP requests to be grouped together for transmission. The grouping element will also contain the target URL of the SOAP server and the value to be passed in the `SOAPAction` HTTP header. Listing 16.3 shows the basic structure of a SOAP batch document such as we are describing.

LISTING 16.3 A SOAP Batch Document

```
<?xml version="1.0" encoding="utf-8"?>
<soap_batch xmlns:SOAP-ENV="http://schemas.xmlsoap.org/soap/envelope/"
    URI="http://localhost/OrderHandler/OrderHandler.wsdl"
    SOAPAction="http://namespaces.strategicxml.com/action/
➥OrderHandler.ProcessOrder">
  <SOAP-ENV:Envelope ...>
```

LISTING 16.3 Continued

```
    <!-- SOAP message body goes here -->
</SOAP-ENV:Envelope>
  <SOAP-ENV:Envelope ...>
    <!-- SOAP message body goes here -->
  </SOAP-ENV:Envelope>
. . .
</soap_batch>
```

This document will serve as the input to our "dumb" SOAP client program.

Implementing a "Dumb" SOAP Client

These are the tasks that need to be performed by our SOAP client:

1. Parse the incoming SOAP batch document.
2. Preserve the SOAP `URI` and `SOAPAction` attributes of the `soap_batch` element.
3. For each SOAP `Envelope` element, perform an HTTP `POST` operation to the specified URI using the `SOAPAction` given. Record the HTTP message results in a specified log file.

Based on the requirement that the resulting program be platform-independent, and the need for XML parsing and HTTP protocol support, Java is a natural selection as the implementation language of this utility.

After Java has been chosen as the implementation language, some thought should be given as to which XML parsing API to use. The two major options that are available are listed here:

- *DOM* *Document-based:* Memory intensive, requires entire document be parsed before processing, provides random access to every element in the document.
- *SAX* *Event-based:* Lightweight, document can be processed as individual elements are recognized, no document data is stored in memory.

Although each technology has its own unique strengths and weaknesses, in this case SAX would appear to be the best alternative. The iterative nature of the application (SOAP `Envelope` element is read, transmitted, and then discarded) lends itself naturally to an event-based API such as SAX. Also, very large documents can be processed without incurring unreasonable memory usage requirements.

Now that the overall application design has been specified, we can move on to the actual implementation.

Implementation Notes

Before we proceed with the actual implementation of the order database to SOAP transformation and the SOAP playback client, a high-level overview of the order submission process is in order. Figure 16.4 shows the flow of information from the original order database document to the SOAP server, and the capturing of the SOAP results into a log file.

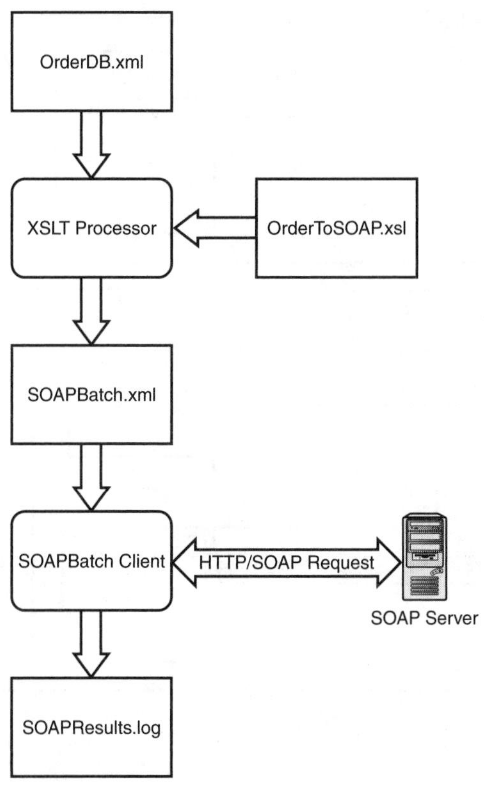

FIGURE 16.4
The overall application data flow.

Because our XSLT will need to construct a valid SOAP request message, it would be useful to see a valid, functional SOAP request that has been generated by an existing SOAP client. Fortunately, the Microsoft SOAP Toolkit provides us with a tool that can do just that.

Using the MS SOAP Trace Tool

The SOAP Trace tool is a simple graphical utility that is installed as part of the Microsoft SOAP Toolkit. It allows a SOAP developer to monitor SOAP message traffic between a SOAP client and a SOAP server. Although it is possible to construct a SOAP request message from scratch using the SOAP specification and a text editor, capturing a "live" message and modifying it can be a real time saver.

Figure 16.5 shows how the SOAP Trace facility inserts itself into the SOAP/HTTP request chain.

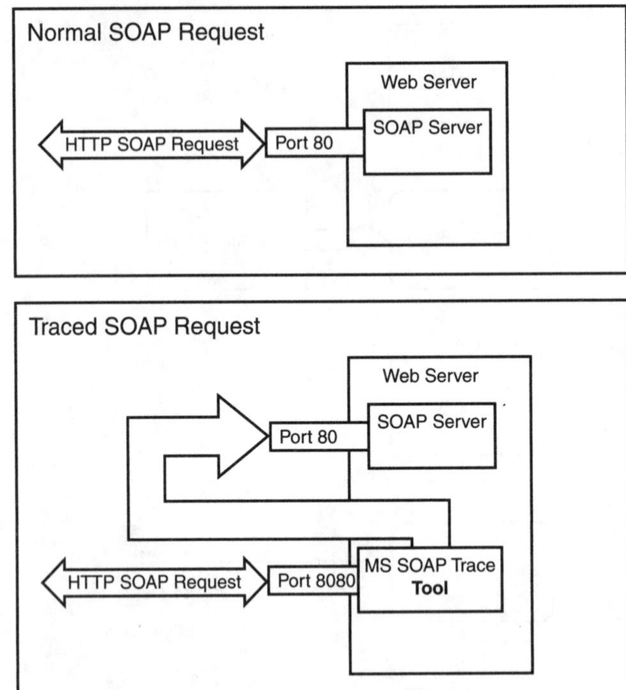

FIGURE 16.5
SOAP request tracing.

One modification needs to be made to the SOAP client application to use the SOAP Trace tool: the SOAP request URL needs to access a nonstandard HTTP port (in this case, 8080) instead of the normal port (port 80). In this case, we will be using the Trace tool to monitor a SOAP transaction between the `OrderHandlerSOAPTest.vbs` script from Chapter 15 and the SOAP service that is declared in `OrderHandler.wsdl` (from Chapter 15 as well). To begin tracing, perform the following steps (assuming that the sample SOAP service from Chapter 15 is installed and running on the current machine):

1. Edit `OrderHandler.wsdl` (in the `OrderHandler` IIS virtual directory). Locate the `<soap:address>` child element of the `<port>` element of the `<service>` element that reads

   ```
   <soap:address location="http://localhost/OrderHandler/OrderHandler.wsdl" />
   ```

2. Modify the URL to read

   ```
   http://localhost:8080/OrderHandler/OrderHandler.wsdl
   ```

3. Run the Trace utility (located in the Start/Programs/Microsoft SOAP Toolkit menu).
4. In the utility, click the File/New/Formatted Trace menu item. The utility will display a dialog box, shown in Figure 16.6.

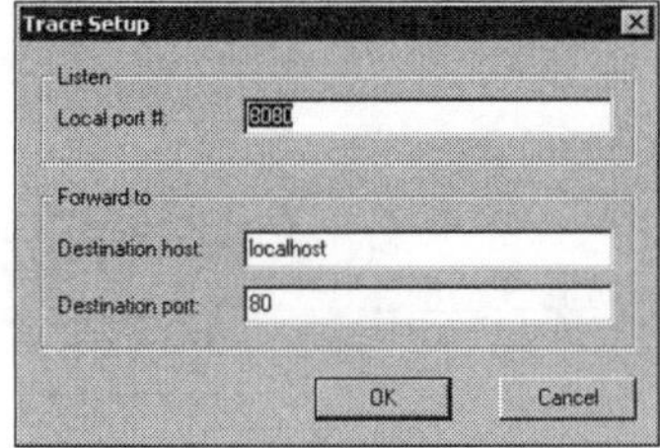

FIGURE 16.6
Creating a new SOAP Trace session.

5. Accept the default options. This will cause the Trace utility to create a new server socket at port 8080 and then forward requests to the server listening at port 80.

The SOAP Trace utility will then show a split window with a tree view on the left side that shows a list of SOAP requests. The top-right panel will show the request as it was sent from the SOAP client, and the bottom-right panel will show the response from the SOAP server. To collect a sample SOAP message, run the `OrderHandlerSOAPTest.vbs` script from Chapter 15. After the request runs, expand the single element in the tree view of the Trace utility and click on Message #1. The Trace application will display the content of the request message in the top-right panel. To capture the message content, right-click on the top-right panel and select View Source from the context menu, as shown in Figure 16.7.

The View Source operation will bring up the contents of the SOAP request in Notepad, where it may be saved to a file or copied to the Clipboard. A sample SOAP message that was captured using the SOAP Trace utility can be found with the source code for this example in `SampleMSSoapMsg.xml`. One thing that becomes apparent when looking at the message that was generated by the SOAP client is that very little optimization is done by the XML generator when it comes to declaring and using namespaces. Although all the elements in the message belong to one of the following 4 namespaces, 15 distinct namespaces are declared and used within the message:

- The default namespace
- `http://namespaces.strategicxml.com/message/`
- `http://www.w3.org/2001/XMLSchema-instance`
- `http://www.w3.org/2001/XMLSchema`

Now that we have a valid SOAP message in captivity, creating an XSLT that will take the input data from the order database document and generate a SOAP request is relatively straightforward.

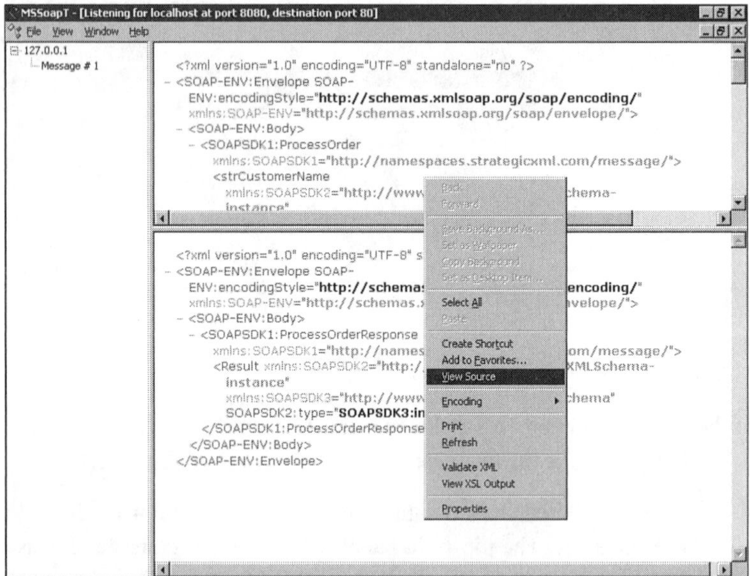

FIGURE 16.7
Viewing the contents of the SOAP transaction.

Writing `OrderToSOAP.xsl`

Constructing the XSLT to generate a batch of SOAP requests from an order database document consists mainly of determining where the data from the order database document needs to be plugged in to the SOAP message data in the output document.

In `OrderToSOAP.xsl`, the first XSL element encountered within the `<xsl:stylesheet>` element is the `<xsl:output>` element:

```
<xsl:output method="xml"/>
```

This tells the XSL formatter to output well-formed XML. If the `method` attribute were set to `html`, for instance, some tags might not be properly terminated (such as <br> or <hr>) based on the assumptions made regarding HTML document structure.

The entire stylesheet consists of two templates. The first template matches the top-level `<orders>` element from the order database document, and emits the top-level `<soap_batch>` element. This element will contain the SOAP client messages that will be transmitted by the Java-based SOAP client we will develop later:

```
<xsl:template match="orders">
  <soap_batch URI="http://localhost/OrderHandler/OrderHandler.wsdl"
      SOAPAction=
      "http://namespaces.strategicxml.com/action/OrderHandler.ProcessOrder">
    <xsl:apply-templates/>
  </soap_batch>
</xsl:template>
```

The `<soap_batch>` element includes the `URI` and `SOAPAction` attributes that will be needed by our SOAP client to connect to the server and send each request.

The other template matches each individual `<order>` element and emits a valid SOAP client message into the target document. It is composed of a series of elements that represent the parameters to the `ProcessOrder()` method on the SOAP server (`<strCustomerName>`, `<strCCNum>`, `<strEmailName>`, and so on).

The most complex transformation that must be performed is in the case of the two array parameters. Because they both follow the same structure, we will look only at the code for the `<astrPartNums>` array here:

```
<xsl:element name="astrPartNums">
  <xsl:attribute name="SOAP-ENV:arrayType"
    >xsd:anyType[<xsl:value-of select="count(items/item)"
    />]</xsl:attribute>
  <xsl:attribute name="xsi:type">SOAP-ENV:Array</xsl:attribute>
  <xsl:for-each select="items/item">
    <SOAP-ENV:anyType xsi:type="xsd:string">
      <xsl:value-of select="@part_num"/>
    </SOAP-ENV:anyType>
  </xsl:for-each>
</xsl:element>
```

The first challenge involves the `SOAP-ENV:arrayType` attribute of the `<astrPartNums>` element itself. The value of this attribute must include the actual number of elements in the array. To create this value using XSLT, we can use the `<xsl:element>` element to explicitly create an element and populate its attributes using the `<xsl:attribute>` element. The attribute value for

`SOAP-ENV:arrayType` uses `<xsl:value-of>` with the XPath `count()` function to return the number of child `<item>` elements of the `<items>` sub-element.

Then, within the `<astrPartNums>` element we must include one `<SOAP-ENV:anyType>` element for each part number. The `<xsl:for-each>` element causes the included transform to be executed once for each `<item>` element in the source document. We first need to extract only the `part_num` attribute from the `<item>` element, then later extract the `quantity` attribute separately. Using `<xsl:for-each>` prevents us from needing to create an awkward duplicate set of templates using `<apply-templates>` along with template modes.

Now that the transformation is complete, we need to write the SOAP batch utility that will send these messages to the SOAP server.

Writing the SOAPBatch Utility

The `SOAPBatch` utility will read a batch of SOAP requests from an XML document and send them to the SOAP server. This is the basic flow of the application:

1. Create a SAX 2.0 parser and new `SOAPBatch` class instance.
2. Register the new `SOAPBatch` class instance to receive events for the `ContentHandler` and `ErrorHandler` interfaces.
3. Parse the SOAP batch document at the URL given on the program's command line (or the input from `stdin`, if no URLs are given).
4. When the top-level `<soap_batch>` element is recognized, preserve the values of the `URI` and `SOAPAction` attributes for use later.
5. When the `<SOAP-ENV:Envelope>` open tag is recognized, begin preserving the XML content using a new `StringBuffer` object instance.
6. When character data is found, append it to the `StringBuffer`, if there is one.
7. When an element close tag is recognized, append it to the `StringBuffer` (if it exists). If it is the `</SOAP-ENV:Envelope>` close tag, transmit the XML content to the SOAP server, capture the results, and set the `StringBuffer` to null (to prevent further content capture).
8. Steps 5–7 repeat until the end of the input document is reached.

The full source code for the `SOAPBatch` class is available on the Web site in the `SOAPBatch.java` file. Although implementing this utility in Java using SAX 2.0 makes certain tasks very easy, there are still a few XML-related issues that require special handling.

Namespaces in SAX 2.0

Unlike SAX 1.0, SAX 2.0 provides explicit support for recognizing and tracking XML namespaces. The old, namespace-ignorant API didn't treat `xmlns` attributes any differently than non-namespace attributes. The new `ContentHandler` interface, however, includes two new methods (`startPrefixMapping()` and `endPrefixMapping()`) that are used to inform the application when namespaces go in and out of scope. The `startElement()` and `endElement()` methods include the element's namespace URI as part of the notification arguments.

For our purposes, the older non-namespace–aware handling would actually make the application much simpler. We need to capture each `<SOAP-ENV:Envelope>` in its entirety, including any namespaces that are active at the time. Because each SOAP message is a standalone XML document, every namespace that is used within the `<SOAP-ENV:Envelope>` element must be declared in it.

One possible approach would be to use the special `setFeature()` method of the `XMLReader` interface. Although SAX 2.0 is namespace-aware by default, it is possible to set the `http://xml.org/sax/features/namespaces` feature to `false`, which would cause the SAX 2.0 library to revert to the old 1.0 namespace behavior.

Although that approach might eventually be made to work, there is another namespace issue that must be dealt with. After the XSLT transformation, the XSL processor moved the declaration of the `SOAP-ENV` namespace to the enclosing `<soap_batch>` element. Although this results in much cleaner XML document, it is necessary that this namespace be declared for each `<SOAP-ENV:Envelope>` message that is transmitted to the SOAP server. Also, every other namespace that is declared must somehow find its way back into an `xmlns` attribute for the trip to the server.

The workaround for this issue is to maintain the current set of namespace prefixes and URIs in a Java `HashMap` object. Each time the `startPrefixMapping()` method is called, the given namespace is added to the `m_hmNamespaces HashMap`. To ensure that all the namespaces declared for the `<soap_batch>` element are propagated to the envelope elements, a separate `m_hmNSBase` member is used to contain the namespaces that were declared in the `<soap_batch>` element. The following code in `startElement()` deals with keeping the namespace hash maps up-to-date:

```
    if (raw.equals("soap_batch")) {
. . .
      m_hmNSBase = m_hmNamespaces;  // preserve the global namespaces for all
      m_hmNamespaces = new HashMap();
. . .
    } else if (raw.equals("SOAP-ENV:Envelope")) {
      m_hmNamespaces.putAll(m_hmNSBase); // add the global namespaces
. . .
    }
```

The contents of the `m_hmNamespaces` hash map include all the namespace prefixes that must be declared to create a standalone XML document from the current element. This is the code in the `echoElement()` method that emits these declarations:

```
if (m_hmNamespaces.size() > 0) {
  Iterator i = m_hmNamespaces.keySet().iterator();

  while (i.hasNext()) {
    String strPrefix = (String)i.next();
    String strURI = (String)m_hmNamespaces.get(strPrefix);

    sb.append(" xmlns:" + strPrefix + "=\"" + strURI + "\"");
  }

  m_hmNamespaces.clear();
```

The final `m_hmNamespaces.clear()` call resets the namespace map to receive any new child namespaces that might be declared within the current element.

Escaping Character Data

Another common gotcha that is encountered when the output from an XML parser is used to feed another XML parser is failing to escape markup characters within character data blocks. The `characters()` notification method uses the `xmlEscape()` method to ensure that XML special characters (`<`, `>`, `&`, `"`, and `'`) are properly escaped using the special built-in entity references (`<`, `>`, `&`, `"`, and `'`).

Using the URL Class

The `sendRequest()` method is the workhorse method of the utility. It takes the XML SOAP message that was collected by the various SAX notification methods and transmits it to the SOAP server using the Java `URL` class. Because the SOAP request must use the HTTP `POST` method to submit the SOAP message body, some extra setup of the URL connection is required:

```
URL url = new URL(m_strRequestURI);

HttpURLConnection huc = (HttpURLConnection)url.openConnection();
huc.setDoOutput(true);

huc.setRequestMethod("POST");
huc.setRequestProperty("Content-Type", "text/xml");
huc.setRequestProperty("SOAPAction", m_strSOAPAction);
```

This code fragment uses the special `HttpURLConnection` subclass of the abstract `URLConnection` class to set the HTTP request method, content type, and special `SOAPAction` header, and to indicate that output will be sent with the request.

The rest of the method uses a `PrintStream` to transmit the SOAP message body from the original SOAP batch document to the server. Then the HTTP response code and the SOAP message body of the return message is written to `System.out`.

Putting It All Together

After the `OrderToSOAP.xsl` stylesheet has been written and the `SOAPBatch` program has been compiled, submitting a new batch to the SOAP server becomes a relatively simple process. The following commands will transform an order database document and then transmit it to a SOAP server:

```
saxon OrderDB.xml OrderToSoap.xsl > soapbatch.xml
java -cp SOAPBatch/classes
➥com.strategicxml.examples.soapbatch.SOAPBatch < soapbatch.xml
```

In a production environment, this task would most likely be automated using a process scheduler (such as the NT/Windows 2000 `AT` command).

NOTE

Although most of the examples in this book use the Saxon XSLT processor, there are a number of other great transformation processors out there. For example, the Apache Foundation's XML Project (`xml.apache.org`) has the Xalan processor

Deployment

These are the steps to deploy this application:

1. Download and unzip the sample files.
2. Ensure that Saxon is properly installed and available from the command line as `saxon`. The following `saxon.bat` file can be used to run Saxon directly from the command line in a Windows environment:

   ```
   @java com.icl.saxon.StyleSheet %1 %2 %3 %4 %5 %6 %7 %8 %9
   ```
3. Ensure that the SOAP application from Chapter 15 is installed and functioning properly on the local system.
4. Use the instructions from the "Putting It All Together" section to submit a test batch using the `OrderDB.xml` document included with the example files.

Conclusion

One of the hallmarks of using XML-based protocols and technologies is flexibility. In this application, a programming API is called on the server using nothing more than a set of recorded commands that were automatically generated from an input document. No specific coding was required, and the resulting solution is just as robust and secure as a more complex solution involving custom programming would have been. As XML blurs the distinction between code and data, our applications can begin to do the same.

Migrating Legacy Data

CHAPTER

17

Let me lay out a frightening little scenario for you: It's 3 p.m. on a Friday afternoon, and most of the IT department is "working from home" already. You're about to join them when your manager rushes in and begins babbling incoherently about batch processes, missing data, and Web interfaces, and, most ominously, the word COBOL is thrown in there somewhere. This is ominous because you know that the only guy who actually knows COBOL is laid up in the hospital from a jousting-related accident he suffered at his last Society for Creative Anachronisms festival.

Unless you're already a COBOL/mainframe programmer (which I'm definitely not), your brain will tend to automatically shut down whenever someone says the "C" word around you. But the fact remains that most of the really critical business systems running today are written in COBOL and running on a mainframe. Learning the bare-bones techniques to gain access to the data from these applications can only help you when you get that unexpected "there goes the weekend" visit from your boss.

Technologies Used:

- **XSLT**
- **COBOL**

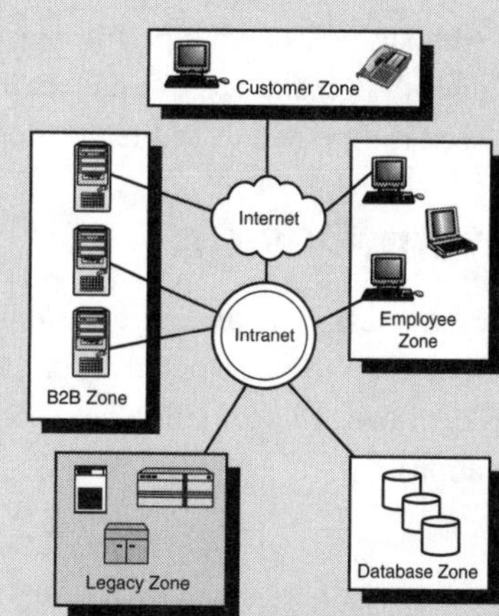

The COBOL programming language has picked up a very bad reputation among the younger, PC-grown crop of programmers. I should know, because I'm one of them. And I used to get in there and make wisecracks with the best of them. But at one point in my career I was forced to actually stop and learn the language, and I came to a startling conclusion: COBOL is not that bad.

Now, it's not the language I would choose to write a new operating system in, and I would rather get a job weighing hibernating grizzly bears than try to write a GUI application in COBOL. But for doing batch processes, generating nice-looking character-based reports, or generally expressing business rules in a clear and readable fashion, COBOL is as good a language as any (and better than most).

Problem Description

A manufacturing company tracks its inventory on a mainframe, using a daily COBOL batch process to update stock levels. A new Internet-based ordering system provides a list of orders as an XML document. These orders must be converted into a format that can be read by the mainframe batch inventory programs.

Also, the Internet-based ordering system must be updated with current stock levels after the master inventory list has been updated. This will require that data from the COBOL inventory file be exported in XML format.

Requirements

This system must meet the following requirements:

- No modifications can be made to the existing inventory processing programs or file formats on the mainframe.
- Any pre- or post-processing that needs to be done to massage the data being transferred with the mainframe may be done either locally (on the Internet application server) or on the mainframe itself.
- Although reasonable performance is always a concern, the batch nature of the processes doesn't demand custom-coded, high-performance solutions. Off-the-shelf tools should be used if they will expedite development.

System Design

Rather than designing an entire system, we are actually designing a data pipeline that will permit information to flow to and from the existing legacy COBOL applications. Figure 17.1 shows the flow of information between the Internet ordering system and the legacy mainframe applications.

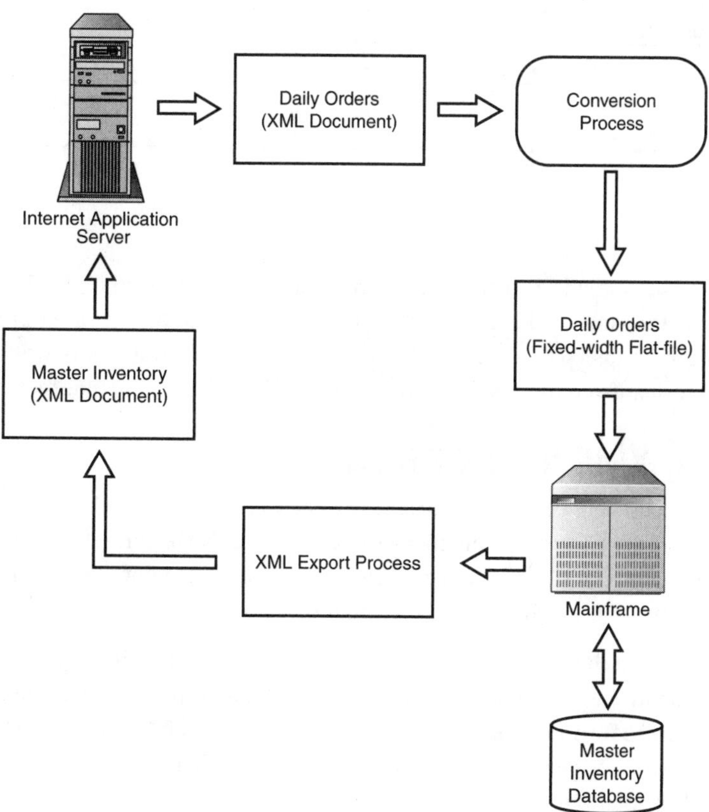

FIGURE 17.1
The Internet/legacy order processing data flow.

Based on this data flow, these are the items that need to be designed and developed:

- The daily order XML to flat-file conversion process.
- The mainframe inventory XML export process.

Also, because there is no real "mainframe" in our scenario, we will develop utilities to simulate the actions that would be performed by the legacy system in a real application.

Converting XML to a Flat-File Format

The documentation we were given for the mainframe daily order update application shows us the actual flat-file format expected by that utility. Figure 17.2 shows the column layout and format of the expected daily update file.

Item Quantity							Part Number														
1	2	3	4	5	6	7	8	9	10	1	2	3	4	5	6	7	8	9	20	1	2
						1	S	C	-	9	3	8									
						1	S	C	-	9	3	8									
						1	S	C	-	9	3	8									

FIGURE 17.2
The daily update file format.

The XML document that will be used to generate this file can be found in `OrderDB.xml`. This document is the same as the document that is created by the offline order processing system that is built in Chapter 14, " Offline Order Processing Using Store-and-Forward." To generate a flat-file format from the XML document, we will use the text output method of XSLT.

Generating XML from COBOL

To close the data loop between the mainframe and the Internet-based ordering system, it is necessary to export the contents of the inventory database in XML format. If the data were stored in a fixed-width flat file on the mainframe, simply downloading the file and using data transformation tools such as Microsoft DTS might be an option.

Unfortunately, because this database is stored as an indexed file, the file format itself is opaque to non-COBOL applications. Most COBOL compilers use a proprietary Indexed/Sequential Access Method (ISAM) format for storing and retrieving data in indexed files. Therefore, writing a COBOL program to retrieve the data records and write them as an XML document is the safest and simplest solution.

Implementation Notes

This project will involve developing the following items:

- The `make_inventory.xsl` stylesheet, which will be used to produce a flat-file representation of the orderable part information from a catalog that follows the document type definition from `OrderCatalog.dtd`.
- The IMPORT-INVENTORY COBOL program, which will take the output of `make_inventory.xsl` and populate a COBOL indexed file with the part database information given.
- The `make_update.xsl` stylesheet, which will be used to convert the orders in `OrderDB.xml` to the flat-file data format described in the "Requirements" section.
- The PROCESS-ORDERS COBOL program will be written to accept the flat file generated by the `make_update` stylesheet and use it to update the inventory file.

- The EXPORT-INVENTORY COBOL program, which will be written to output the contents of the mainframe inventory database as an XML document.

Mapping the Data

We'll start by looking at `make_inventory.xsl`. This stylesheet will accept a product catalog that conforms to `OrderCatalog.dtd` (see Chapter 12, "Web Content Publishing," and Chapter 18, "Unifying Product Documentation," for more information) and generate a flat-file report that conforms to the format shown in Figure 17.3.

Amount in Stock	Part Number	Description
1 2 3 4 5 6 7	1 2 8 9 0 1 2 3 4 5 6 7 8 9 0 1 2	3 3 4 5 6 7 8 9 0 1 2 3 4 5 6
1 0 0	S C - 9 3 8	D C C A R C O R D

Manufacturer
4 5 6 7 8 9 7 8 9 0 1 2 3 4 5 6 7 8 9 0 1 2 3 4 5 6 7 8 9 0 1 2 3 4 5 6 7 8 9 0 1 2 3 4 5 6 7 8 9 0 1 2 3 4 5 6 7 8 9 0 1 2 3 4 5
S H I N D O I N D U S T R I A L C O . , L T D .

FIGURE 17.3
The flat file report format

Each row in this file will represent a single `<item>` element from the order catalog document. The attributes and child elements of the `<item>` element will provide the values to populate the columns in the target file. Listing 17.1 shows the sample `<item>` element that corresponds to the data shown in Figure 17.3.

LISTING 17.1 The Sample Catalog Item

```
<item part_num="SC-938">
  <desc>DC CAR CORD</desc>
  <manufacturer>SHIN DO INDUSTRIAL CO., LTD.</manufacturer>
</item>
```

The `part_num` attribute will be used to populate the Part Number column of the output file. The `<desc>` and `<manufacturer>` elements correspond to the Description and Manufacturer columns. Because the catalog has no inventory information included, each item will be assumed to have 100 units currently in stock.

Now that the data format is understood, it is time to write an XSLT stylesheet that can generate the exact columnar format required.

Writing the Stylesheets

The first element found inside the <xsl:stylesheet> element is the <xsl:output> element:

```
<xsl:output method="text"/>
```

The output element actually supports several different attributes that control various aspects of how the stylesheet processor will format the output document. In this case, the `method="text"` attribute indicates that the output of this stylesheet will be plain text, not markup. When this method is set, the stylesheet processor will not allow markup structures to be generated using the functionality of elements such as <xsl:element>. It also prevents the processor from escaping special markup characters (for example, <, >, &) when they are written to the target document.

The next element is the <xsl:strip-space> element:

```
<xsl:strip-space elements="*"/>
```

The default behavior of an XML parser when parsing a document without a DTD is to consider all whitespace to be significant. Because our application requires fine control over the whitespace that is emitted into the target file, we will notify the XSLT processor to strip any whitespace nodes it may find. The `elements` attribute is either a list of elements to strip space from, or `*`, which matches all elements.

The first template rule may seem a bit confusing at first:

```
<xsl:template match="text()"/>
```

This is necessary because an XSLT processor has a set of default rules that it will automatically apply to the input document if no other rules override them. The rule for text content is to echo it to the output document. Because we will be discarding most of the text from the source document, and will be carefully controlling the text we do emit, this empty template will cause the XSLT processor to swallow any text it encounters in the source document.

The next template matches the <item> element from the catalog document, and this is where the real work is done. Note that the following listing has been wrapped in order to fit on the page. Whitespace and line breaks are significant in this application, so for the next listing the actual hard carriage returns are displayed using the ¶ symbol and spaces are shown using the • symbol.

```
<xsl:template·match="item">····100<xsl: value-of·select="@part_num"/><xsl:value
-of·select="substring('···············',·string length(@part_num)+1)"/> <xsl:va
lue-of·select="desc"/><xsl:value-of·select="substring('···············',·string
```

```
-length(desc)+1)"/><xsl:value-of·select="normalizespace(manufacturer)"/><xsl:va
lueof·select="substring('······································',·string
-length(manufacturer))"/><xsl:text></xsl:text></xsl:template>¶
```

Notice that the first line of the `<xsl:template>` element runs for six lines within this listing. The lack of carriage returns and spaces is necessary to prevent column alignment errors from creeping into the output document. The first string value given is the value `100`, right-aligned in a field that is seven characters wide. This will be the hard-coded inventory level in the output document.

The next value given is the item part number, selected from the `part_num` attribute by the `<xsl:value-of>` element. Referencing Figure 17.3, we can see that the part number needs to be left-aligned in a column that is 15 characters wide. Because most part numbers will be shorter than 15 characters, it is necessary to pad the column with enough spaces to fill the column. That is where the XPath `substring()` function comes in. The `substring()` function returns a subpart of a larger string by accepting a string argument and either a starting position, or a starting position and a length. If no length is given, it returns the remainder of the string including and after the starting position. This function can be used with a constant string that contains exactly as many spaces as there are characters in a particular column, like so:

```
<xsl:value-of·select="substring('········
➥·······',·stringlength(@part_num)+1)"/>
```

This will insert the remainder of the padding string (minus the length of the value string, in this case the `part_num` attribute) into the output document. This same technique is also used to emit the description and manufacturer values.

The last, somewhat mysterious portion of this template is the `<xsl:text>` element that apparently contains nothing. In reality, because the closing tag appears on the next line, this tag contains a carriage return. This is necessary because by default the XSLT processor will collapse carriage returns, linefeeds, and spaces into single spaces. All the characters within the `<xsl:text>` element (including the carriage return) will be echoed verbatim to the output document.

The make_update.xsl stylesheet uses exactly the same techniques to extract information from the <item> element of the OrderDB.xml document and emit the file structure depicted in Figure 17.2.

The IMPORT-INVENTORY Program

The IMPORT-INVENTORY program accepts the flat-file format shown in Figure 17.3 and inserts the inventory items given into an indexed file. The source code for this program is located in IMPORT-INVENTORY.COB and is available on the Web site.

> **NOTE**
>
> All the COBOL sample applications were developed and executed on Windows 2000 Professional using an early release of Fujitsu COBOL version 3.0. They are all COBOL 85 compliant, and they should compile using any other COBOL 85–compliant compiler.

All COBOL programs are separated into distinct areas, called divisions. The four divisions are the IDENTIFICATION, ENVIRONMENT, DATA, and PROCEDURE divisions. Divisions may also be further divided into sections, which are specific to the division they belong to. The IDENTIFICATION division contains program identification information and may contain other optional information (such as the program author's name):

```
000100 IDENTIFICATION DIVISION.
000200  PROGRAM-ID. IMPORT-INVENTORY.
```

Although COBOL is inherently a hardware and operating-system-independent language, the ENVIRONMENT DIVISION is used to associate the abstract file references within a program with the physical files located on the target computer. The ENVIRONMENT DIVISION from the IMPORT-INVENTORY program is used to define two physical files, the INVENTORY-IN-FILE and the INVENTORY-OUT-FILE:

```
000400 ENVIRONMENT DIVISION.
000500  INPUT-OUTPUT SECTION.
000600   FILE-CONTROL.
000700     SELECT INVENTORY-IN-FILE
000800         ASSIGN       TO  INFILE
000900         ORGANIZATION IS  LINE SEQUENTIAL.
001000     SELECT INVENTORY-OUT-FILE
001100         ASSIGN       TO  INVINDEX
001200         ORGANIZATION IS  INDEXED
001300         RECORD KEY   IS  OUT-PART-NUM  OF  ITEM-RECORD
001400         ACCESS MODE  IS  RANDOM.
```

The SELECT statements assign a logical file (INVENTORY-IN-FILE) to a physical file (INFILE) so that the COBOL runtime library can open the correct disk file when the program is executed. Besides specifying the physical file to open, SELECT statements also give other properties of the file. The first SELECT statement declares a file that is organized as a sequence of lines (LINE SEQUENTIAL).

The other SELECT is somewhat more complicated. It defines an INDEXED file, which behaves similarly to a single table in a relational database. It has one or more key columns, and may be accessed either randomly (records are retrieved based on key value) or sequentially (one record after another). This SELECT statement indicates that the file will be accessed randomly.

After the ENVIRONMENT DIVISION comes the DATA DIVISION. This is where all the variable storage areas that will be used by the program must be declared. The two main sections of the DATA DIVISION are the FILE SECTION and the WORKING-STORAGE SECTION.

The FILE SECTION is intrinsically linked with the information provided in the INPUT-OUTPUT section of the ENVIRONMENT DIVISON, which we covered earlier. The FILE SECTION is where the record layouts are defined for use with the physical files that were declared previously using the SELECT statement. The following FILE SECTION contains two file description (FD) entries:

```
001700  FILE SECTION.
001800  FD   INVENTORY-IN-FILE.
001900  01   DATA-RECORD.
002000       02   IN-RECORD.
002100            03   IN-QUANTITY       PIC 9(7).
002200            03   IN-PART-NUM       PIC X(15).
002300            03   IN-DESC           PIC X(15).
002400            03   IN-MFGR           PIC X(45).
002500  FD   INVENTORY-OUT-FILE.
002600  01   INVENTORY-RECORD.
002700       02   ITEM-RECORD.
002800            03   OUT-QUANTITY       PIC 9(7).
002900            03   OUT-PART-NUM       PIC X(15).
003000            03   OUT-DESC           PIC X(15).
003100            03   OUT-MFGR           PIC X(45).
```

The file descriptions give the physical layouts of the records from the INVENTORY-IN-FILE and the INVENTORY-OUT-FILE declared previously. The numbered items below each FD entry declare data items that can be referenced later, from within the PROCEDURE DIVISON of the program.

The data items are preceded by a number (such as 01 or 03). This is called the level number. Items with the same level number are grouped together, and an item with a lower-level number followed by items with higher-level numbers is called a group item. Items that have no children are called elementary items, and they must have a `PIC` keyword that describes their size and layout.

The `PIC` keyword is short for `PICTURE`. The picture clause, as it is called, describes the size, layout, and formatting of data items in a COBOL program. The basic syntax of a `PIC` item is determined by whether the associated data item is numeric or non-numeric.

Non-numeric items are composed of a string of the letter `X`. A four-character field, for instance, would be written like this:

```
PIC         XXXX
```

To simplify the task of writing strings of symbols, any symbol may be followed by a repeat count in parentheses:

```
PIC         X(4)
```

Numeric values are formatted using the character `9` as the character placeholder. Numbers are assumed to be right-justified and integral, unless a decimal point (`.`) character is present.

By comparing the field sizes and layouts, you can see that the record layouts for both files are identical. Because the purpose of this program is to import data from a flat file into an indexed inventory database, this makes sense. Now that the files have been declared and the record layouts have been defined, it is time to do the actual processing. This is done in the `PROCEDURE DIVISION`, as shown in Listing 17.2.

LISTING 17.2 The `PROCEDURE DIVISION` of the IMPORT-INVENTORY Program

```
003300 PROCEDURE DIVISION.
003400* OPEN THE INPUT AND OUTPUT FILES
003500       OPEN INPUT  INVENTORY-IN-FILE.
003600       OPEN OUTPUT    INVENTORY-OUT-FILE.
003700*
003800  LOOP-POINT.
003900* READ THE DATA FROM THE INCOMING FLAT FILE
004000       READ INVENTORY-IN-FILE AT END GO TO TERM-PROC.
004100* UPDATE THE OUTBOUND INDEXED FILE RECORD
004200       MOVE IN-QUANTITY TO OUT-QUANTITY.
004300       MOVE IN-PART-NUM TO OUT-PART-NUM.
004400       MOVE IN-DESC TO OUT-DESC.
004500       MOVE IN-MFGR TO OUT-MFGR.
004600* WRITE THE INDEXED RECORD
004700       WRITE INVENTORY-RECORD INVALID KEY GO TO LOOP-POINT.
004800       GO TO LOOP-POINT.
004900*
```

LISTING 17.2 Continued

```
005000  TERM-PROC.
005100*
005200      CLOSE  INVENTORY-OUT-FILE INVENTORY-IN-FILE.
005300 END PROGRAM IMPORT-INVENTORY.
```

Although the specific keywords and statement structure might be somewhat unfamiliar, the basic logic should resemble that of any batch data processing application you've ever seen (or written).

The first line following the `PROCEDURE DIVISION` statement is actually a COBOL comment. Any line beginning with an asterisk character is a single-line comment.

> **NOTE**
>
> Sometimes I find that the verbose nature of a COBOL program makes it very difficult to tell the comments from the code!

The two `OPEN` statements on lines 3500 and 3600 open the input and output files that are going to be processed. Line 3800 defines a label called `LOOP-POINT` that will serve as the top of the processing loop.

The `READ` statement on line 4000 causes the next record from the `INVENTORY-IN-FILE` to be read into the `DATA-RECORD` area which is declared in the `FILE SECTION` of the `DATA DIVISION`. The `AT END GO TO TERM-PROC` clause provides the escape condition from the read loop. When no more input records are available, the program will jump to the `TERM-PROC` label and complete processing.

The four `MOVE` statements from lines 4200 to 4500 copy the values that were just read from the input file into the storage area for the output file. There are different variations on the `MOVE` statement, and one of them will be shown in a later program.

The data is finally written to the indexed file using the `WRITE` statement on line 4700. The `INVALID KEY` clause is used to return to the top of the loop if an error occurs when writing the record to the inventory database. This could occur if an attempt were made to add the same part number twice.

Line 4800 closes the processing loop and causes execution to resume at the `LOOP-POINT` label.

After the `READ` exhausts the input file and jumps execution to the `TERM-PROC` label, line 5200 closes the input and the output file, and then execution halts at the `END PROGRAM` statement at line 5300.

That concludes a fairly typical COBOL program. The only significance it has from an XML perspective is that the input file was generated by processing an XML document using XSLT. The next program is very similar to this program, but its purpose is to process incoming orders that are presented using the output of the `make_update.xsl` stylesheet.

The PROCESS-ORDERS Program

The PROCESS-ORDERS program accepts a flat file conforming to the structure shown in Figure 17.2 and subtracts the order quantities from the corresponding inventory records in the inventory data file.

The structure and content of this program are very similar to those of the IMPORT-INVENTORY program. In fact, other than the slightly different record layouts between the input and output files, the only significant difference occurs in the `PROCEDURE DIVISION`, as shown in Listing 17.3. This source code is located in the `PROCESS-ORDERS.COB` source file.

LISTING 17.3 The PROCESS-ORDERS Program

```
000100 IDENTIFICATION DIVISION.
000200  PROGRAM-ID. PROCESS-ORDERS.
000300*
000400 ENVIRONMENT DIVISION.
000500  INPUT-OUTPUT SECTION.
000600   FILE-CONTROL.
000700     SELECT ORDER-FILE
000800         ASSIGN       TO  INFILE
000900         ORGANIZATION IS  LINE SEQUENTIAL.
001000     SELECT INVENTORY-FILE
001100         ASSIGN       TO  INVINDEX
001200         ORGANIZATION IS  INDEXED
001300         RECORD KEY   IS  PART-NUM   OF  ITEM-RECORD
001400         ACCESS MODE  IS  RANDOM.
001500*
001600 DATA DIVISION.
001700  FILE SECTION.
001800  FD  ORDER-FILE.
001900  01  DATA-RECORD.
002000      02  ORDER-RECORD.
002100          03  QUANTITY       PIC 9(7).
002200          03  ORDER-PART     PIC X(15).
002300  FD  INVENTORY-FILE.
002400  01  INVENTORY-RECORD.
002500      02  ITEM-RECORD.
```

LISTING 17.3 Continued

```
002600          03  QUANTITY       PIC 9(7).
002700          03  PART-NUM       PIC X(15).
002800          03  DESC           PIC X(15).
002900          03  MFGR           PIC X(45).
003000*
003100 PROCEDURE DIVISION.
003200*
003300      OPEN INPUT  ORDER-FILE.
003400      OPEN I-O    INVENTORY-FILE.
003500*
003600  LOOP-POINT.
003700*
003800      READ ORDER-FILE AT END GO TO TERM-PROC.
003900      MOVE ORDER-PART TO PART-NUM.
004000      READ INVENTORY-FILE.
004100      SUBTRACT QUANTITY OF ORDER-RECORD
004200          FROM QUANTITY OF INVENTORY-RECORD.
004300      REWRITE INVENTORY-RECORD.
004400      GO TO LOOP-POINT.
004500*
004600  TERM-PROC.
004700*
004800      CLOSE  ORDER-FILE INVENTORY-FILE.
004900 END PROGRAM PROCESS-ORDERS.
```

Unlike in the program in Listing 17.2, the `OPEN` statement for the inventory file on line 3400 specifies that the file will be used for both input and output (`I-O`).

Another key difference is how the inventory file is accessed. After the incoming order record is read on line 3800, the `MOVE` statement on line 3900 copies the part number into the `PART-NUM` field of the record associated with the `INVENTORY-FILE`. The subsequent `READ` statement on line 4000 attempts to look up the record using the value currently stored in the key field (`PART-NUM`). The key field was declared using the `RECORD KEY` clause of the `SELECT` statement on line 1300.

After the inventory record has been read into memory, the `SUBTRACT` statement on line 4100 decreases inventory by the amount that was read from the update file. Then the inventory record is rewritten to the inventory file with the `REWRITE` statement.

Although this program is simple, this type of file processing is very common within COBOL programs. The final program will show how the COBOL output facilities can be used to generate a valid XML document.

The EXPORT-INVENTORY Program

As was shown in Figure 17.1, one of the objectives of this project is to make the current inventory data available to the Internet-based ordering system in XML format. This program uses COBOL file output facilities to generate a valid XML document that contains the current contents of the inventory database.

The source code for `EXPORT-INVENTORY.COB` is given in Listing 17.4.

LISTING 17.4 The Source Code for the EXPORT-INVENTORY Program

```
 IDENTIFICATION DIVISION.
  PROGRAM-ID. EXPORT-INVENTORY.
*
 ENVIRONMENT DIVISION.
  INPUT-OUTPUT SECTION.
   FILE-CONTROL.
     SELECT INVENTORY-FILE
         ASSIGN       TO  INVINDEX
         ORGANIZATION IS  INDEXED
         RECORD KEY   IS  PART-NUM   OF   ITEM-RECORD
         ACCESS MODE  IS  SEQUENTIAL.
     SELECT XML-FILE
         ASSIGN       TO  OUTFILE
         ORGANIZATION IS  LINE SEQUENTIAL.
*
 DATA DIVISION.
  FILE SECTION.
  FD  INVENTORY-FILE.
  01  INVENTORY-RECORD.
      02  ITEM-RECORD.
          03  QUANTITY       PIC 9(7).
          03  PART-NUM       PIC X(15).
          03  DESC           PIC X(15).
          03  MFGR           PIC X(45).
  FD  XML-FILE.
  01  PRINT-AREA             PIC X(180).
*
  WORKING-STORAGE SECTION.
  01  OPEN-TAG.
      02                     PIC X(11)      VALUE "<INVENTORY>".
  01  CLOSE-TAG.
      02                     PIC X(12)      VALUE "</INVENTORY>".
  01  ITEM-ELEMENT.
      02                 PIC X(6)           VALUE "<ITEM>".
      02                 PIC X(10)          VALUE "<QUANTITY>".
```

LISTING 17.4 Continued

```
       02  QUANTITY       PIC Z(6)9.
       02                 PIC X(11)          VALUE "</QUANTITY>".
       02                 PIC X(10)          VALUE "<PART-NUM>".
       02  PART-NUM       PIC X(15).
       02                 PIC X(11)          VALUE "</PART-NUM>".
       02                 PIC X(6)           VALUE "<DESC>".
       02  DESC           PIC X(15).
       02                 PIC X(7)           VALUE "</DESC>".
       02                 PIC X(14)          VALUE "<MANUFACTURER>".
       02  MFGR           PIC X(45).
       02                 PIC X(15)          VALUE "</MANUFACTURER>".
       02                 PIC X(7)           VALUE "</ITEM>".
*
 PROCEDURE DIVISION.
*
       OPEN INPUT  INVENTORY-FILE.
       OPEN OUTPUT XML-FILE.
       MOVE OPEN-TAG TO PRINT-AREA.
       WRITE PRINT-AREA.
*
  LOOP-POINT.
*
       READ INVENTORY-FILE AT END GO TO TERM-PROC.
       MOVE CORRESPONDING ITEM-RECORD TO ITEM-ELEMENT.
       MOVE ITEM-ELEMENT TO PRINT-AREA.
       WRITE PRINT-AREA.
       GO TO LOOP-POINT.
*
  TERM-PROC.
       MOVE CLOSE-TAG TO PRINT-AREA.
       WRITE PRINT-AREA.
*
       CLOSE  XML-FILE INVENTORY-FILE .
 END PROGRAM EXPORT-INVENTORY.
```

The program logic behind this program is actually quite simple. It is the constant data that is required to generate the XML document that adds to its apparent complexity.

Unlike the two prior programs, this program declares a `WORKING-STORAGE SECTION` to contain intermediate data values at runtime. This section is where general-purpose variables that will not be read from or written to a file are allocated.

Starting with line 2900, the outermost XML open and close tags (`<INVENTORY>` and `</INVENTORY>`) are declared. Then, the `ITEM-ELEMENT` section declares a series of element open and close tags that bracket named data items that will contain the actual values from the inventory file at runtime.

NOTE

Several data items consist of only a `PIC` clause and nothing else. Unlabeled items like this are referred to as `FILLER` items (because they may each optionally have the name `FILLER`). `FILLER` items may not be referenced directly, but when a higher-level item (such as the level 01 `ITEM-ELEMENT`) is accessed, it implicitly includes all the lower-level items, including the `FILLER` items.

The basic flow of the program is similar to that of the IMPORT-INVENTORY and PROCESS-ORDERS programs. The input and output files are opened on lines 5100 and 5200. Then, the value of the `OPEN-TAG` item is moved into the `PRINT-AREA` and written to the output file. Each time the `WRITE PRINT-AREA` statement is executed, the current contents of the `PRINT-AREA` item are written to the output file and the file is advanced to a new line.

One interesting side effect of the way COBOL sequential file handling deals with fixed-width records is that each line in the output document is exactly the same length. Even the line that contains nothing but the `<INVENTORY>` open tag is 180 characters wide (the size of the `PRINT-AREA` item). The rest of the line is padded by whitespace. Because XML will ignore this additional whitespace, the application is still functional. If the size of the output file is of primary concern, however, it is possible to output lines of varying length by using some of the more sophisticated record-handling facilities of COBOL.

The loop that runs from lines 5600 to 6200 actually reads each inventory record, reformats it, and outputs it to the output file. Most of the `READ`, `WRITE`, and `MOVE` instructions should be familiar from the preceding programs. The one novel feature is the use of the `MOVE CORRESPONDING` statement to prepare the incoming record for output.

The `MOVE CORRESPONDING` statement instructs the compiler to move the values from each elementary data item in the first group item to the elementary data item in the second group item that has the same name. Looking at the child items of `ITEM-RECORD` and `ITEM-ELEMENT`, it becomes apparent that the `QUANTITY`, `PART-NUM`, `DESC`, and `MFGR` items are present in both groups. The compiled code effectively "mixes" the values from the packed `ITEM-RECORD` structure into the interleaved fields in the `ITEM-ELEMENT` structure. This is an extremely useful feature of COBOL that I have not personally seen in any other programming language.

After the individual item element has been populated, it is moved into the `PRINT-AREA` and written to the output file. The loop then continues at the `LOOP-POINT` label.

After the last record has been read, the program jumps to the TERM-PROC, which writes the </INVENTORY> close tag and closes the input and output files. The XML document that results from a sample run of this program can be found on the Web site as INVENTORY-OUT.xml. Even if this XML format is not exactly what is required by the Internet-based ordering system, with our complete grasp of XSLT there should be no formatting challenge that is too great!

Deployment

Here are the steps to deploy this application:

1. Install a COBOL 85–compliant COBOL compiler. The Web site lists links to various commercial and free COBOL compilers that can be found on the Web.
2. Download and unzip the sample files from this book's Web site.
3. Compile and link the three sample programs: IMPORT-INVENTORY.COB, PROCESS-ORDERS.COB, and EXPORT-INVENTORY.COB.
4. Follow your COBOL compiler's instructions for creating associations between the files listed in the SELECT statements of the various programs with physical files on your system.
5. Install an XSLT processor (such as Saxon) on your system.
6. Transform the VCPManual.xml document into a file that can be fed to the IMPORT-INVENTORY program, using make_inventory.xsl.
7. Run IMPORT-INVENTORY on the transformed file. It should create the initial indexed inventory file.
8. Transform the OrderDB.xml document into a file that can be read by the PROCESS-ORDERS program, using make_update.xsl.
9. Run PROCESS-ORDERS a few times, to update the in-stock quantities in the indexed inventory file.
10. Run EXPORT-INVENTORY to generate an XML version of the indexed inventory file, and see whether the quantities have changed as you expected.

Conclusion

When I mentioned to a table full of Internet programmers that I had just finished writing three COBOL programs, I heard comments like "COBOL is evil," and "I've never learned COBOL and I never will." But the one true comment I didn't hear was "COBOL is here and it's not going away." By writing small, carefully targeted import and export systems such as the one described in this chapter, you can harness all the power of more modern systems without giving up the safety and security of the time-proven legacy systems that are in place in a typical large enterprise.

Unifying Product Documentation

CHAPTER

18

About six months ago, I realized that I didn't know how to use one of the more esoteric features of my complicated aviator-style watch. After spending a few futile minutes poking around the manufacturer's Web site, I realized that no documentation was available online. So I located the toll-free telephone number for service, and after waiting on hold for 10 minutes, I spent about 10 minutes giving the customer service rep my address, watch model number, and so on. Then, a mere seven days later I received a hand-addressed envelope with a copy of the manual for my watch.

This experience was expensive for the watch manufacturer, and frustrating for me, the customer. Now, thanks to XML, the goal of publishing documentation simultaneously on paper and on the Web is achievable.

Technologies Used:

- **XML**
- **XSL Transformations (XSLT)**
- **XSL Formatting Objects (XSL-FO)**
- **HTML**

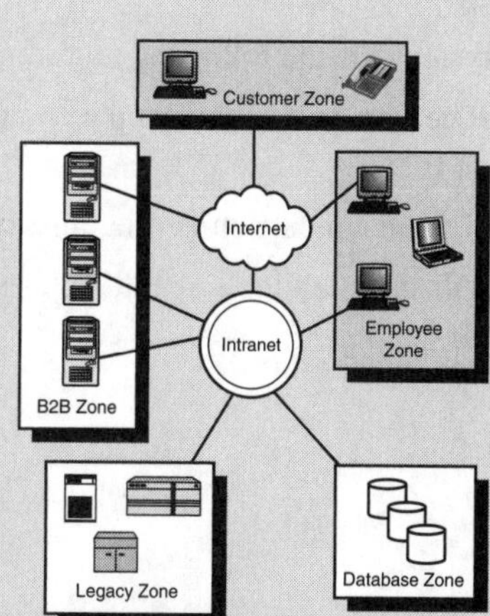

Customer service is one of those thorny problems that face every large company. The sad part is that when the service is done correctly, it is invisible. It's only when it is poor that we really notice it. Applying XML to knowledge management problems can help an organization deliver the information that customers need in a format they can use.

Problem Description

An electronic equipment manufacturer wants to begin simultaneously publishing product documentation on paper and on the Web. The production department must be able to easily author new documents, and the resulting online content must be compatible with the existing corporate web infrastructure. The pilot project to provide a proof-of-concept will be to convert an existing hard-copy document to use the new framework.

NOTE

Before going any further, we would like to thank the LG Electronics corporation for allowing us to use one of their real-life appliance manuals for this project. Not only did they kindly allow us to reproduce significant portions of their manual for this book, but the videocassette player itself has given the author's daughter hundreds of hours of Disney-induced euphoria.

The desired output of this project is

- A document type definition that can be used to create new product documents.
- A system for producing printed output from the XML source.
- The transforms and stylesheets required to display the product documentation on the corporate Web site.

Requirements

This system has the following requirements:

- The system must be simple enough for nontechnical documentation authors and editors to use.
- The document source file must support the creation of HTML and PDF documents.
- Off-the-shelf tools should be used if possible, with little or no custom software development.

System Design

Similar to the Web publishing example (see Chapter 12, "Web Content Publishing"), the basic strategy for this project is to author the primary document in XML, then transform it to produce the final, human-readable product. Figure 18.1 shows the flow of the system, from the human authors and designers to the finished documents.

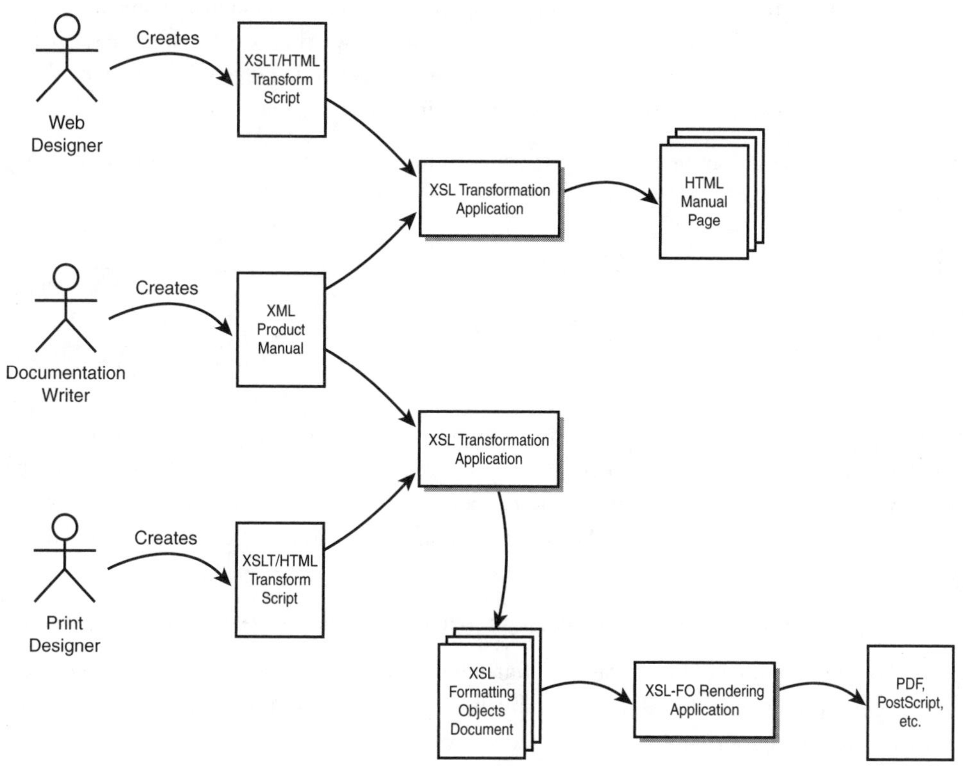

FIGURE 18.1
A single XML manual is transformed into Web and print content.

To do this, you need to carry out the following actions:

- Convert the hard-copy manual into an XML document.
- Develop the stylesheets (XSLT and/or CSS) to display the manual on the Web.
- Assemble the tools and build the stylesheets required to generate printable documentation from the XML source file.

Implementation Notes

The following sections describe the steps taken to build the product-manual production system.

Converting the Hard-Copy Manual to XML

Translating a printed document into XML is a lot more involved than just retyping it into a word processor. XML documents are meant to capture not only the content of a document, but also information about its structure. A typical document in a word processor might have paragraph styles, heading styles, and so on that affect how the text is displayed. This is fine, if the only goal is to produce good-looking output for viewing by people.

A well-designed XML document, however, contains much more information than can be conveyed by simple formatting. For instance, take the following note:

> **NOTE**
>
> XML documents are composed of both structure and content.

On the page, this note appears as a gray box with black text, with a small white box in the upper-left corner that contains the header. This formatting serves to set the note apart from the rest of the text, but it conveys no information about the purpose of the formatted text. If we were to convert this book into XML, however, the note above would be coded as a special XML tag:

```
<note>XML documents are composed of both structure and content.</note>
```

This XML fragment now conveys the actual meaning of the text. Although it doesn't indicate how the text should be displayed, it is a relatively simple matter to transform the original XML document into an appropriate format for the display device.

Building the DTD

The manual we will be converting into XML is for a simple videocassette player (VCP). The scanned version of the original paper manual is available in its entirety on the CD. Converting a basically unstructured document into a structured one is more art than science, but there are some basic steps that make the process smoother.

NOTE

Before you invest a lot of time in building a custom DTD, it is well worth the effort to shop around on the Internet for an existing DTD that will meet your needs. Several sites on the Web attempt to catalog and collect XML DTDs, so be sure to check the resource links listed on this book's Web site. Even if an off-the-shelf DTD doesn't exactly meet your needs, it may help get you started in the right direction.

The final goal of this step is to develop an XML document type definition (DTD) that expresses the structure of valid product manuals. Although it is tempting to go directly from the printed manual to the DTD, in reality it is much easier to convert a paper document into an XML document, then build a DTD for the resulting XML. There are automated tools that simplify this process by building a DTD that matches a well-formed XML document, and we will be using one of them after we have the entire document converted.

The actual process of encoding the printed document in XML format is straightforward, though tedious. There are a few things to keep in mind while encoding the document that can reduce problems later, as described in the following sections.

Isolate the Smallest, Indivisible Elements of a Document

Reduce the document into its atomic elements (images, paragraphs, titles, boxed notes, and so on). After these elements have been isolated, it becomes easier to classify them and group them within the XML document.

Categorize Each Document Element

Looking at each atomic piece of a document, determine whether it serves the same purpose as any of the other pieces. If not, it is necessary to create a new XML element type to contain it. Otherwise, encode it using an existing element type.

Group Related Elements

Frequently in an unstructured document, related material will be scattered throughout a section. Whenever possible, related elements should be grouped into a larger, containing element in XML. For instance, footnotes might appear throughout a technical paper at the bottom of each page. In XML, it would make more sense to place all footnotes in a single container element and include an XLink reference to the specific footnote within the structured document text. This yields a cleaner document format and simplifies transformation scripts.

Use Standard Structured Document Idioms Whenever Possible

Some types of content are so common that the markup used to represent them has become idiomatic. For instance, general-purpose lists and tables are almost always encoded using the basic HTML `<ol>`, `<ul>`, and `<table>` tags. Not only will you save yourself the trouble of reinventing the wheel, but you also will simplify the task of transforming your XML into HTML.

Collapse Duplicated Material

If the same boilerplate material appears in more than one location in your document, you should consider collapsing all the occurrences into a single element. This action will make your document more maintainable, smaller, and more coherent. If you need to incorporate the same material in multiple locations, use XLink to create pointers to the single valid instance of the data.

Exclude Presentational Elements

Drawing the line between true content and presentation can be tricky at times. Here are some examples of presentational elements that should not be included in a content document:

- *List or outline numbers* XSLT provides robust facilities for generating these automatically. Rather than include them in content, then worry about keeping them up-to-date, just remove them and use the order of the elements in the document to maintain relative positioning.
- *Repeated labels or constant text* For example, a long list of addresses in a print document might include labels such as City:, State:, and Zip: for each entry. The correct way to represent this in XML is to create an `<address>` element that includes these values, and then provide the static text labels as part of the transformation step.
- *Hard-coded table of contents or index* Rather than build these manually and keep updating them as the document changes, use XSLT to generate them dynamically. Not only will this approach be easier, but it will make the final document more accurate.

Structural Versus Content Elements

The types of tags we will require in our document fall into two basic classes: structural and content (text). Structural elements exist to organize the document into logical units. Content elements contain the actual character data of the document. The difference between these two types of elements becomes more obvious as we transform the raw XML document into human-readable form for both the Web and print media. Table 18.1 lists a few structural and content elements for comparison.

TABLE 18.1 Structural and Text Element Examples

Structural Elements	*Content Elements*
body	`p`
section	`title`
table	`img`

As a rule of thumb, structural elements are almost never leaf nodes and text elements usually are. Structural elements primarily exist for the purpose of containing and organizing other elements, whereas text elements exist to contain character data.

The completed document is called `VCPManual.xml`. After the original printed manual has been completely encoded in XML, the next step is to create a document type definition for it. The DTD is important because it is what defines what is and what is not a valid product manual (at least according to our system). By formalizing the document structure, we can build generic transforms that should theoretically work not only with the current manual in production, but with any future manuals we would happen to create as well. We can make assumptions about the order of elements within the document, which elements can be nested, and where character data can appear.

To build our DTD, we could manually review the entire document we just created, deduce the relationships between the various elements, and write the entire DTD by hand. This approach would yield a correct DTD, but it is somewhat time-consuming. Several tools are available on the Internet for generating a DTD from an invalid XML document. To build the example, I used the DTDGenerator tool that is available with the SAXON XSLT processor. This tool analyzes the structure of a document and creates a DTD that can be used to validate the document given. Its usage is:

```
java DTDGenerator inputdocument.xml > output.dtd
```

The DTD generated by a tool such as this will not necessarily be completely correct. Because it must infer relationships between elements from a single document, the resulting DTD may tend to be more restrictive than it should be. The automatically generated DTD should be treated as a starting point, and should be reviewed and modified to express the actual rules of the document type in question. A complete and correct DTD can be used by WYSIWYG XML editors (such as SoftQuad's XMetal product) to create new XML documents with a simple drag-and-drop interface. One of the requirements for this project is to use as much off-the-shelf technology as possible, so building a complete and accurate DTD is essential.

Transforming for the Web

There are several approaches for displaying XML data on the Web. Before selecting a particular solution, you should take a few factors into account.

Who Will View the Content?

One of the major problems with developing Web content and applications today is the incredible diversity of consumers of Web content. Millions of users, hundreds of languages, several browsers, and variable bandwidth make delivering useful, high-quality content to every user a difficult problem. In this case, we can't make any assumptions about our audience. Mass-market consumer electronics could be purchased by anyone, so we need to make sure that we don't arbitrarily exclude anyone from viewing our site.

Is the Content Static or Dynamic?

The line between static and dynamic content has become blurry as the Web has matured. Most major commercial Web sites are heavily dependent on active scripting (ASP, JSP, Perl, PHP, and so on). From a site-design perspective, static content is content that will be manually updated by a human being. For example, a page with real-time stock quotes would probably not be a static page. A biography of William Shakespeare, on the other hand, would probably be a good candidate for manual updating. Because our product manual describes an actual physical thing that is not going to change (upgrades or new models would require a new manual), a solution that produces static output will be sufficient.

What Is the Target Server Architecture?

Several different Web server platforms are in use on the Internet, but at the time of this writing Apache Server and Microsoft's IIS together control 80% of the market (according to the Netcraft survey, available at `www.netcraft.com/survey`). Both of these platforms provide integrated support for transforming XML using XSLT on the fly.

Based on these criteria, the content to be displayed should be

- Viewable by as many different browsers as possible.
- Completely static (updated only if errors are discovered)
- Hostable on either Apache or IIS servers.

In this case, generating static plain-vanilla HTML files is a perfectly acceptable solution. The resulting files can be served and indexed efficiently, and can be viewed by most Web clients. The top-down process for generating these files is simple:

1. Define the number, type, and layout of the pages to be generated.
2. Write the XSLT script or scripts to generate the output pages.
3. Use an XSLT transformation tool to create the HTML output.

Although it would be simple to generate a single, monolithic HTML version of the manual, this would place an undue burden on users that have slower connections or limited display capabilities. A better solution would be to create a short table of contents page with hyperlinks to separate pages for each section of the manual. The resulting site layout would resemble what's shown in Figure 18.2.

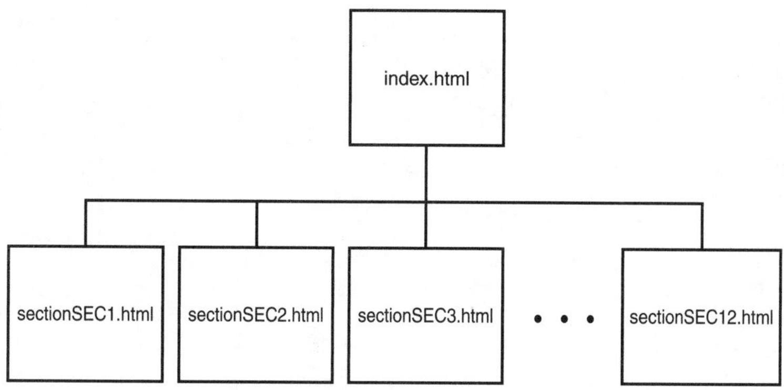

FIGURE 18.2
The desired site map of the HTML pages to be generated from `VCPManual.xml`.

Now the only question is this: What is the best way to generate these pages from the master document? Listing 18.1 shows a condensed version of `VCPManual.xml`, showing only the top-level elements.

LISTING 18.1 A Condensed Version of `VCPManual.xml`

```
<?xml version="1.0" encoding="utf-8"?>
<!--

  VCPManual.xml

  Example for unified product documentation from Sams
  _Strategic XML.

-->
<!DOCTYPE manual SYSTEM "product_manual.dtd" [
<!ENTITY model_num "GVP-C125">
]>
<manual>
  <product_info>
    <manufacturer>
      <company_name>GoldStar</company_name>
```

LISTING 18.1 Continued

```
    <web_site>http://www.lgusa.com</web_site>
  </manufacturer>
  <product_type>Video Cassette Player</product_type>
  <model_num>&model_num;</model_num>
</product_info>
...
<body>
  <section id="SEC1">
    <title>Cautionary Notes</title>
    . . .
  </section>
  <section id="SEC2">
    <title>Features</title>
    . . .
  </section>
  <section id="SEC3">
    <title>Accessories</title>
    . . .
  </section>
  <section id="SEC4">
    <title>Important Safeguards</title>
    . . .
  </section>
  <section id="SEC5">
    <title>Parts and Controls</title>
    . . .
  </section>
  <section id="SEC6">
    <title>Power Sources</title>
    . . .
    <sub_section>
      <title>When using the AC adaptor (Supplied)</title>
      . . .
    </sub_section>
    <sub_section>
      <title>When using the CAR battery</title>
      . . .
    </sub_section>
  </section>
  <section id="SEC7">
      <title>Making the Right Connections</title>
    . . .
  </section>
```

LISTING 18.1 Continued

```
    <section id="SEC8">
        <title>Loading and Unloading</title>
      . . .
    </section>
    <section id="SEC9">
        <title>Precautions</title>
      . . .
    </section>
    <section id="SEC10">
        <title>Pre-recorded Tape Playback</title>
      . . .
      <sub_section>
        <title>SPECIAL EFFECTS PLAYBACK
                (BEST RESULTS AT SP &amp; EP SPEED</title>
        . . .
      </sub_section>
    </section>
    <section id="SEC11">
      <title>Duplicating a Video Tape</title>
      . . .
    </section>
    <section id="SEC12">
      <title>Video Head Cleaning</title>
      . . .
    </section>
    <section id="SEC13">
      <title>Before Requesting Service</title>
      . . .
      <sub_section>
        <title>REPLACING THE FUSE</title>
        . . .
      </sub_section>
    </section>
    <section id="SEC14">
      <title>Specifications</title>
      . . .
    </section>
    <section id="SEC15">
      <title>Warranty</title>
      . . .
    </section>
  </body>
</manual>
```

Generating the Table of Contents Page

Our first task is to write the XSLT stylesheet that will generate the table of contents page (`index.html`). This page should list the title of each section of the document and offer a hyperlink to the related section detail page. Listing 18.2 shows the XSLT template that will produce the HTML table of contents page.

LISTING 18.2 Table of Contents Page Template

```
<xsl:template match="manual">
  <html>
    <head>
      <title>
        <xsl:value-of select="rdf:RDF/rdf:Description/dc:title"/>
      </title>
    </head>
    <link REL="stylesheet" HREF="VCRManual.css" TYPE="text/css"/>
    <body>
      <h1><xsl:value-of select="rdf:RDF/
➥rdf:Description/dc:title"/></h1>
      <h2>Table of Contents</h2>
      <ul>
        <xsl:for-each select="//section">
          <li>
            <a href="section{@id}.html">
➥<xsl:value-of select="title"/></a>
          </li>
        </xsl:for-each>
      </ul>
    </body>
  </html>
</xsl:template>
```

This template loops through each `<section>` element in the source document and emits an HTML unordered list item containing the title of the section. The title is a hyperlink that points to the actual section detail page, which we will be constructing shortly. Notice that the URL of the section detail–relative page is constructed by appending the element ID of the section to the word "section" and then appending the extension `.html`.

Emitting the Section Pages

Although our document has 15 distinct sections, they all follow the same basic pattern. Also, we are trying to build a generic document processing system, and future manuals will most likely have a different number of sections. The XSLT transform for emitting a single section as an HTML page is trivial:

```
<xsl:template match="section">
  <html>
    <head><title><xsl:value-of select="title"/></title></head>
    <link REL="stylesheet" HREF="VCRManual.css" TYPE="text/css"/>
    <body>
      <h1><xsl:value-of select="title"/></h1>
      <p><a href="index.html">Table Of Contents</a></p>
      <xsl:apply-templates/>
    </body>
  </html>
</xsl:template>
```

However, if this template is executed repeatedly within the same XSLT script, the output will be one long file with several complete HTML pages contained in it. Unfortunately, XSLT 1.0 doesn't have a facility for directing output from a single script into multiple output files. If we were to limit ourselves to basic 1.0 functionality, we would be faced with the unappetizing choice of one of the following:

- Creating a separate XSLT script for each section (SEC1.xslt, SEC2.xslt, and so on)
- Resorting to shell scripting and transformation games to automatically generate the required scripts

Luckily, the draft XSLT 1.1 recommendation includes a new element that solves our problem, the `<xsl:document>` element. The SAXON version 6.1 stylesheet processor supports this element, and it can be used to create multiple HTML documents from a single XSLT script. The new transformation for generating a section document would be this:

```
<xsl:template match="section">
  <xsl:document href="section{@id}.html">
    <html>
      <head><title><xsl:value-of select="title"/></title></head>
      <link REL="stylesheet" HREF="VCRManual.css" TYPE="text/css"/>
      <body>
        <h1><xsl:value-of select="title"/></h1>
        <p><a href="index.html">Table Of Contents</a></p>
        <xsl:apply-templates/>
      </body>
    </html>
  </xsl:document>
</xsl:template>
```

Notice that the `href` attribute of the `<xsl:document>` element provides the URL for the output filename. The filename is calculated dynamically by using the attribute value template syntax of XSL (`{@id}`) to insert the ID of the current section.

There is also a link to a Cascading Style Sheet that will be included in the resulting HTML file. This provides basic formatting information such as desired font, foreground & background colors, and other style elements of the page as it should be displayed by the browser.

Now that we have solved the problem of generating multiple output files from a single XSLT stylesheet, the rest of the process is a straightforward transformation of XML elements to appropriate HTML output elements. For a more detailed explanation of how this is done, see Chapter 12.

Transforming for Print Media

Although the entire reason for the existence of XML is to allow programmers and authors to separate content from presentation information, at some point XML data will be presented to a human reader. The XSL specification addresses the need to transform XML into a human-readable format through the XSL Formatting Objects mechanism. XSL-FO defines a vocabulary of XML elements that define how to lay out text on a printed page.

Unlike Cascading Stylesheets, XSL-FO is a complete XML application in and of itself. Although it would be possible to write XSL-FO documents directly, in normal usage an existing XML document is transformed using XSLT into an XSL-FO document. Because no tools (at the time of this writing) natively display XSL-FO, another tool is required to parse the XSL-FO document and render it in a better supported format such as PDF, TEX, or PostScript. The XSL-FO renderer used to develop this application is the Apache XML Project's Fop processor.

The two-stage nature of the rendering process makes solving problems with the output document difficult. There can be errors in the XSLT transform itself, or in the resulting XSLT-FO script. During the development process, it is often useful to take an initial rough cut at the XSLT script, then fix a few errors in the XSL-FO script directly. After the fixes in the XSL-FO script have been verified, the XSLT script can be updated.

Generating a Basic XSL-FO Document

Listing 18.3 shows an XSLT transform that will generate an extremely basic, but functional, XSL-FO document from any XML document. This is the starting point for applying more sophisticated styles to improve the quality of the output document.

LISTING 18.3 A Basic XSL-FO XSLT Transform

```
<?xml version="1.0" encoding="UTF-8"?>
<xsl:stylesheet version="1.1" xmlns:xsl="http://www.w3.org/1999/XSL/Transform"
    xmlns:fo="http://www.w3.org/1999/XSL/Format">
```

LISTING 18.3 Continued

```
  <xsl:template match="*">
    <fo:block><xsl:apply-templates/></fo:block>
  </xsl:template>

  <xsl:template match="/">
    <fo:root>
      <fo:layout-master-set>
        <fo:simple-page-master margin-right="1in" margin-left="1in"
            margin-top="1in" margin-bottom="1in"
            page-width="8.5in" page-height="11in"
            master-name="normal">
          <fo:region-body/>
        </fo:simple-page-master>
      </fo:layout-master-set>

      <fo:page-sequence master-name="normal">
        <fo:flow flow-name="xsl-region-body">
          <xsl:apply-templates/>
        </fo:flow>
      </fo:page-sequence>
    </fo:root>
  </xsl:template>
</xsl:stylesheet>
```


This script will generate an XSL-FO document that displays all the character data from each XML element in its own distinct XSL-FO block.

Completing the Print Layout

The XSL-FO specification is very complex, and at the time of this writing it has still not been approved by the W3C. It would require another book as long as this one to adequately explain the full XSL-FO specification. The XSL-FO transformation provided for this manual can be used as a starting point for other projects. The best way to learn how the transformation works is to visit the book's Web site and download the complete example. Modifying the sample files and viewing the resulting document is a good way to rapidly learn XSL-FO.

Deployment

Because the output of this project is a set of static documents (both HTML and PDF), deployment is simply a matter of distributing the output files to their proper destinations. The HTML files would be deployed to the company's production Web site. The PDF documentation would be printed and duplicated as required.

Conclusions

Moving to an XML-based documentation workflow can provide many benefits to organizations with complex needs. Once the time and effort have been spent to produce the first document, future documents can leverage the generic XML/XSL framework for rapid development. XML finally allows document content, language translations, and presentation information to be separated completely. Being able to develop, translate, and format documents in parallel should take publishing applications to the next level of efficiency.

INDEX

SYMBOLS

A

B

F

G–H

I–J–K

P-Q

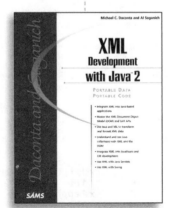